German Jews and Migration to the United States, 1933–1945

Lexington Studies in Modern Jewish History, Historiography, and Memory

Series Editor: Carsten Schapkow, University of Oklahoma

Modern Jewish history is an essentially interdisciplinary field. This series aspires to transcend disciplinary and methodological boundaries, welcoming original scholarship that advances our understanding of the modern Jewish experience. The series will cover all geographical areas and all periods in modern Jewish history by welcoming scholarly contributions including cultural history, intellectual history, transnational Jewish history, global Jewish history, and memory studies. We welcome original monographs and edited volumes as well as English-language translations of manuscripts originally written in other languages.

Titles in the Series

German Jews and Migration to the United States, 1933–1945, edited by Andrea A. Sinn and Andreas Heusler

The Life and Thought of Ze'ev Jawitz: "To Cultivate a Hebrew Culture," by Asaf Yedidya

Rethinking Holocaust Film Reception: A British Case Study, by Stefanie Rauch

Britain, the Bible, and Balfour: Mandate for a Jewish State, 1530–1917, by Jonathan Immanuel

Judaism for Christians: Menasseh ben Israel (1604–1657), by Sina Rauschenbach

Jewish Studies and Israel Studies in the Twenty-First Century: Intersections and Prospects, edited by Klaus Hödl and Carsten Schapkow

Modern Spain and the Sephardim: Legitimizing Identities, by Maite Ojeda-Mata

Eastern European Jewish American Narratives, 1890–1930: Struggles for Recognition, by Dana Mihailescu

Hostile Takeovers of Large Jewish Companies, 1933–1935: Reassessing Aryanization of Jewish-Owned Firms, by William Maurice Katin

German Jews and Migration to the United States, 1933–1945

Edited by
Andrea A. Sinn and Andreas Heusler

LEXINGTON BOOKS
Lanham • Boulder • New York • London

Published by Lexington Books
An imprint of The Rowman & Littlefield Publishing Group, Inc.
4501 Forbes Boulevard, Suite 200, Lanham, Maryland 20706
www.rowman.com

86-90 Paul Street, London EC2A 4NE

Cover image: Loading a lift van in front of the Rosenbaum family's house at Pettenkoferstraße 24, September 1938. The successful Jewish businessman Heinrich Rosenbaum, later Henry Roland (1891–1973) was able to emigrate to the USA via Switzerland in September 1938 with his wife Else Rosenbaum, née Hoffman, his daughter Hilde, and his mother Sophie Rosenbaum, née Lohmeyer.

Ernest B. Hofeller, Munich, 1933–1938. StadtAM, JUD-M-16. Hard copy, 98 pages; written in English in the late 1990s.Selections: pp. 1; 4–7; 21–23; 32–37; 56–58; 64–70; 83–84; 90–96 (with occasional omissions). © Ernest B. Hofeller/Stadtarchiv München.

"Erich Hartmann, StadtAM, JUD-M-15. Hard copy, 13 pages; written in German, 1997; English translation by the editors. Selection: Reprint with two omissions (pp. 2–4, 8). © Erich Hartmann."

"Ein Schülerschicksal, 1933–1945" written for München Mosaik in English translation, typed manuscript, 9 pages; written in German in 1984; English translation by the author. Selection: Full reprint with occasional omissions, supplemented with selected sections from "I live my life in Widening Circles" (hard copy, 4 pages; written in 2004), and "Sweet Sixteen" (hard copy, 4 pages; written in 2006), taken from the same City Archives file.

"Fred Bissinger, The Jaws of the Swastika Tighten. StadtAM, JUD-M-24. Unpublished computer printout, 9 pages; written in English in June 1997. Selection: Full reprint with occasional omissions.© Fred Bissinger/Stadtarchiv München."

This essay was first published in *The Hidden Child 25th Anniversary Issue: Infant Survivors of the Holocaust – The Last Witnesses*. A Publication of Hidden Child Foundation/ADL XXIV (2016): 33 (https://www.adl.org/media/13110/download).

Pesach Schindler, A Jewish Child Growing Up in Nazi Germany. StadtAM, JUD-M-36. Computer printout, 25 pages; written in English in September 2004. Selection: Full reprint with occasional omissions. © Pesach Schindler/Stadtarchiv München.

Schwager Family Letters used courtesy of Dianne Schwager

"Family Blechner "I'm Alive: It's a Miracle!" (StadtAM, JUD-V-99.) Copies of the collection of typed letters of various members of the Blechner Family, written in German; English translation by the editors. Selection: Excerpts of seven letters, all written in 1939. © Courtesy of Anthony and Mark Blechner, the Blechner family Boston, London, Zuerich."

"Inge Moss, My New Life in the U.S. StadtAM, JUD-M-11. Unpublished computer printout, 4 pages; written in English, 1999. Selection: pp. 2–4. © Inge Moss/Stadtarchiv München."

Used with permission of Dana Ulmer Scholle

"Charlotte Haas Schueller, Tossed by the Storms of History: Experiences of a Survivor StadtAM, JUD-M-27.Typewritten English-language manuscript, 110 pages; given to the Munich City Archives by the author during a visit to Munich in 2004. Selection: pp. 45–72, with omissions. © Charlotte Haas Schueller/Stadtarchiv München."

Hanns Peter Merzbacher, Memories (Erinnerungen). StadtAM, JUD-M-32. Printout, hardcover, 92 pages with photos and documents; written in German in 1996; English translation by the editors. Selection: pp. 39–80, with occasional omissions. © Hanns Peter Merzbacher/Stadtarchiv München.

Courtesy of Leo Baeck Institute New York.

Courtesy of Leo Baeck Institute New York.

Published version of letters originally handwritten or typed by various members of the Koppel family, written in German, published in Alfred Koppel, "Dies ist mein letzter Brief…": Eine Münchner Familie vor der Deportation im November 1941, ed. Ilse Macek and Friedbert Mühldorfer (Munich: Volk, 2014); English translation by the editors. © Koppel Family/Ilse Macek.

"Hans Lamm, "Wanderer Between Two Worlds" StadtAM, JUD-V-001 and StadtAM, NL Lamm, Akt 29. Unsorted collection of letters written with typewriter; originals and carbon copies; written in German and English; English translation for German letters provided by the editors. Selection: Excerpts of eleven letters and one postcard, written between 1938 and 1954. © Hans Lamm/ Stadtarchiv München."

British Library Cataloguing in Publication Information Available

Library of Congress Cataloging-in-Publication Data

Names: Sinn, Andrea, editor. | Heusler, Andreas, 1960- editor.
Title: German Jews and migration to the United States, 1933-1945 / edited by
    Andrea A. Sinn and Andreas Heusler.
Description: Lanham, Maryland : Lexington Books, [2022] | Series: Lexington studies in modern
    jewish history, historiography, and memory | Includes bibliographical references and index. |
    Summary: "This collection of mostly unpublished first-person accounts documents the flight
    and exile of German Jews from Nazi Germany to the USA. The thematic and biographical
    introductions by the editors, clear geographic framework, and well-defined time frame make this
    volume helpful to those new to the subject"— Provided by publisher.
Identifiers: LCCN 2021056378 (print) | LCCN 2021056379 (ebook) |
    ISBN 9781793646002 (cloth) | ISBN 9781793646019 (ebook)
Subjects: LCSH: Jews—Germany—Munich—Biography. | Jewish refugees—Germany—Munich—
    Biography. | Exiles—Germany—Munich—History—20th century. | Jews—Persecutions—
    Germany—Munich—History—20th century. |
    Holocaust, Jewish (1939-1945)—Germany. | Germany—Emigration and immigration—
    History—20th century. | United States—Emigration and immigration—History—20th century.
Classification: LCC DS134.36.M86 G47 2022 (print) | LCC DS134.36.M86 (ebook) | DDC
    943/.364004924009042—dc23/eng/20220120
LC record available at https://lccn.loc.gov/2021056378
LC ebook record available at https://lccn.loc.gov/2021056379

Contents

List of Figures

Acknowledgments

We would like to extend our gratitude to many participants in this book project. The editors are thankful to the Munich City Archives for helping to document and reconstruct the Jewish history in the Bavarian metropolis. Our late colleague Brigitte Schmidt played a special role in this work over many years; our publication has benefited greatly from the invaluable results of her work. Also indispensable was the support of David Fletcher, who provided editing of the English texts with great sensitivity. The feedback from Clyde Ellis, Adam Seipp, Hanna Ertl, Barbara Trommeter, and Eva Tyrell gave us important suggestions, especially in the beginning and final phases of the project. You have all helped to bring the manuscript into its final form. Many thanks for this!

Most research is based on archival materials and builds on previous research. This book is no different. We would therefore like to take this opportunity to thank the scholars and archivists whose work inspired us to undertake this project and made it possible. In addition to the Munich City Archives, the following individuals or institutions deserve special mention: Frank Mecklenburg and Michael Simonson (Leo Baeck Institute, New York), Robert Bierschneider (Staatsarchiv Munich), Klaus Lankheit (Institute of Contemporary History, Munich), Timothy Hensley (Virginia Holocaust Museum, Richmond, VA), Daniel Kalman Epstein (Portraits in Faith/ PortraitsInFaith.org), and Rachelle Goldstein (Hidden Child Foundation, New York) have unbureaucratically decided on copyright and reprint rights. For their contributions to the realization of this project, we would like to express our deep gratitude.

All of the authors of the autobiographical texts published here are no longer with us. We have included their texts as they were left to us. Anthony Blechner, Nicholas Hartmann, Dianne Schwager, and Gary Schwager have given us valuable support as descendants. Much assistance and information were also received from the trustees of Al Koppel's estate, Ilse Macek and Friedbert Mühldorfer. The cover photo was given to us by Hilda Yohalem, a former Munich resident. Avital Ben-Chorin made available the correspondence of her late husband, Schalom Ben-Chorin. Our special thanks go to all of them.

Editorial supervision of the series was in the capable hands of Carsten Schapkow. On the publishing side, Judith Lakamper and Mikayla Mislak managed our project with endurance and friendly persistence. Many thanks to all of them for their patience, suggestions, and cooperation.

For the editors, and especially for Andrea Sinn, this book has been a dream project since she began teaching in the United States. Her home institution, Elon University, provided her with a highly appreciated sabbatical leave and an intellectual foundation for all her work. She also wishes to offer her thanks for the generous support of the Historisches Kolleg in Munich, that marvelous Institute for Advanced Study in History founded in 1980 where—as an Honorary Fellow—she was able to devote her sabbatical time in the spring of 2021 to the completion of this collaborative project, a dream now realized.

Introduction

From Hitler's Munich to American Exile

Andrea A. Sinn and Andreas Heusler

They fled over the sea. When the ship reached the open sea, it began to race and maintained this speed until the end of the voyage, constantly zigzagging to avoid attacks from submarines. Their home had become unsafe in the late 1930s, shaken by terror and violence. Their *Heimat*,[1] that familiar place where your heart feels at home, had turned against them. The future was unknown. "It was an end, relentless and almost unbelievable," one of the refugees remembered. "At the last goodbye, a piece of our soul remained stuck in our homeland and will now wander around forever with all the many other souls who have had the same fate as ours, perplexed and searching." The elderly on board had abandoned everything that they had owned, everything that had defined their bourgeois existence. The young people surrendered their dreams. And yet, they all seemed euphoric. Finally, there was a fragment of renewed hope! After the unbelievably fast time of only 4 ½ days, they approached New York.

> The Statue of Liberty suddenly appeared on the horizon, powerful and compelling, and we were overcome by previously unshed tears. Countries and seas had to be crossed to find it—the freedom that had once ruled our faithful homeland and broke our chains. Now, it was gagged and trampled underfoot, and we had to seek in a foreign land that most precious thing, freedom.[2]

Written in 1964, these words describe the experience of Charlotte Stein-Pick, a Jewish refugee from Munich, Germany.[3] Born in the Bavarian capital in 1899, Stein-Pick spent her childhood and youth in her hometown (see figure 0.1), where she experienced not only the outbreak and duration of World War I but also the devastation of post-World War I Germany. Here, she also met her future husband, Herbert Stein, and began her work with the Jewish League of Women, while witnessing the rise of the National Socialist German Workers' Party (or Nazi Party).[4] In 1933, the Nazis succeeded in eliminating the rule of law and transitioned the government to a fascist dictatorship that used terror and extralegal methods. Moreover, the domination of National Socialism, which embraced oppression, persecution, exclusion, and extermination to rule with racism and antisemitism at the center of its ideology,[5] showed in the most alarming way how quickly the comforting concept of *Heimat* may become unstable and unsupportive.

For Charlotte Stein-Pick, as for many German Jews, their Jewish origin in connection with the possession of German citizenship was a self-evident fact. National consciousness, patriotism, and love of one's fatherland were an undisputed part of their identity. Tens of thousands of Jews had fought side by side with their Catholic and Protestant compatriots in World War I, risking or sacrificing their health and lives. For them and their families, it was shocking and incomprehensible that now—after 1933—they were not only denied a sense of belonging to the nation but also accused of having an evil, harmful, even dangerous influence on their homeland.[6] After being increasingly subjected to exclusion and persecution by the Nazis, Charlotte Stein-Pick and her husband were able, with great difficulty, to leave Germany in August 1939. Shortly thereafter, they boarded a ship in France, which carried them to the United States of America, where Charlotte

Figure 0.1   Munich's Main Synagogue in Herzog-Max-Strasse, the Center of Jewish Life in the Heart of the City, Seen from Lenbachplatz, c. 1910. *Source*: Stadtarchiv München.

Stein-Pick died in 1991. It is a familiar story, but Stein-Pick and her husband were hardly alone; the number of Jewish emigrants from German-speaking countries who fled during the Nazi period is estimated at 280,000 persons, with the experiences of Munich Jews being largely representative of urbanized German Jews. Only a minority of these individuals, no more than 4 percent, decided to return to and resettle in their former *Heimat* after the end of World War II.[7]

With its countless catastrophes, most notably regional and international military conflicts with accompanying massive population movements and expulsions, the 20th century is now often referred to as the "century of refugees." The Nazi era illustrated particularly painfully that the loss of personal rights could, and often did, grievously upset life plans and detrimentally affected people's safety, forcing them to face the counterimages to belonging and home which are expulsion and flight (with the hope of secure relocation). Because statistical surveys utilize various terms and methods, it remains unclear precisely how many people were deprived of their homes and sense of community-belonging during the course of the 20th century. However, the Jews of the Nazi era are possibly the most conspicuous example of a group in the 20th century who can be categorized, both in Nazi-controlled regions and when attempting migration, as—to use historian Michael Marrus' term—the "Unwanted."[8] Typically, the "Unwanted" share a common denominator: they are not recognized as individuals but instead are labeled members of a stigmatized group, an unwanted and unwelcome community. Stereotypes are used to justify exclusion; irrational accusations serve to legitimize revocations and expropriations of the right of residence. And then, all too often, biases and racism prevent people of certain cultures who are fleeing war and persecution from becoming established in potential host countries. These forced migrants, who are desperately searching for a place to shelter themselves in their time of emergency, regrettably may find little aid or sympathy abroad.

Evidently, refugee movements can be recorded geographically, sociologically, and statistically. They can be analyzed and classified using recognized scientific methods. But such methods tend to obscure personal emotions and stories associated with forced migration. Experiences of exclusion, expulsion, flight, and the often desperate search for a "safe haven" are all individual. It is arguably the experiences of individuals which make history truly compelling and relevant, and testimonies that reflect them are integral to our understanding of the past and its meaning, both to contemporary participants and all those who lived with and after them. In the case of Germany during the Nazi period, we are fortunate to possess many records of the dramatic, often traumatic, and always momentous consequences of exclusion and loss of one's home. Flight and expulsion force people to make a new start and integrate into an unfamiliar, usually foreign, world. This process is usually associated with feelings of insecurity and fear about the future. Returns to original places of origin after forced migrations are very rare. Vivid examples of these harsh realities comprise the core of this book.

HISTORICAL BACKGROUND

On January 30, 1933, the political and social climate in Germany changed. For countless Germans, the Nazis' assumption of government control ominously foreshadowed the path to legal exclusion, social stigmatization, and violent persecution. Many people followed the events in the capital Berlin and the developments throughout the German Reich with great concern. They witnessed the final and breathtakingly rapid dismantling of democracy and the rule of law, a seemingly unstoppable and state-imposed *Gleichschaltung* or coordination of all aspects of life, and sanctioned violence against political dissidents. But these actions did not fill everyone with unease and horror. A considerable number of Germans placed great hope in the assurances of the new "national" leadership. They openly demonstrated their enthusiasm for the regime in the streets.

The newly appointed head of the German government, Reich chancellor Adolf Hitler (1889–1945), appealed to these excited masses as their long-awaited bringer of salvation, revitalizer of the supposedly humiliated fatherland, and provider of a glorious future. Born in Austria, Hitler moved to Munich in 1913, served in the German army during World War I, and in October 1919 joined a group that would become the Nazi Party. He became its undisputed leader in 1921. After participating in an unsuccessful coup to overthrow the German government on November 9, 1923, the then 34-year-old Hitler was convicted of "high treason" and sentenced to 5 years imprisonment, but he was released in December 1924 after serving less than a year in prison. Within a decade, he became dictator of Germany and the most powerful man in Europe.[9] Modern propaganda techniques, including strong imagery and simple messages, helped transform Hitler from a little-known extremist into a front-runner in the 1932 German presidential election and a candidate for Reich Chancellor a few months later. Nazi propaganda staged Hitler's appointment as chancellor by Reich President Paul von Hindenburg[10] as a "seizure of power." Crowds took pleasure in the obtrusive display of the "national revolution" and in the martial marches and torchlight processions of uniformed Hitler supporters, with their crude hate chants and death threats against Social Democrats, Communists, trade unionists, and especially Jews. Soon, police and judicial despotism became pervasive. These developments made it painfully clear to those excluded from the Nazis' vision of the new state and all nonconformists that they should expect the worst and that personal disaster could come at any time. In view of these alarming political changes, many Jewish Germans began to think seriously about whether their country would or could continue to be their home in the future. The Nazis' antisemitic and deeply misanthropic diatribes, which until then had been spread in newspapers such as the *Völkischer Beobachter* and *Der Stürmer* as well as via countless public rallies, mostly only "rhetorically" thus far, now received official legitimization. Exclusion, persecution, and terror became integrated in state-promoted programs, which were practiced in a highly effective and coldly bureaucratic manner, thanks to countless compliant helpers in offices and government agencies. For example, immediately after the arson attack on the Reichstag building in Berlin on February 27/28, 1933, the perpetrators of which are still disputed today, the Nazi regime used the infamous Reichstag Fire Decree to create a legal framework for the permanent destruction of the democratic constitution and the rapid erosion of fundamental rights.[11]

On the night of March 9, 1933, political leadership also collapsed in Bavaria, the last of the democratically governed German states. On the night of March 10, the longtime Minister of the Interior, Karl Stützel,[12] one of the most active early Nazi opponents and a man who made progress for the Hitler movement as difficult as he could, was dragged through Munich in his nightgown and bare feet before being severely assaulted within the "Brown House" on Brienner Strasse.[13] A short time later, the Jewish lawyer Michael Siegel[14] was also beaten bloody by SS henchmen and chased through the center of Munich, shoeless, and with his trouser legs cut off and a humiliating sign swinging around his neck. The spectacle was witnessed, but his treatment went unchallenged by passers-by, who were shocked and appalled but merely observed without intervening or turned away indignantly. A photo documenting the torture of this respected lawyer (see figure 0.2) was taken by Heinrich Sanden, a press photographer who happened to be present, and was passed on to international newspapers. It circulated around the world shortly thereafter and showed the true face of the new German government, but the incident otherwise passed without consequences for the perpetrators.[15]

The Siegel case clearly shows that the stability and functioning of the Nazi system of rule were based on the passivity of a large segment of the population. It was the many silent observers, often referred to as "bystanders"— those who did not intervene and who studiously averted their eyes when compassionate attitudes and civil courage were called for, who made the perpetrators' unjust actions possible. Their nonaction, for whatever reasons, suggested approval or even applause and contributed to a steady escalation of violence against "community strangers" and minorities.[16]

Jewish Germans, in particular, were soon made social outcasts by a fast-paced, precise, and systematic government-approved effort. As early as April 1, 1933, for example, a nationwide "boycott campaign" spread fear and terror

Figure 0.2   Without His Shoes and with Cut-off Trouser Legs, SS Men Drove Michael Siegel through Munich on March 10, 1933. *Source:* Stadtarchiv München.

among the Jewish population.[17] In Munich, SA men took up positions in front of lawyers' and doctors' offices and before stores owned by Jews (see figure 0.3). Customers, patients, and clients were insulted and prevented from entering the buildings. Only a few days earlier, the new Munich police chief Heinrich Himmler[18] had ordered the establishment of a concentration camp in nearby Dachau. In addition to numerous political opponents of the Nazi Party—especially Communists, Social Democrats, and trade unionists—Jews were among the first prisoners to be incarcerated and to lose their lives there. The Dachau concentration camp became a National Socialist model facility for its routine implementation of persecution, humiliation, and violence. This treatment of prisoners occurred at the beginning of the Nazis' official period of political and social control and would develop into an unprecedented record of moral baseness and murderous malice.[19]

For men and women who had publicly exposed their identities in the fight against National Socialism and thereby risked much to prevent the Nazis' rule, considerations about their future were pressing. Remaining in Germany might prove to be life-threatening for them, and so many believed, that the only option left was a hasty escape abroad. Dissenting intellectuals—including writers, artists, musicians, theater people, filmmakers, scientists, journalists, and publicists—realized that in this "new Germany" both their careers

Figure 0.3   The SA Boycotting the Bamberger & Hertz Store, Munich, April 1, 1933.
Source: Stadtarchiv München.

and even their lives were in grave jeopardy. Jewish citizens in particular saw not only their economic livelihoods placed at risk; they also felt physically threatened by the new circumstances.

In 1933, the Jewish Community of Munich officially counted 10,737 members.[20] The actual population of men, women, and children of Jewish origin living in Munich was considerably higher because not all of them belonged to the Jewish community. Many had converted to the Christian faith years before or described themselves as having no religion. Despite this, by late 1935, they were included among the victims of Nazi persecution as a result of the Nuremberg Laws which defined love relationships and marriages between Jews and non-Jews as criminal offenses. "Race defilement" became punishable by imprisonment or incarceration in concentration camps. Jewish Germans were degraded to second-class citizens.[21] These inhumane measures marked the beginning of the second phase of antisemitic persecution in Germany.[22] Nazi anti-Jewish policy caused the first major wave of emigration from Munich as early as 1933 when 565 Jewish citizens left the city.[23] Most of them tried their luck in Palestine because they were mainly supporters of the Zionist movement and had already considered moving to Eretz Israel during the Weimar Republic. The Nazi threat now provided the decisive impetus to emigrate. Those not familiar with the ideals of Zionism were more likely to move to the neighboring German-speaking countries Austria or Switzerland; others emigrated to England or the United States.[24]

Those who stayed clung to the hope that Hitler's regime would be only a temporary episode and that conditions eventually would return to normal. Surely, rational political forces would once again regain the upper hand. Pogroms against Jews, uninhibited violence, and unbridled murder seemed unimaginable in a country that invoked cultural icons like Bach, Beethoven, Goethe, and Schiller. Many thought in the same way as Emil Goldschmidt, a successful Munich merchant, who had served in the German army during World War I and been seriously wounded on the front lines. Despite the aggressive rhetoric of the Nazi rulers, Goldschmidt did not believe that the safety of his family could be endangered in this country for which he had risked his life and which was his home. Only much later, in September 1939, did the Goldschmidts decide to emigrate to Switzerland and then to Palestine.[25]

Unlike today, a time in which national borders typically have a high degree of permeability due to liberal travel laws and international travel is commonplace, foreign travel in the 1930s was hampered by a multitude of national regulations. Many people did not regard travel (especially permanent relocation) to a "foreign land" as an opportunity for an exotic adventure. Instead, they were compelled to face the worrisome challenge of many unknown factors and uncertainties that were difficult to assess and end-gains even more difficult if not impossible to calculate. Also, only a small percentage of the people confronted with this decision had knowledge of foreign languages, which today are more commonly studied, thanks to modernized school systems. All this caused many who were persecuted to initially postpone their decision to leave Germany. But news of the outrageous measures enacted against Jews, political dissidents, Social Democrats, Communists, and trade unionists did not diminish. On the contrary, the brutal ruthlessness of the Nazi state became more obvious and shocking. This gradually encouraged an increasing number of hesitant optimists and cautious fence-sitters to reconsider.

Year after year, hundreds of Jewish residents of Munich left their hometown. By the end of 1939, nearly 6,000 had emigrated abroad, and the Jewish community had lost more than half of its members.[26] The social structural change of the Jewish community due to emigration was serious for those who remained. The majority of those who left were able-bodied and well-educated young people. For them, the risks of an uncertain future in a foreign country were easier to bear than for the older generation. A new start in an unfamiliar country requires courage, strength, optimism, and assertiveness— qualities that are more typical of younger people. The potential host countries, imposing strict and increasingly restrictive immigration regulations, ensured that not only the elderly but also the sick, noncontributors, and the asset-less were barred from crossing their borders. In June 1938, potential host countries discussed their future receptivity to Jewish refugees at a conference in Évian-les-Bains, France. An understanding in the sense of a humanitarian and generous, general immigration policy failed to materialize.[27] The hurdles to emigration remained high and were insurmountable for many in Germany, which caused fear tantamount to a death sentence.[28] Among those who remained behind in Munich, the proportion of the elderly, the sick, and those in need of support increased. Added to this was a sharply declining birth rate since 1933, which further exacerbated the already dramatic aging of the Jewish community in the Bavarian capital.[29] The community's welfare system and inner-Jewish solidarity were put to the test by these developments because the financial resources of the religious community, which was harassed by the Nazi authorities, simply could not meet the growing needs of those who were suffering from the state's systematic campaigns of economic, political, and ethnic persecution. The municipal welfare office, under its director Friedrich Hilble,[30] acted as a pioneer for Reich-wide legal frameworks to exclude Jews from state aid.[31] Munich's political leadership was also particularly in a hurry to demolish synagogues. The initiative for the demolition of the main synagogue in Herzog-Max-Strasse, built in 1887 in the center of the city and at that time the third largest in Germany, came from Hitler himself in early June 1938—months before the night of pogroms in which most synagogues fell victim to the Nazis' destructive fury. The act of destruction was carried out by the Bavarian Minister of the Interior and Gauleiter Adolf Wagner[32] and by the City of Munich (see figure 0.4). Again, the Nazis used Munich as a test case to assess public attitudes concerning the city's Jewish population. The result was clear. In 1938, the hostility toward Jews—or rather the degree of indifference—was so high that the pogroms on November 9th and 10th could be initiated without resistance from the German population.[33]

In order to escape the pressure of persecution, increasing disenfranchisement, and social and economic exclusion, and to be able to lead a self-determined and secured life abroad—free from the German police and bureaucratic arbitrariness—emigrants accepted considerable sacrifices and restrictions. To obtain permission to leave the country, for example, they had to pay high taxes to the Nazi state. Already in 1931 Germany had enacted a *Reichsfluchtsteuer* or Reich Flight Tax to prevent capital flight abroad. The Nazi government abused this instrument for the plundering of Jewish emigrants by requiring them to hand over a quarter of their assets to German tax authorities. Even emigrants to Palestine were made to pay through the Ha'avara Agreement,[34] which required them to deposit at least 1,000 pounds sterling. And that was not all. Many were unable to avoid selling large parts of their property at dumping prices to "Aryan" interested parties. Businesses, law firms, and medical practices were ceded for small amounts of money to non-Jewish successors who profited from the plight of those willing to

Figure 0.4 On Adolf Hitler's Personal Orders, Munich's Main Synagogue Was Demolished in the First Days of June 1938. It was the first synagogue to be destroyed in Nazi Germany. *Source:* Stadtarchiv München.

emigrate. This "Aryanization" of assets from Jewish property, carried out between 1933 and 1945, was surely one of the largest state-legitimized extortions in modern history.[35] While the economic pressuring and plundering of Jewish citizens was initially a process that took place without any significant official regulation, the state increasingly took the lead as the most important actor and profiteer in this "Aryanization" from 1938 onward. But state-organized transfers of assets took place largely out of public sight. The covetousness was directed not only at businesses and commercial enterprises but also at private assets. Bank deposits, securities accounts, jewelry and objects made of precious metals, art collections, libraries, furniture and household goods, houses, apartments, and land were gradually seized from their Jewish owners.

Such favorable opportunities for exploiting Jewish assets generated an opportunist mood among many members of the *Volksgemeinschaft.* This "national community" was an idea envisioned by the National Socialists for the reorganization of society as a racially unified and hierarchically organized body, in which the interests of individuals would be strictly subordinate to those of the nation, or *Volk,* and to which only the "hereditarily valuable" and "racially pure" Germans would belong. "Foreign peoples" and "aliens to the community," above all the Jews, were to be excluded. In this hunt for profits, state institutions, party officials, and ordinary citizens developed into shameless "bargain hunters." The transfers of assets favored countless Munich citizens, companies, institutions, and administrations who actively promoted or knowingly profited from these expropriations targeting Jewish neighbors, Jewish companies, and Jewish competitors.

After 1933, the intensification and escalation of murderous Nazi persecution directly increased Jewish emigration. The connection is unmistakably reflected in emigration statistics (see figure 0.5).[36] Like the seizure of power in 1933 and the state-led "boycott action" in April of that year, the passing of the Nuremberg Laws[37] in 1935 led to a gradual increase in emigration. However, the greatest impact was from the escalation of violence that occurred during *Kristallnacht*,[38] the night of November 9–10, 1938, when Jewish persons and properties were attacked with unprecedented brutality throughout the German Reich. Despite the organized nature of these state-sponsored pogroms, Nazi propaganda portrayed the violence as an outburst of "spontaneous national rage." In the months following these acts of terror, which signified an open and public demonstration of the Nazis' brutal anti-Jewish policies, more people than ever before left the country.[39] In 1939, nearly 2,300 men, women, and children who faced persecution as Jews turned their backs on their hometown of Munich, which no longer seemed their home.[40]

Though emigration saved their lives, the German-Jewish refugees lost a lot in the process. By fleeing Germany, they left behind nearly their entire social and cultural frame of reference. Leaving their own cultural circle went hand in hand with largely silencing their mother tongue. This loss was felt

Figure 0.5   Emigration from Munich, 1933–1943. *Source:* Created by Editors.

particularly by poets, publicists, and academics, for whom language was at once a marker of identity, a means for expression, and an indispensable instrument of professional communication. For Schalom Ben-Chorin,[41] the poet and religious philosopher born Fritz Rosenthal in Munich in 1913, who emigrated to Palestine in 1935, this was the definite and most sobering aspect of his flight:

> One can leave a country, break off relations with its people, but language is so much a part of our own existence that there can be no separation from that. [. . .] I never forsook my [native] language, and I write these memoirs even today in that language which did not wither within me.[42]

The Nazi regime wanted to get rid of the Jewish Germans as quickly as possible, but grueling bureaucratic harassment made it difficult for those willing to emigrate to leave the country. Countless visits to the authorities had to be completed, applications had to be filed, forms had to be filled out, and evidence had to be provided. And despite the support of friends and relatives as well as Jewish charities, concerns loomed about securing a livelihood in a new homeland. Professional qualifications acquired in Germany would not guarantee an easy new start in every case. Lawyers moving to Anglo-Saxon countries, for example, were forced to familiarize themselves with an unfamiliar legal system; this also required perfect language skills. A look at the advertising pages of the *Bayerische Israelitische Gemeinde-Zeitung* (Bavarian Jewish Community Newspaper) from the 1930s shows that, in addition to teaching skills that could prove useful in the new environment, a wide range of language courses and vocational training programs were being offered. In mid-October 1938, for example, a "New York teacher" in Munich advertised "United States English and American Stenography classes." This was listed alongside numerous other language courses, a six-month "training course for radio technicians," and – as a "foreign occupation for ladies"– training in "making made-to-measure corsets," and an intensive course in "marcelling, water waves, and perms" and manicures.[43] Two weeks later, in addition to language and conversation courses, more posts appeared to advertise cooking and baking classes, "training in arts and crafts, metal, wood, leather," and "tailoring and sewing courses."[44]

In this context, it is important to highlight two institutions that were especially significant for many Munich emigrants at the end of the 1930s: The *Kochschule Albert Schwarz* (Albert Schwarz Cooking School) and the *Jüdische Anlernwerkstätten* (Jewish Vocational Training Workshops). Both were committed to providing young people and adults with basic skills for popular professions to prepare them for a new career abroad. Albert Schwarz,[45] the founder

Figure 0.6 **"Apprentices" of the Albert Schwarz Cooking School during a Break, 1938.**
Source: Stadtarchiv München.

of the cooking school, had run a kosher restaurant in Munich's Schlosserstrasse until the end of 1937. In 1938, he applied to the municipal school department for approval of a baking and cooking course for Jewish participants. Although the authorities rejected new Jewish institutions as a matter of principle, this application was approved because it was hoped that the training measures would encourage Jewish emigration and build professional qualifications required for their entry into many host countries.[46] While Schwarz was in charge of the training program, a former business trustee Richard Baum,[47] who was a silent partner in the school, took over the management of the company. When the training center opened in April 1938, demand was enormous, despite substantial tuition costs (see figure 0.6). For September and October 1938 alone, 240 people from all over Germany registered. The courses offered by the school consisted of one cooking course each for cold and hot dishes, two confectionery courses, a praline course, a serving and waitressing course, a butchering course, a baking course, and an ice cream preparation course, which was only held in the summer. Course fees varied from RM 50 for the cold food preparation course to as much as RM 95 for the cooking course. After *Kristallnacht*, the cooking school was officially closed, but it was reopened shortly thereafter and continued for a few months (until mid-1939), despite adverse circumstances and harassment by the authorities. By then, the school was under a non-Jewish trustee but was still conducted in the spirit of its founders, thus enabling many more people willing to emigrate to acquire culinary knowledge and training.[48]

Manual skills were particularly important for emigration to South America, where, unlike the United Kingdom or United States, demand remained high for locksmiths, electricians, carpenters, and other manual trades.[49] As early as the summer of 1936, the Association of Bavarian Jewish Communities applied for the establishment of a "training school for the education of Jewish youths as craftsmen" in an abandoned leather factory at Biederstein. Despite lack of official approval, teaching began in August 1937. Modern machines for metal and wood processing were available as well as an abundant stock of materials. In addition to their practical training, the apprentices received 12 to 15 hours of instruction per week in arithmetic, tools, materials, technical drawing, accounting, business correspondence, and economics. In the 1938/1939 school year, 91 young people attended the institute. Adults willing to leave the country were also taught welding and furniture making. In 1939, however, the building was confiscated and the training workshops closed. Following instructions from the Munich *Stapoleitstelle*,[50] the facility was moved to the former synagogue on Reichenbachstrasse, the interior of which had been destroyed during *Kristallnacht*. In the next two years, about 100 Jewish youths received training

Figure 0.7 **Jewish Apprentices in the Training Workshops at Reichenbachstrasse 27, ca. 1941**. *Source:* Stadtarchiv München.

there (see figure 0.7). At the beginning of 1942, the facility was dissolved by the Gestapo; the tools and machines were given to a Hitler Youth school.[51]

A survey of the emigrants' destination countries from Munich reveals a striking picture. Almost half of all Jewish Munich emigrants sought a new life in Europe. The most important European host country was Great Britain, where around 15.43 percent of all Munich emigrants[52] found a temporary or permanent home.[53] This remarkably high number was due to changes in immigration policy in the UK as well as the *Kindertransporte* or children's transports, with which the British government and various aid organizations rescued persecuted minors after the violent excesses of *Kristallnacht*.[54] In Palestine, the restrictive immigration policy of the British mandate authorities was responsible for a highly regulated influx of persecuted German Jews. Immigrants were expected above all to have agricultural or domestic skills and a command of the Hebrew language, which meant that many emigrants interested in settling in Palestine had little prospect of doing so without attending appropriate *Hachshara* courses. These were classes that focused exclusively on agricultural or vocational training in preparation for emigration, usually in the form of compact courses. Nonetheless, as many as 11.31 percent of all the emigrants from Munich[55] were able to settle in Palestine.[56]

While most of the Jewish emigrants from Nazi Germany initially fled to other European countries and Palestine, the United States increasingly became the preferred country of immigration as Nazism tightened its hold. For those desperately seeking refuge in the 1930s, the United States stood for freedom and democracy. The country's credo promised liberty, safety, and well-being. Yet, grave domestic problems in the United States, together with a public opinion that was, at best, largely indifferent to international problems, resulted in a restrictive immigration policy that stood in stark contrast to the years preceding the 1880s, when practically all who sought entry to the United States were welcomed.[57]

Researchers often argue that World War I marked sudden discontinuation of the age of Jewish mass migration and led to increased sedentarism. In the case of the United States, the process was more gradual and closely tied to the passage of three immigration laws that fundamentally changed the legal basis for immigration. The first act, passed in 1917, defined basic restrictions on immigration and specified the various categories of aliens who should be excluded: for example, physical, mental, or moral defects (however defined) could bar entry, as well as political or economic factors.[58] Next, major steps were taken toward overturning the traditional open-door policy and essentially closing the gates to all but a favored few during the years 1921 and 1924, when the United States introduced a quota system that regulated immigration according to its own national population as of 1890. This was a new means of regulation, which defined "wanted" and "unwanted" migrants by national origin. This policy also required that emigrants had to arrange to be admitted at an American consulate in the country of origin before they left.[59]

The Great Depression amplified demands for additional requirements and reductions. This explains why even after Hitler's rise to power in Germany, when a growing number of applications were made for entry to the United States due to antisemitic events in the German Reich, American policy continued to focus on a gradual and limited wave of emigration rather than on solving a refugee crisis. For example, a stricter interpretation by the State Department of the "likely to become a public charge" (LPC) clause (first included in a law in 1882) was initiated during the autumn of 1930. The clause stated that no visa should be issued to anyone who was "unlikely to obtain a job under current market conditions." This proved to be an extremely effective tool for preventing the entry of refugees without the need for legislative action. Indeed, these new rules were among the most effective means by which the US State Department, through the American consuls, could administratively regulate the extent of immigration. For the thousands of Jews who began to seek escape from Nazi Germany, this rigorous enforcement of the LPC clause presented an enormous challenge. It also vividly illustrates that the Roosevelt administration, while publicly expressing sympathy for the victims of Nazi persecution, in practice did everything it could to restrict immigration.[60]

It was not only US refugee policy in the 1930s and 1940s, however, that determined the fate of those who had been declared targets of Nazi hatred, persecution, and terror. Much depended on the inner workings of American consulates in Nazi Germany, as it was the US consuls abroad who were given, as specified in the 1924 act, sole responsibility for issuing visas. Those officials thus played a crucial role in implementing immigration policy between 1933 and 1941. The fact that the United States did not distinguish between immigrants and refugees meant that those desperately trying to escape Germany had to go through a deliberate and slow immigration process and often experienced great difficulty in persuading a consul to assess the financial, political, and moral reliability of the applicant. In order to obtain a visa, the prospective immigrant was required to present a valid passport, a police clearance certificate, a certificate from the health department, duplicates of all relevant personal information, and a thorough financial statement, as well as an affidavit from relatives or a friend listing the total assets of the immigrant's guarantor and the specific percentage of support expected from that sponsor. For Munich's Jews, the procurement of visas and quota numbers was additionally complicated by the fact that those wishing to emigrate from Munich had to go to the US consulate in Stuttgart, which entailed time-consuming and costly trips to Württemberg, often in vain. Only in late 1938, after the *Anschluss* of Austria in March, the failed Évian Conference in July, and *Kristallnacht* in November, did the US government allow more flexibility in granting temporary permits for visitors and in the handling of paper requirements by the consuls. Notwithstanding these measures, the consuls, who aimed to prevent immigration as much as possible, acted as "gatekeepers." They held the keys to the path toward security for those seeking refuge, for it was the consul's interpretation of the law that determined who qualified for an immigrant visa.[61]

Nevertheless, the United States remained a strong option for Jews seeking emigration from Munich. As many as 31.98 percent of all the Jewish emigrants from the Bavarian capital[62] managed to meet the strict American entry requirements. In total, the United States granted immigrant visas to 129,600 people from Germany and Austria between 1933 and 1941, of whom 81,500 (or 68 percent) self-identified as Jews by religion.[63] It was, however, not until 1938–1939 that the US immigration quota for Germany and Austria was filled, mainly because of the many limiting rules and regulations regarding who was allowed to immigrate and the bureaucratic obstacles imposed by the consuls. Between 1938 and 1941, some 55,000 Jewish refugees from Germany and Austria entered the United States.[64] In fact, the mostly German and Austrian Jews who made it to the United States in 1939 accounted for more than 50 percent of the general immigration to the country that year.[65]

It seems that immigrants who sought swift integration into new homes had a very different experience than those who fled Germany but did not initially seek to remain abroad. The absorptive process of integration is most closely associated with the United States and was particularly successful with the first wave of refugees who left following the ascension of the National Socialists. The fact that most of the German immigrants who arrived in the middle of the 1930s had been educated beyond the elementary school level (nearly half had attended college or graduate school) was one significant feature that distinguished them from former immigrants. Their educational backgrounds combined with their generally cosmopolitan outlook—many had traveled widely and knew languages other than their own—also might have aided them in their integration. A second wave of refugees followed at the end of the 1930s. Unlike the earlier wave of immigrants, those who came to the United States in the years immediately preceding the war and later from German-occupied countries generally did not fare as well. This was primarily because of their demographic and economic profiles and the adverse circumstances. Many refugees had only a few dollars in their pockets when they arrived in their host country, and very few of them were able to immediately find a job in the profession they had learned (most had to settle for low-paying, entry-level jobs). Most of the new arrivals were dependent on help from relatives and aid organizations, at least for a while. Younger people generally found it easier to deal with uprooting than older people. In the United States in particular, many

who immigrated as children or youths were able to eventually build successful careers. It should also be noted that, overall, women found it easier than
men to gain an economic foothold in the new environment.[66]

For many newcomers to the United States, the fact that their place of refuge
was (not without reason) considered the immigration country *par excellence*
may have contributed to their integration. US integration processes had a
different dynamic, proceeded more smoothly, and were less prone to conflict
than in the classic European nation-states, with their largely homogeneous
linguistic and cultural populations. In addition, a fairly well-organized
American Jewish communal system and other relief and welfare organizations were present and willing to support the newcomers. Despite some
publicly stated concerns expressed by various interest groups about this wave
of immigration, particularly focused on rising unemployment (especially in
the professions and white-collar industries), a coalition of long-established
Jewish charities, non-Jewish organizations, and the government created an
emergency system to absorb German-Jewish mass immigration. The overall intent was to facilitate integration while avoiding harm to the American
economy.[67]

What this overview of the emigration destinations of Jewish Munich residents
between 1933 and 1942[68] does not show is the fact that hardly any emigrants
were able to determine the destination of their journey themselves. Against
the background of steadily increasing numbers of emigrants from Germany,
many countries tightened their entry regulations and set admission quotas.
Those who had only modest financial means, who could not name relatives or
contact persons as guarantors or sponsors in the emigration countries, or who
were old, sick, or did not have the professional qualifications required by the
destination countries were confronted with great, and sometimes insurmountable, difficulties when attempting to obtain the necessary entry documents. For
nearly 3,000 Jewish residents of Munich, an escape abroad thus remained out
of reach. Many were targets when the Nazi regime worked to systematically
remove Jewish tenants from their apartments. In Munich, a large barracks camp
was built on the northern outskirts of the city for this purpose and also in preparation for the deportations (see figure 0.8). Starting in November 1941, Jewish
residents of Munich were deported to concentration and extermination camps.[69]

Some Jews resisted the orders for deportation. But only a few Jews survived in Munich in hiding or by assuming a false identity.[70] Others did not
have to go into hiding to escape deportation, but they could never be sure
whether their stay in the Reich would be cut short. Even the German rulers
were not in agreement about the fate of intermarried Jews and *Mischlinge* and
Geltungsjuden, which meant that the lives of those so classified were marked
by constant fear and uncertainty.[71] By now, we know from recent research
that life in a "privileged" and supposedly protected "mixed marriage" was

Figure 0.8   Jewish Men Were Forced to Help with the Construction of the Barracks Camp at Knorrstrasse 148, 1941. *Source:* Stadtarchiv München.

also associated with considerable stress and grave uncertainties for both Jewish and their non-Jewish spouses.[72] For others, fleeing to other European countries was only a temporary solution. For many Munich residents, permanent safety in France, Belgium, the Netherlands, or Italy was merely an illusion. The invasion of German troops and the collaboration of local administrations with the occupiers meant a death sentence for countless exiled German Jews.[73]

For those who found refuge in a safe third country, the term "home" took on a new quality. The bitterness with which one remembered one's roots and the time before one was expelled from Germany was in many cases closely linked to a longing for that place which once was "home" and simultaneously was perceived as painful. In addition, the ever-widening war in Europe and the growing fear for relatives and friends who had not (yet) been able to escape from Germany burdened many Jewish Germans in exile. Just like non-Jewish emigrants, many followed current developments in their former homeland with skepticism and concern, but at the same time emphasized that they never wanted to set foot on German soil again because of the exclusion they had experienced, the loss of their prior property, and the deprivation of rights and degradation they had suffered in their homeland. Only a few decided to actively participate in the fight against the "Third Reich." These volunteered for military service and returned to Germany as soldiers, clergymen, or field rabbis with the Allied forces.[74]

After the Allied victory over the Nazi regime, one of the main reasons (and for many, the sole reason) for fleeing to another European country or overseas had disappeared. A return to the old homeland was suddenly within the realm of possibility.[75] European Jews who had fled their homes and found a safe haven abroad were thus confronted with another, initially unsettling situation. Would the host countries that had accepted refugees on the premise that they would return to their place of origin when the Nazi regime fell expect them to leave or move on? Could one, as a former outcast, trust the Germans again after all that had happened and relocate to mostly destroyed postwar Germany? Was it time to tear up the roots they had put down or grow them deeper into the soil of their second *Heimat*? Was there an obligation for those who had persevered in exile to fill the voids created by their departure and contribute to the establishment of democratic structures in post-1945 Germany?[76]

Exiles not only had to continue to negotiate the emotional difficulties, practical problems, and existential issues associated with starting over; the postwar challenges emigrants faced were as diverse as their exile experiences. After all, many refugees found themselves at the end of the war without a clear sense of where they belonged. Family issues dominated the postwar adjustment, and even those who were fortunate enough to find relatives often had great difficulty putting the family back together. For a variety of reasons, family reunification and the resumption of family life did not always succeed, just as there was no "solution" to the finality of death.[77]

As was the case for the majority of German Jews who escaped to the United States between 1933 and 1945, the number of Munich Jews who fled to the United States and wanted to settle back in their former homeland after the end of the war was small. At the same time, however, it was impossible for most of them, as for many emigrants, to completely detach themselves from their former homeland. Some returned as members of the Allied forces and employees of international aid organizations; it was primarily interpreters, lawyers, and journalists (some of whom later worked at the Nuremberg Trials[78]) who were initially granted permission to enter and resettle within the Allied occupation zones.[79] It was only a few years later, after the founding of the Federal Republic, that further developments occurred, for example, the passing of the federal laws on compensation (*Wiedergutmachung*) for victims of Nazi persecution (1953 and 1956),[80] which saw many German and German-Jewish emigrants return to their old homeland for varying lengths of time. The legal proceedings made possible on the basis of these laws were often lengthy and emotionally very stressful for those affected. About 45 percent of Jewish emigrants returned to Germany temporarily during the period of reparation negotiations. The so-called sojourners, most of whom returned to the country of exile after completing their personal restitution proceedings, had a significant impact on this period.[81] From 1960, Jewish emigrants also repeatedly traveled back to their old homeland at the invitation of the cities from which they had been expelled. Munich, for instance, was the first West German city to organize visitation programs for emigrants starting in 1960—an example that was to be followed by numerous other cities and that still makes it possible for former Munich residents to visit their hometown today. Interestingly, it was sometimes these visits that connected former Munich residents with the city archive and inspired them to write memoirs.[82]

What personal narratives illustrate more than almost any other source is the fact that the story of refugees is one of adaptation and adjustment, often marked by anxiety and fear as well as loss and loneliness. Moreover, the experiences of individual refugees show that emigration is not limited to the moment when groups and individuals move from one place to another, but is a complex, ongoing process that is also characterized by the dynamics of transmigration, the dominance of migrant networks, and the complex relationship between national politics and migrants' agency. Many Jewish refugees fleeing Nazi Germany lost their homes, language, families, roots, and sense of belonging to their homeland, and managed the unbelievable: they survived, moved on, built lives.[83]

Today, the voices of those able to share their personal experiences of persecution, flight, expulsion, deportation, and new beginnings have almost fallen silent. However, more than 75 years after the end of World War II and the liberation of the extermination camp at Auschwitz, we may readily find that the history of Nazi Germany and the monstrous crimes against humanity during the *Shoah* remain very prominent in current political and remembrance-cultural discourses. Moreover, though those historical events have come to an end, and politicians and historians have incorporated them into the canon of a broader historical narrative, for younger generations of people who lived (and continue to live) among and after the victims, these historical events painfully remain a part of their own history. Those temporally distant events continue to define, to some extent, living people's positions in society.

But it is not only historians and politicians who shape a community's image of history and its culture of remembrance. Often, an interested and critical public become the protagonists, especially historically interested individuals and civil society groups. They develop central questions, many falling outside the mainstream of academic-university interests, and confront political agendas with demands for adequate answers to historical entanglements. Any public discourse on the right way to deal with the Nazi past and the challenges of (forced) migration and refugee integration is also an expression of a developed civil society that strives for historical competence and historical sensitivity. However, there is no automatic guarantee that the maintenance of specific aspects of history will be continued and presented responsibly. In view of the dwindling number of eyewitnesses, we all have a special responsibility to keep asking ourselves how we want to deal with this particular history at the beginning of the 20th century and what lessons we can learn from the history of refugees' daily lives and emotions with regard to refugee crises, whether historical or contemporary. We owe this ongoing effort especially to those who were excluded and forcibly expelled from their *Heimat* after 1933. Their voices can be heard in this book.

ABOUT THE BOOK

German Jews and Migration to the United States, 1933–1945 brings together a collection of first-person narratives of flight and exile, many never before published.[84] Unlike comprehensive studies on the topic,[85] this volume contains a concise selection of 16 autobiographical primary source texts by German Jews on their migration to the United States in the years 1933–1945. Readers may study these firsthand accounts to understand the often traumatic, life-changing, and individual experiences of forced migration, expulsion, displacement, and new beginnings in the United States—the country that welcomed the largest number of refugees from Nazi Germany and Austria, about 129,000 to 132,000 people in total.[86]

When examined critically, personal testimonies such as the letters and memoirs included in this volume can serve as valuable historical sources. Fortunately, they have gained in importance since the 1990s, especially with regard to research on everyday life during the "Third Reich."[87] These accounts illuminate the experiences of Jewish women, men, and children, each focusing on recollections that other types of sources, especially records handed down by the perpetrators, cannot provide. Given the many shortfalls associated with more traditional documentary sources for analyzing events from the perspective of the persecuted, letters and memoirs written by German Jews who lived during the 1930s and Holocaust survivors fill innumerable gaps. Aside from personal information, the individual impressions, informal mannerisms, and relationships between individuals that may be discerned help historians and all interested readers to better understand what it was actually like to be the victims. There is usually little human information about them in official (i.e., party, perpetrator, communal, or state) sources.[88]

Due to the challenges posed by Holocaust memoirs that are associated with hindsight and potential distortions of memory, editors oftentimes have opted to center their collections of contemporary witness statements on reports, memoranda, letters, diaries, poems, and photographs. Because of their subjectivity and the narrative constructions that arise in retrospective writing, memoirs in particular have been repeatedly criticized by scholars and questioned as to how reliable such accounts are, especially those written many years after the events they describe.[89] Certainly, a point worth emphasizing here is that personal recollections are not an analytical or conceptual history of the Holocaust (nor can they substitute for that historiography); they rather serve as a reservoir of testimonial information. Scholars also widely agree that personal accounts, though presented as a retelling of private experiences, may contain information about events that the author did not directly witness; they are often supplemented with information drawn from the stories of others, newspaper articles, or monographs; and they may contain contradictions regarding chronology, persons, and/or details within an "established" course of events. This is not always a bad thing, though corroboration of stated "facts" can be difficult (as with any unique historical source). But despite these (and other) challenges, the study of Holocaust memoirs as a form of Holocaust history and memory is important because, at the least, the emotional content and human interest of the testimonies is a useful record of attitudes amid and toward hard events.[90]

To partly fill an information gap in existing published sourcebooks, this volume therefore focuses exclusively on Holocaust memoirs and intentionally juxtaposes selected passages from those recollections written later in life with excerpts from contemporary correspondence. Letters from those who successfully emigrated are among the most valuable and reliable sources of information about the journey, the new places encountered, and the experiences and social and economic conditions for the newcomers in the foreign land. Letters from those trapped in Nazi Germany, though subject to strict censorship, are among the most telling testimonies of conditions "at home." They provide details about the increasing persecution and threat to life for those persecuted as Jews and their increasingly desperate efforts to find a means of emigration or escape, especially since the outbreak of the war, more and more often without success. Although usually a two-way exchange, when letters were sent in both directions, often only one side of the exchange survived. But even with omissions in the surviving records, it is clear that these letters held great personal significance for those who exchanged them and helped both the writers and recipients alike, at least in part, to overcome the isolation experienced in the foreign country and/or to make the enforced separation from loved ones somewhat less painful. We should be aware that many times, information conveyed in letters was already outdated by the time they arrived or was simply factually incorrect. But again, even though letters alone do not paint the whole picture of the related events befalling the parties involved, their special value lies in the preservation of the contemporary emotions and daily-life details which enhance the modern reader's view of those times. It also is always best to keep in mind that we may now know the fate of the writers and their subsequent life situations (the collection of biographies presents some of this), but that such knowledge was as yet unknown to the original correspondents. The letters, if not the memoirs, are snapshots of moments during a flow of time.[91]

For easier accessibility, all personal accounts included in this book have been carefully edited, extensively annotated, and provided with a biographical introduction about the author. Brief historical explanations of the context in which the memoirs and letters were written are also offered. This book emphasizes the fact that Holocaust survivors wrote under conditions that differed greatly from those of their pre-exile lives, and that the authors were burdened by the enormity of all that befell or was currently happening to them, and to the Jewish people more broadly. The inclusion of letters with contemporary descriptions of Jewish responses to persecution is intended to remind readers that for much of the Nazi era, observers amid these events had no idea where things would lead.

The selection presented in this reader was not made to favor one source over another, but to present documents that both speak for themselves and also relate to each other. This is one of the main reasons why all the authors of these ego-documents share two key similarities. They all had close ties to the Bavarian capital Munich, and they all emigrated from that cultural hub in the south of Germany during the Nazi regime to the United States, though some traveled there via detours and/or following stays of varying lengths in other places of refuge. It is the special significance of Munich and the United States in the history of 20th-century migration that led to the decision to highlight these two geographical areas. No other German city was as closely associated with the rise of National Socialism as the former seat of the party leadership and "capital of the movement."[92] Using the party organizations controlled from Munich, the Nazi state achieved a high degree of efficiency in penetrating and bringing society into line. The party bureaucracy, prominently located in Munich, was not a redundant administration but a powerful instigator with considerable influence in shaping society. The more than 10,000 Jews who lived in Munich felt this very strongly. They sat in the front row, so to speak, and were important witnesses who reported from their own experiences both the rise of the National Socialists as a politically effective force and the persecution measures they implemented against Jews. Munich was a key area during the rise of the Nazi Party, and the United States was one of the most important countries of exile for Jewish refugees from the German Reich as well as a driving force in 20th-century immigration policy. Thus, this regionally focused primary source collection provides readers an in-depth introduction to a specific place of origin and a significant place of refuge, and offers a set of personal accounts to provide detailed, case-specific information.

The accounts are by former Munich residents and were mostly compiled by the Munich City Archives.[93] Since the early 1990s, the Munich City Archives has built a "Judaica" collection, which now offers considerable scope. More than 3,000 photographs of people, families, and places from the second half of the 19th century to the present provide exciting insights into family life and the everyday lives of former Munich residents. Of special interest are the personal materials of various provenance that are preserved here: correspondences and diaries, as well as papers and other donations from survivors and descendants of people who once lived in Munich. These collections can help to generate new perspectives on the diversity of Jewish life and are an important set of sources for reconstructing the everyday reality and results of Jewish persecution in Munich during the Nazi regime. The handwritten manuscripts, typewritten texts, and digital memoirs (archived in more recent years) came to the City Archives in very different ways. Some Munich emigrants or their descendants were prompted to write their personal memoirs by a visit to their former homeland or after holding conversations with staff working in the City Archives. Others felt the need to record their experiences in English for their children and grandchildren while still in their place of refuge. Many also used their familiar German mother tongue to record their experiences for posterity. The contributions collected in this volume are as diverse as the memoirs and letters in the collection of the archives. They vary in length, and the thematic foci are diverse; there is also a wide range in the timing of recording the authors' experiences and their ages.

The individual memoirs and correspondences collected in this volume are reproduced either in full or, in the case of extensive manuscripts, as excerpts. The primary themes of part I are childhood and youth in Munich at the beginning of the 20th century and exclusion, discrimination, and persecution during the Nazi regime. Part II largely addresses the years of emigration and new beginnings, which the writers encountered as part of their exile. In their diversity, these autobiographical testimonies represent a broad spectrum of individual experiences. Arranged chronologically according to the birth date of the authors, the collection depicts their testimonies about losing one's homeland, flight, expulsion, arriving in a foreign country, and also living, working, marrying, and raising a family. Also conveyed are their sadness, loneliness, joy, and hopes, which will enable readers to relate in a personal way to these events of the past and will promote a deeper understanding of this history as a series of human events.

Eleven of the texts printed here were originally written in English; this demonstrates a remarkable linguistic integration of the authors into their new homeland. The original German-language texts, both memoirs and letters, appear in English translation.[94] Editorial interventions in the texts were avoided wherever possible. In order not to interfere with the peculiarities and unique characteristics of autobiographical writing, only obvious spelling errors have been corrected. This explains, among other things, the different spelling of proper names and holidays as well as foreign-language terms. Supplementary explanations and further information can be found in the notes at the end of each chapter and the glossary inserted at the end of the book (see Appendix 1). Unless otherwise noted, the explanations of persons mentioned in the texts are based on information derived from the memoirs themselves or from the database of the *Biografisches Gedenkbuch der Münchner Juden 1933 bis 1945* (Biographical Memorial Book of Munich Jews), maintained by the Munich City Archives.[95] Since this volume uses the database of the Munich City Archives as a source of data, it defines as "Jewish"—following the definition of the Memorial Book—anyone who was persecuted as a Jew under the National Socialists' racial legislation. Although this approach adopts the perpetrator definition and disregards the self-attributions of the individuals, this method seems necessary to depict the situation of persecution under National Socialist rule. A "Munich resident" is defined as someone who had lived in the city for at least 12 months. People who only stayed in Munich temporarily, for example, to prepare for their emigration or to complete a short training course, are not included. In some exceptional cases, personal names mentioned in the text have been anonymized by the editors to protect personal rights. Detailed information on the published memoirs and pictorial materials as well as references to translations and copyrights are summarized in the source commentary and picture credits (see Appendix 2).

Compared to the approximately 8,000 Jewish citizens who emigrated from the Bavarian capital, the number of memoirs preserved in the Munich City Archives—66 autobiographical testimonies—seems small. The vast majority of emigrants remained silent or shared their exile experiences only with family or friends. Their life stories remain hidden to scholars and the public. This underscores the importance of the memoirs published in this book. These individual accounts of experiences, personal snapshots, and subjective assessments and evaluations draw our attention to an aspect of the history of persecution that has long been unjustly marginalized: the experience of exile. Ultimately, and in line with trends in the fields of American Jewish history and Jewish migration history more generally,[96] this book is intended to inspire readers to critically evaluate the dynamics and significance of transmigration, the role of migrant networks, and the complex relationship between national policies and the migrants' agency, both then and now. Currently, the relative freedom of global movement has once again vanished, and heated debates focusing on issues of immigration and integration are not only bringing this issue back into the public eye but also back into our homes and university classrooms.

NOTES

1. The German term *Heimat* literally translates to "home" or "homeland," but it implies a much deeper idea and describes a feeling, a strong sense of belonging. It is a place, village community, landscape, and so on where one feels comfortable, where one is understood, and for which one longs when away. It can also describe political or social milieus. See Peter Blickle, *Heimat: A Critical Theory of the German Idea of Homeland* (Rochester: Camden House, 2002); Friederike Eigler and Jens Kugele, eds. *Heimat: At the Intersection of Memory and Space* (Berlin: De Gruyter, 2012).

2. Charlotte Stein-Pick, "Die verlorene Heimat." Unpublished Memoir [1964]. In *Leo Baeck Institute New York*, ME 619, MM 73, 000201092, DTLPID: 416859.

3. Personal testimonies such as memoirs and letters are an important source for research on the everyday life and persecution of Jews during the Nazi era. Age, gender, and time of writing are three central factors that shape the character of subjective memory. And even within a source genre, as in the case of memoirs, differences can be found depending on whether they were written before or after 1945 (i.e., whether the author still experienced the events or reported them retrospectively), the degree of emotionality (which is typically stronger the closer the writer is to the experiences recounted in the memoir), and the level of factual knowledge (often stronger if the memoir was written after years of reflection, as in the case of Charlotte Stein-Pick). For more information, see, for example, Anna Ullrich, *Von "jüdischem Optimismus" und "unausbleiblicher Enttäuschung": Erwartungsmanagement deutsch-jüdischer Vereine und gesellschaftlicher Antisemitismus 1914–1938* (Berlin: DeGruyter Oldenbourg, 2018); and Nicole Marrenbach, "Memoiren Münchner Juden als Quelle für die 'Arisierungs'-Forschung," *zeitenblicke* 3, no. 2 (2004), last modified September 13, 2004, http://www.zeitenblicke.historicum.net/2004/02/marrenbach/index.html.

4. Dietrich Orlow, *The Nazi Party, 1919–1945: A Complete History* (New York: Enigma, 2010).

5. For a short history of the "Third Reich," see, for example, Joseph W. Bendersky, *A Concise History of Nazi Germany*, 5th ed. (Lanham: Rowman & Littlefield Publishers, 2020); and Thomas Childers, *The Third Reich: The History of Nazi Germany* (New York: Simon & Schuster, 2017).

6. Victor Klemperer impressively describes these experiences in his diaries *Ich will Zeugnis ablegen bis zum letzten: Tagebücher, 1933–1945* (Berlin: Aufbau, 2015).

7. The estimate refers to those Jews whose return was recorded by Jewish communities in Germany. Monika Richarz, "Juden in der Bundesrepublik Deutschland und in der Deutschen Demokratischen Republik seit 1945," in *Jüdisches Leben in Deutschland seit 1945*, ed. Micha Brumlik et al. (Frankfurt/Main: Jüd. Verl. bei Athenäum, 1988), 19; Herbert A. Strauss, "Introductions: Jews in German History. Persecution, Emigration, Acculturation," in *International Biographical Dictionary of Central European Emigres 1933–1945, Vol. II/Part 1*, eds. Herbert Strauss and Werner Röder (Munich: Saur, 1983), esp. XV and XX–XXII.

8. Michael R. Marrus, *The Unwanted: European Refugees in the Twentieth Century* (New York: Oxford Univ. Press, 1985).

9. Ian Kershaw, *Hitler*, 2nd ed. (Harlow: Longman, 2001); and A. N. Wilson, *Hitler: A Short Biography* (London: HarperPress, 2012).

10. Paul von Hindenburg (1847–1934), German field marshal during World War I and second president of the Weimar Republic (1925–1934).

11. Sven Felix Kellerhoff, *Der Reichstagsbrand: Die Karriere eines Kriminalfalls* (Berlin: be.bra Verlag, 2008); Benjamin Carter Hett, *Burning the Reichstag: An Investigation into the Third Reich's Enduring Mystery* (Oxford: Oxford Univ. Press, 2014); and Molly Jean Loberg, *The Struggle for the Streets of Berlin: Politics, Consumption, and Urban Space, 1914–1945* (Cambridge: Cambridge Univ. Press, 2018), 199–242.

12. Karl Stützel (1872–1944), German politician of the Bavarian People's Party (Bayerische Volkspartei, BVP).

13. The "Brown House" (German: *Braunes Haus*) was the name of the Nazi party's headquarters building in Munich, Brienner Straße 34, which existed from 1930 to 1945. Andreas Heusler, *Das Braune Haus: Wie München zur "Hauptstadt der Bewegung" wurde* (Munich: DVA, 2008), 164ff.

14. Michael Siegel (1882–1979), lawyer. In August 1940, Michael Siegel and his wife fled to Peru via Los Angeles. Already in 1939, their children had emigrated to England, their daughter with a *Kindertransport* and their son with a study visa.

15. Heinrich Sanden, "'Das Foto ist von mir ...'," in *Die Gleichschaltung der Bilder: Zur Geschichte der Pressefotografie 1930–1936*, eds. Diethard Krebs, Walter Uka and Brigitte Walz-Richter (Berlin: Fröhlich & Kaufmann, 1983), 122–126.

16. Raul Hilberg, *Perpetrators, Victims, Bystanders: The Jewish Catastrophe, 1933–1945* (New York: HarperCollins, 1992); Robert M. Ehrenreich and Tim Cole, "The Perpetrator-Bystander-Victim Constellation: Rethinking Genocidal Relationships," *Human Organization* 64, no. 3 (2005): 213–224; Kristen Renwick Monroe, "Cracking the Code of Genocide: The Moral Psychology of Rescuers, Bystanders, and Nazis during the Holocaust," *Political Psychology* 29, no. 5 (2008): 699–736.

17. Saul Friedländer, *Nazi Germany and the Jews: The Years of Persecution, 1933–1939* (New York: HarperCollins, 1997), 17–26; Moshe Gottlieb, "The First of April Boycott and the Reaction of the American Jewish Community," *American Jewish Historical Quarterly* 57, no. 4 (June 1968): 516–517, 519–556; Christoph Kreutzmüller, *Final Sale in Berlin: The Destruction of Jewish Commercial Activity 1930–1945* (New York: Berghahn, 2015).

18. Heinrich Himmler (1900–1945), leading member of the Nazi Party; Reichsführer-SS (from 1929), Chief of the German Police (from 1934), also Reich Minister of the Interior (from 1943), and Commander of the Reserve Army (from 1944). He committed suicide after being captured by the Allies in 1945.

19. Wolfgang Benz and Angelika Königseder, eds., *Das Konzentrationslager Dachau: Geschichte und Wirkung nationalsozialistischer Repression* (Berlin: Metropol, 2008); Barbara Distel, *The Dachau Concentration Camp, 1933 to 1945: Text and Photo Documents from the Exhibition* (Munich: Lipp, 2005); and Harold Marcuse, *Legacies of Dachau: The Uses and Abuses of a Concentration Camp* (Cambridge: Cambridge Univ. Press, 2001).

20. Staatsarchiv München, Polizeidirektion 7006.

21. The infamous "Nuremberg Laws" of September 1935 (esp. the "Reich Citizenship Law" and the "Law for the Protection of German Blood and German Honor") severely restricted the civic rights of Jewish Germans. In particular, the ban on marriages between non-Jews and Jews deeply interfered with the privacy and personal autonomy of those concerned. Sexual intercourse between non-Jews and Jews, judged as "racial defilement," could now be prosecuted under criminal law. For more information, see Cornelia Essner, *Die "Nürnberger Gesetze" oder Die Verwaltung des Rassenwahns 1933–1945* (Paderborn: Schöningh, 2002).

22. Essner, *Die "Nürnberger Gesetze."*

23. According to calculations by the Munich City Archives (database for the Biographical Memorial Book of Munich Jews 1933–1945).

24. For more information and comparative analysis of policies regarding the refugees from Nazi Germany, see Frank Caestecker and Bob Moore, eds., *Refugees from Nazi Germany and the Liberal European States* (New York: Berghahn, 2010); Debóra Dwork and Robert Jan van Pelt, *Flight from the Reich: Refugee Jews, 1933–1946* (New York: Norton, 2009); Marion A. Kaplan, *Between Dignity and Despair: Jewish Life in Nazi Germany* (New York: Oxford Univ. Press, 1999); and Hagit Lavsky, *The Creation of the German-Jewish Diaspora: Interwar German-Jewish Immigration to Palestine, the USA, and England* (Berlin: DeGruyter, 2017).

25. Emil Goldschmidt (1878–1957) and his wife had two children. Following *Kristallnacht*, they applied for a visa to the United States but were given a waiting number much too high to get a visa in the foreseeable future. Palestine was only possible because relatives who were already living there spoke up for them.

26. According to calculations by the Munich City Archives.

27. Jochen Thies, *Évian 1938: Als die Welt die Juden verriet* (Essen: Klartext Verlag, 2017); Yehuda Bauer, *Jews for Sale? Nazi-Jewish Negotiations, 1933–1945* (New Haven: Yale Univ. Press, 1994), 30–43; Eva Schöck-Quinteros, Matthias Loeber, and Simon Rau, eds., *Keine Zuflucht. Nirgends: Die Konferenz von Evian und die Fahrt der St. Louis, 1938/39*, 2nd corr. and exp. ed. (Bremen: Institut für Geschichtswissenschaft, 2019).

28. Those Jews who did not find a way to leave the city before the borders of the Nazi state and the immigration host countries closed were later in mortal danger when deportations of Jewish residents from Munich began in November 1941. Stadtarchiv München, ed., "…verzogen, unbekannt wohin": Die erste Deportation von Münchner Juden im November 1941 (Zurich: Pendo, 2000).

29. According to calculations by the Munich City Archives.

30. Friedrich Hilble (1881–1937), Munich administrative officer and professional city councilor.

31. Florian Wimmer, *Die völkische Ordnung von Armut: Kommunale Sozialpolitik im nationalsozialistischen München* (Göttingen: Wallstein, 2014), 306–316.

32. Adolf Wagner (1890–1944), high-ranking Nazi party functionary, *Gauleiter* (regional leader) of the *Gau* (district) Munich-Upper Bavaria and, from March 9, 1933, Minister of the Interior in Bavaria.

33. Stadtarchiv München, ed., *Beth ha-Knesseth: Zur Geschichte der Münchner Synagogen, ihrer Rabbiner und Kantoren* (Munich: Buchendorfer Verlag, 1999).

34. Avraham Barkai, "German Interests in the Haavara-Transfer Agreement 1933–1939," *Leo Baeck Institute Yearbook* 35 (1990): 245–266.

35. Avraham Barkai, *From Boykott to Annihilation: The Economic Struggle of German Jews, 1933–1943* (Hanover: Univ. Press of New England, 1989), 13–138; Angelika Baumann and Andreas Heusler, eds., *München arisiert: Entrechtung und Enteignung der Juden in der NS-Zeit* (Munich: Beck, 2004).

36. According to most recent calculations (as of June 2021), at least 6,685 Jewish residents from Munich emigrated between 1933 and 1943, and their emigration destinations are known. Low or nonexistent emigration figures after 1941 are directly related to the emigration ban issued by the Nazi government in October 1941. Apart from 19 individual cases, Jews still living in Munich at that time had no possibility of circumventing this ban. For more information, see Katharina Bergmann, *Jüdische Emigration aus München: Entscheidungsfindung und Auswanderungswege (1933–1941)* (Munich; DeGruyter Oldenbourg, 2021).

37. Essner, *Die "Nürnberger Gesetze"*; Peter Longerich, *The Nazi Persecution and Murder of the Jews* (Oxford: Oxford Univ. Press, 2010), 52–89.

38. In nationwide pogroms in Germany between November 7 and 13, and especially on the night of November 9 to 10, 1938, half of the synagogues in Germany were subjected to vandalization and arson, 7,500 shops were demolished, and 30,000 Jews were arrested and sent to prisons or concentration camps. These measures were mainly directed against young and wealthy men, who were taken into "protective custody" to force them to emigrate and renounce their assets. The vast majority of prisoners, especially those who could produce a visa to leave the country or had surrendered their properties during protective custody, were released by the beginning of 1939. Andreas Heusler and Tobias Weger, *"Kristallnacht": Gewalt gegen die Münchner Juden im November 1938* (Munich: Buchendorfer Verl., 1998); Emanuel Marx, "Messages from a Present Past: The Kristallnacht as Symbolic Turning Point in Nazi Rule," in *Marking Evil: Holocaust Memory in the Global Age*, eds. Amos Goldberg and Haim Hazan (New York: Berghahn Books, 2015), 319–344; and Alan E. Steinweis, *Kristallnacht 1938* (Cambridge: Havard Univ. Press, 2009).

39. Kaplan, *Between Dignity and Despair*, chapter 5; and Longerich, *The Nazi Persecution*, 90–130.

40. According to calculations by the Munich City Archives. Cf. also the informative statistical analysis by Werner J. Cahnman, "The Decline of the Munich Jewish Community, 1933–1938," *Jewish Social Studies* 3, no. 3 (July 1941): 285–300.

41. Schalom Ben-Chorin (1913–1999), poet, German-Israeli journalist, and religious scholar.

42. Schalom Ben-Chorin, *Jugend an der Isar* (Munich: List, 1974), 185f. [Original in German; English translation by the editors.]

43. *Jüdisches Gemeindeblatt für den Verband der Kultusgemeinden in Bayern*, October 15, 1938, 318.

44. *Jüdisches Gemeindeblatt für den Verband der Kultusgemeinden in Bayern*, November 1, 1938, 334.

45. Albert Schwarz (b. 1880), restaurateur, emigrated with his wife Flora Schwarz, née Baer (b. 1876), to Prague on December 29, 1938; they were deported from there to Theresienstadt in 1942 and were murdered in Maly Trostinec.

46. Stadtarchiv München, JUD-V-69.

47. Richard Baum (1881–1941) graduated in national economics from the Trade College (*Handelshochschule*) Frankfurt am Main and did military service from 1914 to 1916. He lived in a "mixed marriage."

48. See "Kochschule Albert Schwarz," accessed June 4, 2021, https://gedenkbuch .muenchen.de/index.php?id=kochschule_schwarz.

49. Christine Hohnschopp, ed., *Exil in Brasilien: Die deutschsprachige Emigration, 1933–1945* (Leipzig: Deutsche Bibliothek, 1994); and Jeff Lesser, *Welcoming the Undesirables: Brazil and the Jewish Question* (Berkeley: Univ. of California Press, 1995).

50. The regional office of the Secret State Police (Gestapo) responsible for the district of Upper Bavaria and at times the district of Swabia; see Marita Krauss and Erich Kasberger, eds., *Rechte Karrieren in München von den Weimarer Jahren bis in die Nachkriegszeit* (Munich: Volk Verlag, 2010), 202–206.

51. See "Jüdische Anlernwerkstätten," accessed June 4, 2021, https://gedenkbuch .muenchen.de/index.php?id=anlernwerkstatt.

52. Based on information recorded in the database of the Municipal Archives, it was possible to identify 1,235 people (among the 6,685 emigrants whose emigration destinations are known) who found temporary or permanent refuge in England. This information is derived from data collected by the city as part of the deregistration process required when moving out of Munich, from data collected by the host country, and/or from information provided by the emigrants themselves. For the statistical calculation above (c. 15.43 percent), an estimated total number of 8,000 emigrants from Munich is assumed, which includes people whose destinations are not known; the estimate provided here is therefore an informed approximation, not a conclusive statement.

53. For more information, see Marion Berghahn, *Continental Britons: German-Jewish Refugees from Nazi Germany*, rev. ed. (Oxford: Berghahn, 2007); Louise London, *Whitehall and the Jews, 1933–1948: British Immigration Policy, Jewish Refugees and the Holocaust* (Cambridge: Cambridge Univ. Press, 2000); Werner E. Mosse, ed., *Second Chance: Two Centuries of German-Speaking Jews in the United Kingdom* (Tübingen: Mohr, 1991); and Ari J. Sherman, *Island Refuge: Britain and Refugees from the Third Reich, 1933–1939*, 2nd ed. (London: Frank Cass, 1994).

54. Claudia Curio, "Were Unaccompanied Child Refugees a Privileged Class of Refugees in the Liberal States of Europe?" In *Refugees From Nazi Germany and the Liberal European States*, eds. Frank Caestecker and Bob Moore (New York: Berghahn, 2010), 169–189; Vera Fast, *Children's Exodus: A History of the Kindertransport* (London: I. B. Tauris, 2010); and Andrea Hammel, ed., *The Kindertransport to Britain 1938/1939: New Perspectives* (Amsterdam: Rodopi, 2012).

55. Based on information recorded in the database of the Municipal Archives, it was possible to identify 905 people (among the 6,685 emigrants whose emigration

destinations are known) who found temporary or permanent refuge in Palestine, later Israel. For the statistical calculation above (c. 11.31 percent), an estimated total number of 8,000 emigrants from Munich is assumed, which includes people whose destinations are not known. For more details on the statistical calculation, see note 53.

56. For more information, see, for example, Rebecca Boehling and Uta Larkey, *Life and Loss in the Shadow of the Holocaust: A Jewish Family's Untold Story* (Cambridge: Cambridge Univ. Press, 2011); and Joachim Schlör, *Endlich im Gelobten Land? Deutsche Juden unterwegs in eine neue Heimat* (Berlin: Aufbau, 2003).

57. More than 2.5 million Jews found a haven in the United States during the late 19th and early 20th century. Bat-Ami-Zucker, "American Refugee Policy in the 1930s," in *Refugees from Nazi Germany and the Liberal European States*, eds. Frank Caestecker and Bob Moore (New York: Berghahn, 2010), 151–168; Ulla Kriebernegg et al., eds., *"Nach Amerika nämlich:" Jüdische Migration in die Amerikas im 19. und 20. Jahrhundert* (Göttingen: Wallstein, 2012), here esp. 7–22. For an overview of Jewish involvement in shaping American Immigration policy, see Kevin MacDonald, "Jewish Involvement in Shaping American Immigration Policy, 1881–1965: A Historical Review," *Population & Environment* 19, no. 4 (1998): 295–356.

58. The act, "Regulating Immigration of Aliens to, and Residence of Aliens in, the United States," was passed on February 5, 1917 and was considered the new cornerstone of American immigration policy. An Act to Regulate the Immigration of Aliens to, and the Residence of Aliens in, the United States, 1917; Public -- No. 301 -- 64th Congress, H.R. 10384, in Immigration Collection of Prescott Farnsworth Hall (Harvard College Library), accessed June 2, 2021, https://id.lib.harvard.edu/curiosity /immigration-to-the-united-states-1789-1930/39-990100032410203941.

59. The National Origins Immigration Act of 1924—also known as the Johnson-Reed Act—was enacted on May 26, 1924. This federal law perpetuated the basic restrictions on immigration to the United States that had been established in 1921 and modified the "National Origins Formula," an American system of immigration quotas that had been first introduced in that year. Its most basic purpose was to preserve the ideal of US homogeneity by limiting the number of immigrants allowed into the United States. The quota provided immigration visas to 2 percent of the total number of people of each nationality in the United States as of the 1890 national census. (In fact, setting quotas by national origin proved to be a difficult task and was not accepted and finalized until 1929.) It completely excluded immigrants from Asia. In conjunction with the Immigration Act of 1917, it governed US immigration policy until the passage of the Immigration and Nationality Act of 1952, which completely revised it. John Bond Trevor, *An Analysis of the American Immigration Act of 1924* (New York: Carnegie Endowment for International Peace, 1924); and Michael C. LeMay, *U.S. Immigration Policy, Ethnicity, and Religion in American History* (Santa Barbara: Praeger, 2018), 129–151.

60. Richard Breitmann and Alan M. Kraut, *American Refugee Policy and European Jewry, 1933–1945* (Bloomington: Indiana Univ. Press, 1987); LeMay, *U.S. Immigration Policy*, 152–165.

61. As a result of strict immigration policies based on economic considerations that did not expand the quota or introduce a refugee category, only 580,000

immigrants entered the United States in the decade 1931–1940, which is fewer than in any previous decade. Lavsky, *The Creation*, 16–19; Bat-Ami Zucker, *In Search of Refuge: Jews and US Consuls in Nazi Germany, 1933–1941* (London: Valentin Mitchell, 2001).

62. Based on information recorded in the database of the Municipal Archives, it was possible to identify 2,559 people (among the 6,685 emigrants whose emigration destinations are known) who found temporary or permanent refuge in the United States. For the statistical calculation above (c. 31.98 percent), an estimated total number of 8,000 emigrants from Munich is assumed, which includes people whose destinations are not known. For more details on the statistical calculation, see note 53.

63. It appears that a majority of the remainder were Jews by racial descent according to the Nazi definition, who were not characterized as "Hebrews" (those registered as Jews in general) by US immigration authorities. Lavsky, *The Creation*, 71–75; and Maurice R. Davie and Samuel Koenig, *The Refugees are now Americans* (New York: Public Affairs Committee, Inc., 1945), 7–9.

64. In the early years of the Nazi regime, the total number of immigrants allowed to enter each year under the quota for Germany (25,557) and Austria (1,413) was not exhausted. From 1933 to 1938, the United States received approx. 27,000 Jewish immigrants (which corresponds to 16 percent of the total Jewish emigration from Germany during this period). Lavsky, *The Creation*, 71–75.

65. Tobias Brinkmann, "Transnational Ties: The Longue Durée of Jewish Migrations to the United States," *American Jewish History* 101, no. 4 (October 2017): 566.

66. Helga Embacher, "Die USA als Aufnahmeland von jüdischen Verfolgten des NS-Regimes und Holocaustüberlebenden," in *"Nach Amerika nämlich!" Jüdische Migrationen in die Amerikas im 19. und 20. Jahrhundert*, eds. Ulla Kriebernegg et al. (Göttingen: Wallstein, 2012), 111–134; Lavsky, *The Creation*, 90–94, 113–125; Judy Tydor Baumel-Schwartz, "The Rescue of Jewish Girls and Teenage Women to England and the USA during the Holocaust: A Gendered Perspective," *Jewish History* 26, no. 1–2 (2012): 223–245; and Sibylle Quack, "Changing Gender Roles and Emigration: The Example of German Jewish Women and Their Emigration to the United States, 1933–1945," in *People in Transit: German Migrations in Comparative Perspective, 1820–1930*, eds. Dirk Hoerder and Jörg Nagler (Washington: GHI, 1995), 379–397.

67. Embacher, "Die USA"; Lavsky, *The Creation*, 113–125.

68. According to calculations by the Munich City Archives. The first emigration destination is mentioned in this table; in many cases, emigration to a third country took place later.

69. Maximilian Strnad, *Zwischenstation "Judensiedlung": Verfolgung und Deportation der jüdischen Münchner 1941–1945* (Munich: Oldenbourg, 2011).

70. Susanna Schrafstetter, *Flucht und Versteck: Untergetauchte Juden in München – Verfolgungserfahrung und Nachkriegsalltag* (Göttingen: Wallstein, 2015), 11f.; on the everyday life of Jews during the Holocaust, see, for example, Andrea Löw, Doris L. Bergen and Anna Hájková, eds., *Alltag im Holocaust: Jüdisches Leben im Großdeutschen Reich 1941–1945* (Munich: Oldenbourg, 2013).

71. The word *Mischling*—a pejorative legal term used in Nazi Germany to denote persons of both "Aryan" (Nazi pseudoscientific delineation for Germanic) and Jewish ancestry—means "half-caste, mongrel, or hybrid." Two years after seizing power, the Nazis implemented laws to separate *Mischlinge* from "Aryans." In 1935, the Nuremberg Laws created two new "racial" categories: the half-Jew (Jewish *Mischlinge* first degree) and the quarter-Jew (Jewish *Mischlinge* second degree). According to the Nuremberg Laws, a Jew was a person—regardless of religious affiliation or self-identification—who had at least three Jewish grandparents. A person who had two Jewish grandparents was classified as a Jewish *Mischling* of the first degree and was legally considered a "Jew" (so-called *Geltungsjude*) if that person was a descendant of a mixed marriage who belonged to the Jewish community after 1935; was a descendant of a mixed marriage who was married to a Jew after 1935; or was an illegitimate child of a *Geltungsjude* born after 1935. A person with only one Jewish grandparent was classified a *Mischling* of the second degree. Maria von der Heydt, "Möglichkeiten und Grenzen der Auswanderung von 'jüdischen Mischlingen,' 1938–1941," in *"Wer bleibt, opfert seine Jahre, vielleicht sein Leben": Deutsche Juden, 1938–1941*, eds. Susanne Heim, Beate Meyer, and Francis R. Nicosia (Göttingen: Wallstein, 2010), 77–95.

72. Maximilian Strnad, *Privileg Mischehe? Handlungsräume "jüdisch versippter" Familien 1933–1949* (Göttingen: Wallstein, 2021); and Nathan Stoltzfus, "The Limits of Policy: Social Protection of Intermarried German Jews in Nazi Germany," in *Social Outsiders in Nazi Germany*, eds. Robert Gellately and Nathan Stoltzfus (Princeton: Princeton Univ. Press, 2001), 117–144.

73. See, for example, Insa Meinen, *Verfolgt von Land zu Land: Jüdische Flüchtlinge in Westeuropa, 1938–1944* (Paderborn: Schöningh, 2013); and Bergmann, *Jüdische Emigration*, 186–189.

74. Wolfgang Benz, *Das Exil der kleinen Leute: Alltagserfahrungen deutscher Juden in der Emigration* (Munich: Beck, 1991), 7–37; Marita Krauss, *Heimkehr in ein fremdes Land: Geschichte der Remigration nach 1945* (Munich: Beck, 2001), 42–49.

75. Age and/or poor health, language problems, economic and professional difficulties while in exile, political reasons, and finally a general though rarely admitted feeling of homesickness were among the most important motives mentioned by those Jewish Germans who resettled in the two German states founded in 1949. By 1959, Harry Maòr identifies about 9,000 Jewish remigrants, that is, less than 2 percent of emigrants. Harry Maòr, *Über den Wiederaufbau der jüdischen Gemeinden in Deutschland seit 1945*, Diss. Phil. (Mainz: [s.n.], 1961), 31–50.

76. On the relationship between German Jews fleeing Nazi Germany and their places of origin, see Michael A. Meyer, "Looking Back: American Jews' Relationship to Their Places of Origin," *Modern Judaism* 37, no. 2 (2019): 143–164.

77. Dwork and van Pelt, *Flight*, 315–339; and Andreas Lixl-Purcell, ed., *Women of Exile: German-Jewish Autobiographies since 1933* (New York: Greenwood Press, 1988).

78. The Nuremberg Trials comprised the International Military Tribunal (IMT) under the authority of the 4 main victorious powers, which took place from November

20, 1945, to September 30, 1946, and 12 successor trials under US authority, which took place between October 25, 1946, and April 14, 1949. Michael R. Marrus, *The Nuremberg War Crimes Trial, 1945–46: A Brief History with Documents*, 2nd ed. (Boston: Bedford/St. Martin's/Macmillan Learning, 2018); and Kim Christian Priemel, *The Betrayal: The Nuremberg Trials and German Divergence* (New York: Oxford Univ. Press, 2016).

79. A notable example was that of the "Camp Ritchie Boys," graduates of the US Army's Military Intelligence Training Center, or "Camp Ritchie." The participants were mainly young emigrants from Germany and Austria, mostly Jews who had found a new home in the United States who used their native language skills and knowledge of their home countries to help America to victory in World War II. After the war, Ritchie Boys interpreted during the Nuremberg war crimes trials, filled important liaison positions in the US military government, or helped build a democratic press landscape in West Germany. See Beverley Driver Eddy, *Ritchie Boy Secrets: How a Force of Immigrants and Refugees Helped Win World War II* (Guilford: Stackpole Books, 2021); and Bruce Henderson, *Sons and Soldiers: The Untold Story of the Jews Who Escaped the Nazis and Returned with the U.S. Army to Fight Hitler* (New York: William Morrow, 2017).

80. Hans Günter Hockerts, "Wiedergutmachung in Deutschland: Eine historische Bilanz 1945–2000," *Vierteljahrshefte für Zeitgeschichte* 49 (2001): 167–214; Constantin Goschler, *Schuld und Schulden: Die Politik der Wiedergutmachung für NS-Verfolgte seit 1945* (Göttingen: Wallstein, 2005); Jay Howard Geller, *Jews in Post-Holocaust Germany* (Cambridge: Cambridge Univ. Press, 2005); and Andrea Sinn, "We Have the Right to Exist Here: Jewish Politics and The Challenge of *Wiedergutmachung* in Post-Holocaust Germany," in *Rebuilding Jewish Life in Germany*, eds. Jay Howard Geller and Michael Meng (New Brunswick: Rutgers Univ. Press, 2020), 30–47.

81. Scholars generally refer to this period, from the conclusion of the Reparation Treaty between Israel and Germany in 1952 to c.1960, as the second phase of Jewish remigration. See, for example, Krauss, *Heimkehr*, 13f., 127; and Meron Mendel, "The Policy for the Past in West Germany and Israel: The Case of Jewish Remigration," *Leo Baeck Institute Yearbook* 49 (2004): 121–136.

82. Lina Nikou, *Besuche in der alten Heimat: Einladungsprogramme für ehemals Verfolgte des Nationalsozialismus in München, Frankfurt am Main, und Berlin* (Berlin: Neofelis Verlag, 2020).

83. These remarks closely follow the reasoning of Dwork and van Pelt, *Flight*, 360–380.

84. The focus of this volume is exclusively on emigrants and refugees who had to leave their homes because their lives were threatened. It is not on migrants who left their homes for a variety of other reasons and by their own free will. For a careful discussion of the terminology, see Andreas Kossert, *Flucht: Eine Menschheitsgeschichte*, 2nd ed. (Munich: Siedler, 2020).

85. The full story of Jews who fled Nazi Germany and of Jewish migration to the United States is well documented in a number of excellent books and articles by historians such as Gur Alroey, Tobias Brinkmann, Joseph Edelman, Donald Fleming, Libby

Garland, Peter Gay, Claus-Dieter Krohn, Rafael Medoff, Werner Röder, Herbert A. Strauss, Frank Wolff, and David S. Wyman. Two outstanding studies are Dwork and van Pelt's *Flight from the Reich*—a comprehensive survey of various countries' responses to the refugee crisis and their often self-serving motives—and Barry Trachtenberg's *The United States and the Nazi Holocaust: Race, Refugee, and Remembrance* (London: Bloomsbury, 2018)—an invaluable synthesis of US policies and attitudes toward the Nazi persecution of European Jewry from 1933 right up to the modern day.

86. This publication was inspired by source readers such as the carefully annotated volumes featured in the groundbreaking series *Documenting Life and Destruction: Holocaust Sources in Context*, published since 2010 by the Mandel Center for Advanced Holocaust Studies of the United States Holocaust Memorial Museum. It is intended as a locally focused addition to existing collections of primary sources on the "Third Reich," World War II, and the Holocaust. One of the earliest and most extensive publication projects focused on the history of the Holocaust, which amplified the perspective of victims and survivors, is *The Holocaust: Selected Documents in Eighteen Volumes*, edited by John Mendelsohn (New York: Garland, 1982). Other examples of translations of sources documenting the destruction of Jewish communities under the Nazis, which outline the history of the Holocaust, are Michael Berenbaum, ed., *Witness to the Holocaust* (New York: HarperCollins Publishers, 1997); Yitzhak Arad, Israel Gutman, and Abraham Margaliot, eds., *Documents on the Holocaust: Selected Sources on the Destruction of the Jews of Germany and Austria, Poland, and the Soviet Union* (Lincoln: Univ. of Nebraska Press, 1999); Steve Hochstadt, *Sources of the Holocaust* (New York: Palgrave Macmillan, 2004); and Jeff Hill, *The Holocaust* (Detroit, MI: Omnigraphics, 2006). For statistics see Herbert A. Strauss, "The Immigration and Acculturation of the German Jew in the United States of America," *Leo Baeck Institute Year Book* 16, 1 (1971): 63–94.

87. For details on the role, importance, and problematic nature of first-person documents in historical research, see Mary Fulbrook and Ulinka Rublack, "In Relation: The 'Social Self' and Ego-Documents," *German History* 28, no. 3 (2010): 263–272; and Winfried Schulze, ed., *Ego-Dokumente: Annäherung an den Menschen in der Geschichte* (Berlin: DeGruyter, 1996).

88. For details on the role and significance as well as use of first-person documents in the writing and teaching of Jewish and Holocaust history, see Kaplan, *Between Dignity and Despair*, esp. 3–7; Saul Friedländer, *Nazi Germany and the Jews: The Years of Persecution, 1933–1939* (New York: HarperCollins, 1997) and Saul Friedländer, *Nazi Germany and the Jews: The Years of Extermination, 1939–1945* (New York: HarperCollins, 2007); Jeffrey C. Blutinger, "Bearing Witness: Teaching the Holocaust from a Victim-Centered Perspective," *The History Teacher* 42, no. 3 (2009): 269–279; and Laura J. Hilton and Avinoam J. Patt, eds., *Understanding and Teaching the Holocaust* (Madison: Univ. of Wisconsin Press, 2020).

89. For instance, historians Jürgen Matthäus and Emil Kerenji, editors of *Jewish Responses to Persecution, 1933–1946: A Source Reader* (London: Rowman & Littlefield, 2017), argue convincingly for the value of contemporary accounts "for imbuing historical periods and topics with a sense of immediacy." Moreover, they excluded retrospective accounts from inclusion in their collection because, as they stated, "when it comes to understanding the Holocaust [. . .] contemporary documents, and especially those that come from victims rather than perpetrators, have a

meaning and significance that goes beyond the general rule. They help to recover the individuality of those who are all too often seen only as objects of Nazi policy" (2). See also John K. Roth et al., eds., *Remembering for the Future: The Holocaust in an Age of Genocide, Vol. 3: Memory* (Basingstoke: Palgrave, 2001).

90. On the specificity of Holocaust memoirs, see Andreas Lixl-Purcell, "Memoirs as History," *Leo Baeck Institute Year Book* 39 (1994): 227–238; Jeremy D. Popkin, "Holocaust Memories, Historians' Memoirs: First-Person Narrative and the Memory of the Holocaust," *History & Memory* 15, no. 1 (2003): 49–84; and Robert Rozett, "Published Memoirs of Holocaust Survivors," in *Remembering for the Future: The Holocaust in an Age of Genocide, Vol. 3: Memory*, eds. John K. Roth et al. (Basingstoke: Palgrave, 2001), 167–171.

91. On the importance of personal letters in research and education, see Marion Kaplan, *Hitler's Jewish Refugees: Hope and Anxiety in Portugal* (New Haven: Yale Univ. Press, 2020); Michael Mascuch, Rudolf Dekker, and Arianne Baggerman, "Egodocuments and History: A Short Account of the Longue Durée," *Historian* 78, no. 1 (2016): 11–56; and Dalia Ofer, "Personal Letters in Research and Education on the Holocaust," *Holocaust and Genocide Studies* 4, no. 3 (1989): 341–355.

92. The term "capital of the movement" (German: "Hauptstadt der Bewegung") is an honorary title that Adolf Hitler bestowed on Munich for its significance as the founding site of the Nazi Party. Münchner Stadtmuseum, ed., *München—"Hauptstadt der Bewegung"* (Munich: self-published, 1993).

93. With the exception of two sources, all the first-person documents printed here are held by the Munich City Archives (Stadtarchiv München, StadtAM). The memoirs of Lotte Bamberger and Charlotte Stein-Pick are part of the collection and have been reprinted with the permission of the Leo Baeck Institute New York. For more information, see the sources commentary and picture credits at the end of this book (Appendix 2).

94. The German-language recollections are the memoirs of Erich Hartmann, Hanns Peter Merzbacher, and Charlotte Stein-Pick. In all the letter collections, at least some, if not all, of the writing was in German and has been translated by the editors.

95. The *Biografisches Gedenkbuch der Münchner Juden, 1933–1945* includes the most important life data of all the women, men, and children who lived in Munich between 1933 and 1945, who were persecuted and murdered as Jews by the National Socialists. The database has a total number of 14,294 recorded individuals; of these, at least 6,685 emigrated to known emigration destinations. For several hundred other Jewish Munich residents, the emigration destination cannot be clearly reconstructed. The memorial book is available in a revised online version, which is continuously updated, at https://gedenkbuch.muenchen.de/.

96. Libby Garland, "State of the Field: New Directions for American Jewish Migration Histories," *American Jewish History* 102, no. 3 (2018): 423–440; and Frank Wolff, "Global Walls and Global Movement: New Destinations in Jewish Migration, 1918–1939," *East European Jewish Affairs* 44, no. 2–3 (2014): 187–204.

Part I

HEIMAT—JEWISH LIFE IN GERMANY AND NAZI PERSECUTION

Munich, the capital of Bavaria, is home to centuries-old buildings and numerous museums. Located on the Isar River, the city is known for its annual Oktoberfest and its beer halls, including the famous Hofbräuhaus, founded in 1589. The admiration for Greece shown by Ludwig I (1786–1868), king of Bavaria from 1825 to 1848, is still visible in the cityscape and architecture and earned Munich the honorary title "Isar-Athens" in the early 19th century. In the first decades of the 20th century, the Bavarian capital became an important source of inspiration for artistic and literary modernism. The artists' group "Der Blaue Reiter" (The Blue Rider), centered on Franz Marc and Wassily Kandinsky, represented the art world's *avant-garde*. The names Thomas and Heinrich Mann, Bertolt Brecht, and Lion Feuchtwanger signify Munich's rank as a center of famous literature. But Munich was also where, following World War I, the Nazi Party formed, developed, and consolidated itself as a politically effective force. Growing from a splinter group in Munich's confusing far-right and nationalist spectrum, the Nazi Party became the strongest party in Germany after the Reichstag elections of 1932 and soon after destroyed the fragile foundations of the Weimar Republic in 1933, without any significant resistance. Those who lived and worked in Munich at that time, among them more than 10,000 Jewish residents, experienced firsthand how democratic structures could be quickly and systematically destroyed and fundamental rights literally trampled underfoot. Munich played a key role in the implementation of the totalitarian dictatorship of the Nazi regime. As the "capital of the movement," the city was a role model for the implementation of the "national revolution." Within that program, the exclusion, disenfranchisement, deprivation, and eventual expulsion of Jewish Munich residents were top priorities for the fanatical antisemites who controlled Munich's city hall from 1933 to 1945.

The personal testimonies included in this part of the book, all from the Judaica collection of the Munich City Archives, draw attention to the tremendous pressure exerted by the persecutors and the suffering which the Jewish community in Munich endured. However, they also represent the "Unwanted" in Germany as a whole because, in most German cities and communities, radical antisemitism based on the Munich model soon also became firmly established. The memoirs and letters presented here contain detailed descriptions of everyday life and specifically Jewish life in Munich. They additionally include reports of noticeable changes in society and politics following Hitler's appointment as Germany's chancellor, document individual experiences of exclusion and increasing persecution, and provide insights on significant decisions and steps taken in preparation for eventual emigration. Most importantly, while official sources in the archives reveal the persecution of Jewish people from the perspective of the perpetrators and as a Nazi success story, these accounts reveal the consternation, concern, and despair of the oppressed in the face of what would eventually prove to be a hopeless situation.

The noticeable changes in the character of the city of Munich that followed Hitler's appointment as Reich Chancellor are described most vividly by Ernest B. Hofeller and Erich Hartmann, who experienced the rise of the National Socialists as adolescents in Munich. The contributions by Fred Bissinger and Pesach Schindler, children at the time of these events, illuminate in detail the often-lengthy preparations for emigration and the significance of *Kristallnacht* to their families' emigration efforts. Christine Roth-Schurtman and Hugo Holzmann write about their experiences as *Mischlinge* in Munich and how emigration took place in stages in their families; in both cases, the emigration of a Jewish parent took place well before the other family members were able to follow. The correspondence between the members of two families, the Blechners and Schwagers, who were scattered over several continents, demonstrates how difficult it was to find a way to emigrate and, with emotional immediacy, adds an important perspective regarding that time. In short, the memoirs and letters selected for this first part showcase—bluntly and irrefutably—the worsening discrimination, marginalization, and persecution of German Jews that culminated in the destruction of one of the most vibrant centers of Jewish life in Germany.

Chapter 1

Munich, 1933–1938

Ernest B. Hofeller

Ernest (Ernst) Bernhard Hofeller was born in Munich on September 22, 1921, the second child of banker Alfred Hofeller and his wife Hildegard, née Unikower. His father was the owner of the banking business A. Hofeller & Co. at Maximiliansplatz 13. Ernest Hofeller celebrated his Bar Mitzvah in Munich's main synagogue on September 15, 1934. Like his three-year-older sister Leonore (Lore), he attended a boarding school in Vevey, Switzerland, in 1938. His sister had returned to Munich in 1937, after studying French for a year in the French part of Switzerland. Between 1938 and 1941, she and the parents tried unsuccessfully to obtain visas to leave the country for England, the United States, and the Dominican Republic. Three years after the father's business was deregistered on September 6, 1938 (retroactive as of April 1, 1938), in the course of the progressive "Aryanization," she and the parents finally received an entry permit to the Dominican Republic in September 1941, and in early November the visa was entered into all their passports. However, their emigration could no longer be implemented, as their deportation order had already arrived. Instead of finding refuge abroad, the sister and parents were deported on November 20, 1941, and were murdered in Kovno (Kaunas).

Ernest Hofeller, alone in the family, managed to escape in 1940. Initially, he made his way from Switzerland via Portugal to the Dominican Republic, where, like several hundred German-Jewish refugees, he settled temporarily in the agricultural settlement of Sosúa. After receiving an affidavit in August 1945 from the former Munich community rabbi, Dr. Leo Baerwald (1883–1970), he moved to New York, USA, on January 12, 1946. He died on July 16, 2008, in Pembroke Pines, Florida (USA).

Ernest Hofeller wrote his memoirs in English at the end of the 1990s. The excerpt printed here provides an insight into his experiences during his childhood and youth in Munich.[1]

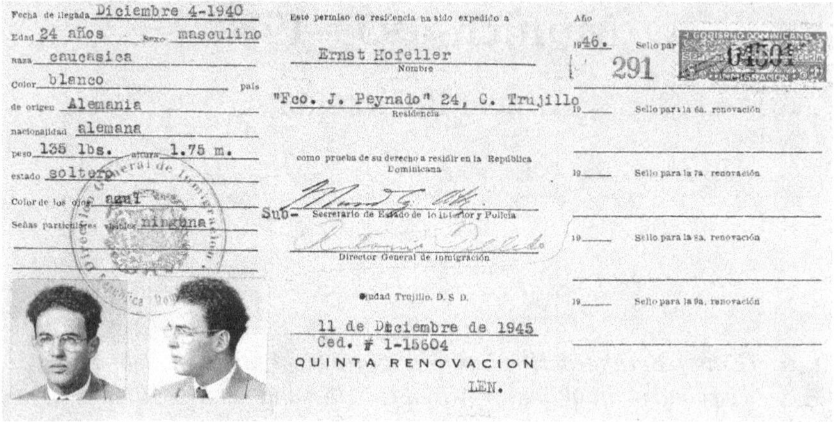
Fecha de llegada Diciembre 4-1940
Edad 24 años Sexo masculino
Raza caucasica
Color blanco
país de origen Alemania
nacionalidad alemana
peso 135 lbs. altura 1.75 m.
estado soltero
Color de los ojos azul
Señas particulares visibles ninguna

Este permiso de residencia ha sido expedido a
Ernst Hofeller
Nombre
"Fco. J. Peynado" 24, C. Trujillo
Residencia
como prueba de su derecho a residir en la República Dominicana
Sub- Secretario de Estado de lo Interior y Policía
Director General de Inmigración
Ciudad Trujillo, D. S. D.
11 de Diciembre de 1945
Ced. # 1-15604
QUINTA RENOVACION
LEN.

Año
1946.
Sello par
291
GOBIERNO DOMINICANO
INMIGRACION
04501
19____ Sello para la 6a. renovación
19____ Sello para la 7a. renovación
19____ Sello para la 8a. renovación
19____ Sello para la 9a. renovación

Figure 1.1 Residence Permit for Foreigners, Issued by the Dominican Immigration Service to Ernst Hofeller on December 11, 1945. *Source:* Courtesy of Leo Baeck Institute New York.

The day Hitler was appointed chancellor of Germany, my father[2] came home for a late lunch from the stock exchange with the following comment: "We give him six weeks."

It was January 30, 1933; I was 11 years old and we lived in Schwabing, a part of Munich to which the minuscule Jewish population was partial. [. . .]

The first two months of Hitler's assumption of power[3] passed rather uneventfully, as far as I was concerned. I had attended the first grade of the Gymnasium and, as half the class was Jewish, we were in charge. The first recollection that something was wrong came on Saturday, April 1, 1933, "Boykott Day." The boycott, as all other Nazi activities, was organized by the "S.A.," the abbreviation of *Sturmabteilung*. These were the brown-shirted, paramilitary Nazis who had put Hitler into power. At all of the party meetings in Nuremberg, you could see every year thousands upon thousands of S.A. men, and all of the top Nazis always wore brown uniforms. The "S.S." (*Schutzstaffel*) was dressed all in black and was originally founded as a personal protection group for Hitler. Later it expanded into police, secret police and camp activities.

The Nazis had complete and accurate lists of every Jewish store or enterprise and marked their windows or signs with a yellow star. My father sent down his manager [. . .] to take a picture of the firm's name (Alfred Hofeller

& Co.) with a yellow star on it. He thought it was some kind of amusing oddity which one could show to people once the Nazis had disappeared, which undoubtedly would happen very soon. [. . .] The Nazis tried to persuade the Christian customers from buying in Jewish places, but many people disregarded this and crossed just as you would pass a picket line and be called a scab. My father otherwise was not interested in the effect this boycott might have on his Christian clientele, but he sarcastically remarked various times that at least the Jews would now know who he was, because based on our German-sounding name, they assumed this was a Christian business, something that annoyed him very much. By 1938, when *Kristallnacht* took place, his attitude had changed completely. [. . .]

Something like a reverse boycott took place when the gentiles tried to exclude the Jews from using their facilities. There were many picturesque villages and spas in the foothills of the Bavarian Alps, only about an hour by train from Munich, which were very popular with the Jews. One of them was Bad Toeltz,[4] where very early on a big billboard appeared at the entrance of the village, with the caricature of a Jew with a suitcase, saying: "Jews not wanted." The Jews immediately stayed away. The same, however, did not apply to the Cafe Luitpoldt at the Lenbachplatz[5] where the Jewish bankers and businessmen met in the afternoon to have coffee, gossip, discuss politics or business. In later years, a small gold-lettered sign appeared at the bottom of the glass door, stating that Jews were not welcome. In this case the Jews decided to ignore it and continue to visit the coffee house, without any incident, one might add.

Soon after the Nazis came to power, Saturday morning classes were cancelled and the time was used to train the Hitler Youth boys, presumably in paramilitary exercises with political indoctrination. The Jewish parents decided that as we did not have to go to school any more, we should go Saturday morning to synagogue. Their goal was probably less due to religious fervor than to their desire to get us out of the house. For a time therefore, we spent Saturday morning in temple. [. . .] Although I hated school, the teachers and my classmates—all of them fervent Nazis—I was not particularly afraid to go there. I do not recall ever having been beaten up or chased down the street, even though street fighting or brawling had been quite common for me when I attended grade school before the arrival of the Nazis. [. . .]

When you wanted to go on a vacation or on a business trip abroad, you applied for permission to take out or convert a specific amount of money, which caused no particular problem as long as you were a banker like my father and had the necessary connections. However, if you wanted to emigrate and leave for good—assuming that you had received a visa from a foreign country—there were stringent restrictions that prevented people from taking along or transferring their capital, no matter if it was cash, real estate, jewelry, stocks, bonds, or any other financial holdings.

You were permitted to take all of your household goods, packed in a lift-van which had to be—"stuffed" was the proper word—under the supervision of a Nazi official. [. . .] I do not know the exact amount of money you were officially permitted to take with you in the first few years of Nazi rule, but I recall a discussion at lunch sometime in 1936. Father said that if they would let him take out 15 percent of his money, he would gladly give 10 percent to charity. My mother and I did not understand this calculation, by which we thought he would be left with 5 percent, until he explained that he would give away 10 percent of the 15 percent.[6] After 1937, you were legally permitted to take with you no more than 10 marks per person, the equivalent of two and a half dollars.

When you left Germany you often had to undergo a "*Leibesvisitation*" at the border, which meant that some travelers were called out of the train into the station where they had to strip to be checked by the police to see if they were hiding or smuggling any valuables. The Nazis put a large red "J" on the first page of your passport so that at the border they did not have any great difficulty in identifying who was a Jew. In this way they could immediately turn back Jews at the border. The "J" was also quite convenient for other languages because not only did it stand for "Jude" in German, it also fitted "Jew," "Judio," and "Juif."

As soon as the regulations prohibiting the transfer of monies went into effect, German Jews became obsessed with finding ways to beat them. It was a regular mania, and the name the Nazis had given it was *Devisenschieben* (smuggling of foreign exchange). It was not only illegal but also highly dangerous. If caught, the least you could end up with was prison and the worst was being sent to a concentration camp. Nevertheless there were numerous attempts to transfer money or jewelry illegally, some of which I recall vividly. My father used to take an old coat, fill it with good cigars, and hang it in the corner of the train compartment. If found, they were not his. If not found, he did not have to smoke the awful Italian cigars.

Another of the more harmless tricks was to wrap the remnants of a cold lunch together with some money, put them in a paper bag, and throw them under a seat or in the corner far away from you. More sophisticated methods were used by people who went to Switzerland for skiing and took along ski wax, more or less in the form of a bar of soap. They melted the wax at home, inserted a nugget of gold and molded the wax again around it to take it abroad, where the gold was removed and sold. Then there was the story my mother told, of the man who had hidden a large amount of money under the paper towels in the washroom of the express train to Switzerland. When he went to the toilet after the train had crossed the border, someone else had been there before him and the money was gone.

One of the truly imaginative ways involved a Munich Jew who put an ad in the *Voelkischer Beobachter*, Hitler's own paper. He advertised some real estate at a very advantageous price under a box number. Then he mailed about fifty envelopes in different colors and sizes to his own box number. In each one he put a 1000 mark bill. After that he left for Switzerland, and when safely abroad, he asked the newspaper to forward any replies to him, as he now was on vacation. The paper obliged and mailed the letters in a wrapper with a big swastika. What censor would have dared to open the correspondence from Hitler's own newspaper? [. . .]

Obviously many of these stories did not have such happy endings, and the papers were full of names of people who went on trial having been caught when smuggling money abroad. There was, however, one sure way to get your money out. It was discreet, reliable, prompt, and foolproof. Behind the Cathedral in Cologne was a coffeehouse where one went to make contact with one or another of the people waiting there. For a fee of 50 marks, they would take your money across the nearby border into Holland or Belgium. The people who did this were S.A. men, or brown shirts. In short, Nazis. I can make this statement without qualification, because when I left for school in Switzerland, my father gave me a list of monies that, up to then, had been smuggled abroad and he told me that this was the way some of the more had been taken out.

Another of my father's business friends was the director of one of the largest and most famous Munich breweries, who was universally known as "Uncle Julius."[7] A bachelor, who spoke with a heavy Bavarian dialect, he wore a cap indoors and out because he was completely bald. In November 1932, two months before Hitler took over, he decided that he had seen and heard enough, left Munich and, with all his money, installed himself in the Dolder Hotel,[8] overlooking the Lake of Zurich in Switzerland. He later told me that he had had an arrangement with my father that if he did not return to Germany within two or three months, my father would follow. This must have been a very one-sided agreement, because I do not recall my father ever making the slightest move in the early 1930s to leave Munich. Uncle Julius, on the other hand, never returned; he ended up in New York, alive and with money. Later, when I went to school in Lucerne, the money that had been on deposit for me there ran out and friends contacted Uncle Julius, who offered to help me with a monthly remittance. Many years after the war had ended an aunt of mine who had moved to Chile came to visit. My father had, much earlier, put her husband into business in Munich. I told her about the kindness of Uncle Julius. She looked flabbergasted and then said: "But Ernest, that was not his money, that was your father's money." [. . .]

We spent a good many vacations before and after 1933 in either Switzerland or Italy. Austria had been declared off limits by the Nazis, in order to punish the country by withholding sorely needed income from tourism. Not only was the money for these expensive trips available without any discussion, but the equally difficult task of obtaining very scarce foreign exchange during the Nazi times seemed to present no problem. My father apparently must have had some excellent connections from which he legally obtained the francs and lire needed for these trips.

At Easter time in 1936, we were preparing to go to Montreux, Switzerland, to inspect the boarding school my sister[9] was to attend in Vevey[10] for the next year. There were 300 private schools around Lake Geneva and the choice was large. If you were anybody at all, you saw to it that your son or daughter went to one of these finishing schools. (I attended school there two years later.) It was morning: father had left for work and we were at home packing. Around 10 o'clock, the call came from my father: The Gestapo was on the way to pick up the passports of the Jews. I was told to come to the office immediately where both of us would walk around town until the train was leaving. If the Gestapo looked for him at his business, they would not find him there either. My mother and sister rushed to finish packing. Half an hour later the bell rang, and the maid, who had previously been instructed, told the agents that no one was home. We met at the railroad station, traveled abroad, and had a good time for the next two weeks. The only problem arose when my father realized that banks in Switzerland were closed from Good Friday until the following Tuesday. The concierge at the hotel was accommodating enough to advance us money. When we returned home, a letter from the police was on hand asking for our passports. I never found out whether my father had been tipped off or how he guessed that we would be among the first to be visited by the Gestapo.

In the fall of 1937, my mother and sister went to the Isle of Capri, where my sister was to recuperate from one of her frequent illnesses. They had afternoon coffee on the hotel terrace and next to them sat Rudolf Hess,[11] surrounded by a group of flunkies. In what can only be described as a display of mind-boggling stupidity, one of these Nazis started to flirt with my decidedly Jewish-looking sister. My mother, who sometimes had a very particular sense of humor, thought this was hysterically funny. [. . .]

The next year, when I was in school in the mountains behind Lac Leman, in February 1938, my parents took their last trip abroad. We met in Lausanne, and I tried to convince them to stay abroad but that was out of the question. I still have a letter from my mother in which she recalled that I had suggested that they take a trip around the world to see where they wanted to live, even though I have no recollection of such a conversation. They never got out again and neither did my sister Lore, who had returned home after attending her Swiss school. [. . .]

The first thing I ever learned about the United States was in a Nazi school in Munich. For the school year 1937, which started at Easter, we had a new

English teacher. He came into the room, ordered us to take out our notebooks, and dictated the following in English: "The flag of the United States has 48 stars and 13 stripes." From then on, all lessons dealt strictly with American customs and America. He loved the U.S. and told us he had been working at the German Embassy in Washington prior to 1933. The date was easily established because according to his story, he once stood next to President Hoover[12] at a reception and Hoover had ordered some official to come over and see him and in the process had called him "that boy." That made a big impression on the teacher and on us.

German schools were completely influenced by the British when teaching English. We learned, for instance, that every Englishman had his own little house, that there was a two-day weekend something unheard of in Germany where everyone worked at least half a day on Saturday—we knew about Hyde Park and soap box speakers at Marble Arch and naturally about the English monarchy and "The City." [. . .] We knew much less about the U.S. It was the custom to give books at Bar Mitzvah time as gifts, although "Tom Sawyer and Huckleberry Finn," a book we all owned, would not have helped a newcomer too much. [. . .] Around the same time Margaret Mitchell's *Vom Winde verweht*[13] became extremely popular, an enormous bestseller. I recall the books very well, but I hardly can remember any American films. Probably very few were being shown because many of the actors, directors, or producers were not only Jews but former German Jews.

The English teacher was a small, middle-aged man who wore a swastika in his buttonhole and never at any time showed any preference for or against the Nazis. While he was obliged to start each class with the Nazi salute and "Heil Hitler," his greeting was formal and disinterested and did not have the religious fever some of his colleagues invoked when mentioning their beloved Fuehrer. He continued relentlessly with his always favorable instruction about America, and his job in Washington must have been fairly high up. When exactly he retired or was recalled was not quite clear, but presumably it was shortly after the new administrations came in, both in the U.S. and in Germany. The German ambassador in Washington had been the only diplomat who resigned when Hitler took over.

Things went without a problem until one day he read us a story by Helen Keller.[14] It was about a little girl and he translated it as he went along. At the end he tested us on what we had learned. It turned out that no one, not one of the 32 or so pupils, had paid the slightest attention to what he was reading, and no one was interested in the story of the little girl. Everyone had pursued his own interest: some had read Wild West stories spread out on their knees under the desks; some had played tic-tac-toe; some had done homework for other classes and others like me had just daydreamed. He now wanted to know what the little girl said when she saw the back of the old-fashioned pocket watch as it was opened. No one had an idea. The teacher, a quiet and polite man, flew into a frightening rage. [. . .] The class sat in dumb silence because this meek little man had suddenly turned into someone to fear. Unable to get any response at all, he changed tactics and offered to lend the book to anyone who wanted to borrow it. No one moved. No hand went up. Finally, I raised my hand, not because I had the remotest interest in what this little girl wanted to see or say, but out of a sense of duty to support this man.

Our family had recently—much too late—applied for registration number at the American consulate, so I had to show some solidarity to such a fervent America-lover. He told me to pick the book up at his house on one of the next afternoons. This was a deliberate breach of rules, because no teacher had ever openly invited one of the students to his house. The temptation to let drop some information regarding the date or the subject of the next test was too great. But here, not only did he openly and in front of the whole class invite a pupil to his house, but a Jew at that. Undoubtedly, the Hitler Youth boys, who for years had been indoctrinated to denounce anyone showing the slightest divergence from the Nazi credo, would report this immediately to other teachers, who would bring it to the attention of the principle. Or so I thought.

A few days later, I passed by his apartment in the Franz-Josephstrasse, the same street of apartment houses where we lived. My father always claimed that all teachers were poor, so I was in for quite a shock. This was an old, graystone apartment building with only one apartment per floor, indicating that each was very large. When opening the door to the building, after the buzzer admitted you, one faced a beautiful winding staircase covered by an oriental runner and a gleaming, wooden banister smelling of fresh pine. I walked up one flight, where another surprise awaited me. The door was opened by a maid in full regalia: black, shiny dress; white, starched full-length apron and cap on the head. While I was accustomed to maids, I never had seen one dressed up like this at three o'clock on a weekday afternoon. I told her why I was there. She closed the door in my face and reappeared some minutes later with the book, which she handed to me. I don't recall how I returned it but I know I did not go to the teacher's house again.

When my arm went up in class requesting the book, the teacher had a number of choices. He could have ignored me completely, as the Jews were sitting all in a row by themselves, or he could have acknowledged me and then just forgotten about the whole thing or he could have brought the book to school and handed it to me there. But he chose not to. Not only had he asked a Jew to come to his house to borrow a book whose author was Helen Keller, a writer whose books were burned by the Nazis in 1933 for having written: "How I Became a Socialist."[15] The book borrowing occurred in 1937, more than four years later—and even though the class had no idea that Helen Keller was considered a subversive anti-Nazi, some of the other teachers, all dedicated Nazis, might have known about it, particularly as there were only two or three American authors whose books were burned.

There was absolutely no doubt in my mind that the story would spread like wildfire through the school. I waited to see if anything would happen next, but nothing did. No investigation. No sarcastic comments from any of the other pupils about my being "teacher's pet," for which position there were a number of less flattering descriptions. No comment from any other teacher. The whole incident was wiped from everyone's memory. After having seen where he lived in the Franz-Josephstrasse it was quite clear to me that the teacher had no need to earn a salary at our school, so that he had taken the job either to keep himself busy or as a front for other activities. Probably he had not taken a teacher's examination but had been appointed to the job, which in turn would have entailed meeting the approval of the principle, [. . .] a very strict and fervent Nazi at this Bavarian state school. Anyone there needed an impeccable reputation as a Nazi. The teacher might have been a big shot in the Foreign Service, he might have had very good connections and lots of money, but that would not have saved his neck from what appeared to be behavior not conforming to the rules. People of high standing with influential friends had been shot left and right in the 1934 purge[16] and a majority of the prisoners in Dachau and Buchenwald were still German Christians at that time.

Years later, after the war, I came across a slim volume of recollections by the Reuters correspondent who had been stationed in Munich in the 1930s. He wrote that the Gestapo had listened in on all the telephone conversations of the English or American residents and newspaper correspondents. Naturally, for such a job they needed people with a very good knowledge not only of the language but also of the country. The Gestapo office, the Reuters correspondent wrote, that overheard these conversations had been located in the Franz-Josephstrasse. [. . .]

Somewhere around 1936, perhaps a little before, but not afterward, the general attitude changed. It became clear the joke was over. The guy with the Roman salute and the Chaplin mustache as he was described, was not going to disappear. The rush was on to join him and his gang. The large number of hard-core Nazis increased by millions including tens of millions of former Democrats, Socialists, Communists, and Catholics, who as late as 1932 had voted against Hitler. In the intervening years, they found out that there were jobs, appointments and money to be had if you became a Nazi. As Bertold Brecht says in "The Three Penny Opera": *"Erst kommt das Fressen, dann kommt die Moral."* (First you eat, then come the morals.)[17] And the Jews lost every shred of respect. [. . .]

Our chemistry professor had polyps, a rather common sickness then, which made him snort every few seconds and talk in an unpleasant way. His dream was to visit Bali, as he once told the surprised class.

Shortly before the Christmas vacation around the middle of December 1937, I was trying to follow some experiment. Each pupil had his own table with Bunsen burner, vials and other paraphernalia for chemistry lessons. I started to laugh because I had very little, if any idea as to what I was supposed to do. The teacher came over, planted himself right in front of me and screamed: "You, Hofeller, have nothing to laugh about. You are a Jew and we are going to kill you." Actually he used the word *umbringen* which was gangster jargon for "to do you in." I left the classroom and the school, went home, and announced that I would not return.

Nevertheless, I had to go back [the] next day to obtain my graduation diploma, which was being prepared in a rush and which was a required document to continue my schooling abroad. I recall that I said good-bye only to two teachers—who by now had naturally heard the story—one of them the old party member who once had stopped me on the staircase for not saluting. He asked where I was going. When I told him: Switzerland, he grabbed my hand, shook it vigorously and said: "Very good. Much, much better for you." When I picked up my clothes from the gym locker, my class by coincidence was there. No one took any notice of me or said good-bye, except one boy whose father was a baker and who came over to wish me well. I had the feeling he had heard a different song at home when he had told his parents about the incident the day before.

There were only four grades, which were: excellent, good, satisfactory, and unsatisfactory. I received a "good" in English, but only a "satisfactory" in German. Apparently the teacher felt that a Jew was not entitled to a better grade in the language in which he had been brought up.

The main synagogue in Munich was the first one to be destroyed by the Nazis.[18] It was located in the Herzog Max Strasse directly across from a fashionable Nazi meeting place, the *"Deutsches Kuenstlerhaus."*[19] On a visit in June 1938, either Hitler or Goebbels[20] had ordered that the synagogue had to disappear [. . .]. My father was called and rushed there to take part in the final services, but when he arrived the workmen were already throwing down benches from the women's section in the balcony into the main hall where the male congregation used to assemble. Therefore, when November came, the Munich synagogue had already disappeared and in its place was a parking lot. [. . .]

It is the middle of September 1938 and I have returned from Switzerland to Munich for summer vacation. The Nazi saber rattling about Czechoslovakia is becoming more and more ominous, and I am getting very nervous and trying to get back to Switzerland. I have already asked my former Swiss teacher to send me an invitation to come and see him if this would become necessary to show to the German authorities.

What I do not know and did not count on are the delays connected with obtaining the necessary papers to leave Germany. Although I have a valid

German passport, I need a certificate from the tax office and some other documents and then at the last moment, comes an additional requirement. Everyone up to a certain age has to have permission to leave the country, which is getting ready for war and does not want anybody to go abroad. This results in my having to go to [the] Hitler Youth Headquarters, which, contrary to expectations, is not located in a grey office building with long, barren corridors and endless doors, but in a two-story villa at the outskirts of town. The regular office building with all the records was probably somewhere in the city, but the top leadership likes to live well. It is a quiet elegant place with a receptionist at the door, an open, beautiful staircase, and a skylight. I'm sent to the second floor where a uniformed high Hitler Youth official questions me at the landing.

When asked why I am not a member, I tell him I am Jewish. There is great embarrassment all around, and he rushes apologetically to get me the paper, stating that as a Jew, I am not required to be a member of the Hitler Youth.

A few days later, after hearing Hitler's speech that starts the Czech crisis,[21] I go to my room and finish packing. Very early the next morning my parents take me to the train to Zurich. They think I will be back for the next school vacation, but I know I will never return.

It is always exciting and a great adventure to take these trains which rumbled for about four hours through the Bavarian countryside. They have corridors with windows that can be lowered, and when the train stops there are signs in every station: "Do not spit on the tracks." The locomotives are coal driven, and when you lean out the window into the wind, every so often you get a cinder into your eye which then has to be carefully removed with a clean handkerchief.

This trip is different. I sit in the corner of the compartment which has its own door and is big enough for eight people. But this time there is only one other passenger: a blonde, young, good-looking woman who sits at the window, reading a book. I am afraid of being alone with her. I always remember the story of the Jew who opened the streetcar door for a woman and found himself in a concentration camp, accused of "Defilement of the race." The train gets to Lindau, the border town, built on a small strip of land reaching into Lake Constance. The passport and custom control passed without incident. The officials have more important things on their mind than a teen-age schoolboy.

Outside on the platform across the adjoining tracks stands a regiment of storm troopers, lined up in military formation. All are in brown uniforms, with swastika arm bands, black boots with flags, and a brass band. They also carry their own standards with swastikas of cloth on top of a pole. The cloth is pulled tight showing a black swastika on white with red borders and the words: "Deutschland erwache" (Germany awake). All around the banners are gilded rods with little bells hanging on the four sides. In the wind or when being carried they do what bells are supposed to do. They tinkle.

The Nazis are waiting for the train in the opposite direction, which will take them inside Germany. It is hot. There is no shade at midday and they are perspiring. It is an enormously colorful scene. The devil is not always dressed in black.

The train is slowly starting to get up steam and going toward the Swiss border which is a few minutes away. Suddenly, the blonde gets up, lowers the window, and while the train passes the long line of S.A. men, she screams at them. She calls them a bunch of stupid idiots who deserve nothing better than to stand in the broiling sun, and she has a few uncomplimentary words about their Fuehrer which leaves them stunned. Even if they had not been taken by complete surprise, there is nothing they can do, because the train is already speeding toward Switzerland. When we get out of the station, the blonde closes the window, sits down and resumes reading, apparently eminently satisfied with what she had done.

NOTES

1. The photograph printed in this chapter has been obtained from the Leo Baeck Institute New York, Ernest B. Hofeller Collection, 1928–2001, AR 5413, Box 1, Folder 4, digital images signature f002_004 und f002_005.

2. Alfred Hofeller (1889–1941), banker in Munich; married to Hildegard Hofeller, née Unikower (1889–1941), since February 6, 1917. Together with his wife and daughter Leonore (1918–1941), Alfred Hofeller was deported on November 20, 1941, and murdered in Kovno (Kaunas).

3. Adolf Hitler had been appointed Reich Chancellor by Reich President Paul von Hindenburg (1847–1934).

4. The spa town of Bad Tölz is located on the Isar River about 50 kilometers south of Munich.

5. The correct spelling is Cafe Luitpold. Lenbachplatz is a public square on the northwestern edge of Munich's city center.

6. As of December 8, 1931, all emigrants who gave up their domestic residence and whose assets exceeded RM 200,000 or whose annual income exceeded RM 20,000 had to pay 25 percent of their assets as Reich Flight Tax. In 1934, the exemption limit was reduced to RM 50,000. Those who could not or would not pay did not receive the documents necessary for emigration.

7. This probably refers to Julius Schülein (1881–1959), who emigrated with his wife Mina Schülein, née Kahn (1893–1970), to the United States in December 1938.

8. Built in 1899, the Dolder Grand (formerly known as the Grand Hotel Dolder) is a five-star hotel in the Swiss city of Zurich.

9. Leonore (Lore) Hofeller (1918–1941), sister of Ernest Bernhard Hofeller, was deported on November 20, 1941, and murdered in Kovno (Kaunas).

10. Vevey is a Swiss town on Lake Geneva (or Lac Léman).

11. Rudolf Heß (1894–1987), leading Nazi politician and, from 1933, Reich Minister without portfolio and deputy to Adolf Hitler. He was one of the defendants in the Nuremberg trial of major war criminals; he was sentenced to life imprisonment and died by suicide in Spandau War Crimes Prison in 1987.

12. Herbert Clark Hoover (1874–1964), 31st president of the United States (1929–1933).

13. Margaret Mitchell's novel *Gone with the Wind* was published on June 30, 1936, and became one of the biggest bestsellers in the history of American literature.

14. Helen Keller (1880–1968), American author, educator, and disability rights advocate, who was blind and deaf from early childhood.

15. Helen Keller's letter "How I became a Socialist" was first published in the *New York Call*, a socialist daily newspaper published in New York City from 1908 through 1923, on November 3, 1912.

16. This is a reference to the "Night of the Long Knives," a purge of Nazi leaders ordered by Adolf Hitler on June 30, 1934.

17. Bertolt Brecht (1898–1956), German playwright and lyricist. The National Socialists banned his works and their performance, whereupon Brecht left Germany as late as 1933; in 1948 he returned to the Soviet occupation zone, later the GDR.

18. The main synagogue, built in 1884/87 in the neo-Romanesque style by Albert Schmidt, was demolished in June 1938 by the Munich construction company Leonhard Moll on Hitler's personal orders.

19. The *Künstlerhaus at Lenbachplatz* is a former social gathering place of Munich artists.

20. Joseph Goebbels (1897–1945), German Nazi politician who was Nazi Gauleiter of Berlin, chief propagandist for the Nazi Party, and then Minister for Public Enlightenment and Propaganda for the German "Third Reich".

21. On September 26, 1938, Adolf Hitler gave a speech in which he announced his territorial demands concerning Czechoslovakia, which was home to some three million ethnic Germans, most of them living in the Sudetenland. The German occupation of Czechoslovakia (1938–1945) began with the German annexation of the Sudetenland in October 1938 and continued with the invasion of the Czech lands in March 1939.

Chapter 2

The Munich Years

Erich Hartmann

Erich Hartmann was born in Munich on July 29, 1922. His parents, Max Simon and Irma Hartmann, had been the owners of a manufacturing and fashion store in downtown Passau since 1922. The couple had three children. In 1933, the Hartmanns fled to Munich, where Max Simon Hartmann secured the family's finances with a small store for office supplies at St.-Pauls-Platz 7. They sought invisibility in the big city until the political terror was over, but the persecution continued and intensified. In the course of the "Aryanization" enforced by the National Socialists, the small business was liquidated in May 1938. And so, the family—father, mother, Erich at 16 being the eldest son, and his 2 younger siblings Kurt and Ruth—fled again shortly thereafter via Berlin and Hamburg to the United States.

The only English-speaking member of the family, Erich Hartmann worked in a textile mill after the family settled in Albany, New York. He attended night school and, later, night classes at Siena College on the side. In 1943, he volunteered for the American military and returned to Germany in 1945 as a GI, where he was temporarily stationed in Augsburg and was, at the war's end, assigned as court interpreter at Nazi trials in Cologne. After returning to the United States, he began training as a photographer in New York in 1946, and in 1952 he became an employee of the prestigious Magnum photo agency, founded by Robert Capa in 1947. In the 1960s, Erich Hartmann was a member of the Magnum board of directors, and in 1985/86 he served as president of the agency. In 1993/94, he and his wife, the writer Ruth E. Bains (b. 1924), to whom he had been married since 1946 (they had two children), undertook a trip to former concentration camps, which Erich Hartmann documented in the book and traveling exhibition "In the Camps."

Erich Hartmann, who was renowned for his poetic approach to science, industry, and architecture and emphasized their human cultural and geographic contexts, died in New York on February 4, 1999. He wrote the biographical text printed here in parts in his native German in 1997 after a visit to the Munich City Archives. The following excerpt focuses on his every-day life in Munich and changes for the family after 1933.

Figure 2.1   Erich Hartmann, ca. 1938. *Source:* Staatsarchiv München.

Shakespeare's King Henry the Fifth says to his officers before the Battle of Agincourt, "Old men forget; yet all shall be forgot. But he'll remember . . ."[1] The following pages do not speak of martial heroic deeds, but of retrospectives on childhood and youth, in which the child and the boy experienced courage and cowardice, good and bad deeds, and saw battles fought not with tangible weapons, but against fear and trepidation and a merciless opponent, a battle in which it was not about the conquest of ground, but about the right to stay alive in the "Third Reich."

Today, I am also an old man and forgetful, but not everything is forgotten. Even if not all the details are sharp anymore (it was a long time ago), my memory of the basic experiences of my childhood and youth is still clear—what I felt, what inner scent I carried away and preserved from people and events.

I thought long and hard about whether there might be a more than selfish purpose to reminding myself in writing of my beginning—how important is one life among the more than 10 billion today?[2] The question answered itself: thinking of my own life, I had to think at the same time of the many millions of people who had to lose their lives, unlived and unfinished, under the Nazis. I have also therefore tried to live my life in the full sense of being alive. Whether this was successful or not is not important here. In any case, this memoir is dedicated to the memory of the many unlived lives.

Munich is my birthplace, but my hometown is Passau[3] because my parents, Max and Irma Hartmann, née Blättner,[4] lived there. But when it came to the birth of their first child, the Passau Children's Hospital was not good enough for my father (it was regarding my two siblings, four and eight years later), so he took my mother to Munich, to Uncle Max and Aunt Regina,[5] and when the time came, my aunt took my mother to the Women's Hospital[6] near Sendlinger Tor. It was not a simple doctor, but a *Sanitätsrat*,[7] who transported me to the outside world on July 29, 1922. After a few weeks, the two of us were back in Passau, only now I was no longer—let's say, "in boarding" with my mother.

My childhood in Passau was protected and orderly. [. . .] Then came January 30, 1933, my mother's 35th birthday and the day the newly elected German National Socialist government came to power.[8] A torchlight procession marched past our apartment. I heard a rock smash into one of the windows in my parents' bedroom and a gruff voice yell up, "Judas verrecke!"[9]

I had believed that our parents could protect me against darkness and all evil, but I quickly understood that the dangers were much greater than those that often followed me to sleep from fairy tales and stories. It was the beginning of the hard time, whose intentions and extent seemed incredible at first, but not for long. I was ten years and six months old, and my childhood was over.

On the first day of April 1933, the Nazis organized a general boycott against Jewish stores.[10] An SA man stood in front of the store doors, and my parents and siblings and I, along with other Jewish merchants in Passau and their families, went for a walk because no one dared go near their own store. A few days later, when my father returned to his store,[11] the door was locked with a new lock to which his key no longer fit. His Christian partner told him that the business would quickly go to ruin with a Jewish co-owner and presented him with an ultimatum: accept my price for your share of the business or go away empty-handed. My father accepted the ridiculously low price offered and was out of a job and out of income. The partner took over the business as sole owner and remained faithful to his Jewish wife throughout the Nazi years.

I have never found an explanation for why my father was not also immediately sent to a concentration camp like many others—he was a Jew, successful in his work, a lifelong if passive Social Democrat. Perhaps he was not immediately arrested because he served as a volunteer and front-line fighter in World War I and was awarded the Iron Cross. For that, at least in the beginning, the Nazis still had respect, even for Jews.

We moved to Munich. That's a big city, and people were more open-minded there than here. We had relatives there; dad found customers there among the many Jewish companies; and we weathered this storm of hatred and anger there—[but] it couldn't stay like this for long. My mother found us a garret apartment on St. Paulsplatz. My father, a trained letterpress printer, brokered complicated printing work between Jewish customers and small print shops and thus earned enough for us. I found Munich even more beautiful than Passau and more interesting. The streetcars! I went to the Ludwigsrealschule,[12] past the BMW shop windows in Sonnenstrasse with their glittering machines and the racing driver Ernst Henne,[13] who was adored by all the boys and who sometimes stood at the window; also passed a large gray building, an SS barracks, which is said to have once been a monastery.[14] I could see down into the kitchen; it was steaming from the big kettles, and through the open window, it smelled of meat and dumplings. After school, we played on the meadow next to our house: soldiers and Indians in the Wild West, which I knew from the Karl May books.

Soon I didn't like going to school anymore. Learning was easy for me, and this led to trouble with classmates: "How come a Jew gets the best grade in German history?!" The teachers learned the new "law" quickly, and many of the students—to call them "schoolmates" would be wrong—had fun with "the Jew boys."

When I was thirteen, I was able to leave school. My father got me a trainee position (being an apprentice was already forbidden to us at that time) in a small cliché factory[15] on Schwanthalerstrasse—an encounter with photography that was to have lasting consequences to this day. The work was interesting in parts, but the vocational school I had to go to once a week was much more interesting. Looking back, it was the people at work that I remember from those three years: one owner was a big man with hands like a peasant from the mountains; he had little to say and was friendly. The other owner was a small restless man, son of a pious Jewish father, whom I sometimes saw praying in the synagogue, married to a Christian woman and with a baby. They also had a huge German shepherd that bit me once because I got too close to the baby. The longest-serving worker—a front-line fighter like my father—didn't talk to anyone; did his work, read his newspaper during the break, went home. The two photographers were friends and argued amicably and incessantly. The etcher was an enthusiastic leica photographer and mostly talked about skiing and his girlfriend. There was a second Hartmann in my class at vocational school. Not only were we not related; he came from an officer's family and for a long time had no idea what a Jew was. He tried to teach me to smoke, but I already knew how.

One of my daily duties was to buy snacks for the people in the company by bicycle—rolls with *Leberkäs*[16] or cold cuts and beer, everything in a big bag and on top of it the liver cheese and the roll, which one of the friendly saleswomen slipped to me almost every day. Then back, past the German Theater, to the waiting people.

My Bar Mitzvah took place in the Great Synagogue on Herzog-Max-Strasse (the synagogue no longer exists, of course, it was demolished after Kristallnacht to build a "necessary" parking lot).[17] I must have said my Torah paragraph correctly, maybe even sang it well; my parents were proud. I remember better the priestly blessing pronounced over me by Rabbi Dr. Kessler,[18] with his hands on my bowed head. There was a lunch in the then still existing Jewish restaurant Schwarz in Sonnenstrasse, where I also gave a "speech." I still have the card on which I wrote it; it was not a good speech. I received many gifts, including the Philo-Lexicon, "Handbook of Jewish Knowledge,"[19] which has since wandered with me and stands before me.

The measures against us Jews—decrees, laws, deprivations—became harsher and more dangerous—and more humiliating—with each passing month. I began to believe what newspapers and radio and speakers claimed and exclaimed daily—that every Jew is a parasite, who is not to be trusted and with whom the German people should have as little to do as possible. But I was lucky; I joined the "Bund der Deutsch-Jüdischen Jugend" (Association of German-Jewish Youth),[20] from whose name the Nazis soon deleted the word "German." The camaraderie of open-minded young people who knew more than I did, and the feeling that we belonged together and could and would stand by each other as long as we were (still) together, encouraged and comforted me and gave me the faith that I still carry within me today: that I, too, have a right to the cultural heritage of this country in which I was born, that Schiller and Beethoven and the revered Johann Sebastian Bach also spoke to me. We made Sunday excursions and once a week-long bicycle trip through the foothills of the Alps, slept in hay barns (had to give our matches to the farmer's wife beforehand), looked at the royal castles from the outside. Nobody knew us, the mountains showed no hostility. [. . .]

Due to the Nuremberg Laws, our Anna had to leave us. Shortly after my birth, as a very young girl in Passau [. . .], my mother brought her into our apartment and into our family as a nanny. She cried for a week, my mother and little sister too. Again and again she said softly, "I don't know where to go." But she fought her way through, survived the war, which killed her husband early and cruelly. Today, she lives quietly and peacefully in Lutherstadt Wittenberg, a grandmother of great age. We write Christmas letters to each other.

In the large synagogue, there was now a symphony orchestra consisting of Jewish musicians, including professors who had been dismissed from their positions and pensions in opera and theater orchestras. They were allowed to play only "Jewish music"—Mendelssohn, Goldmark, Mahler, Schoenberg, others. The concerts were widely attended, but the then 15-year-old remembers that many faces were no longer devout or solemn, but were pale and dark, marked by fear. The camp gate to the concentration camp had long been visible in the inner eye, and for many it became a reality; it came closer and closer to all of us. The choice became clear: no authority, no court, no one here can or will help us out of persecution. We must leave Germany, or they will destroy us. The concern among the adults became urgent and more pressing. I felt it too—wordless, relentless, always present.

A small accident brought me into contact with Dachau for the first time. I fell off my bicycle on a rain-soaked street, and my parents sent me to the clinic near our apartment. When I got to the waiting room, two men were already there; one was standing, the other sitting on the bench. The one standing wore the black skull uniform and pistol of the SS, the other the blue and gray striped clothing and wooden slippers of a prisoner. His head was shaved, his face was gaunt and showed dark spots. No one spoke; I don't know why they were there. The SS man looked out at the spring garden, the prisoner at the ground. They did not look at each other. Once the SS man looked over at me and away again, without interest. In his eyes I saw the calm based on pure physical strength; in the prisoner's eyes I saw something I had never seen before in a face—no expression, no expectation, no hope, an empty, a blank face. I was called, the knee was quickly treated, and on the way out, the two were no longer there. I didn't see them again, but I would still recognize the inmate today.

From adventure stories I knew the expression "the blood ran like ice in his veins." Now, for the first time, I knew what that meant—I felt immediate, tangible terror as never before. I began to understand what the Nazis had begun to make of the Germany that was the land of my birth and that I loved—an icy hell, as one Dachau survivor later wrote. In those few minutes in the clean and antiseptic clinic room, I got an inkling of what it must have meant to be a prisoner of the SS, and much later I realized that I had looked into the two faces of Nazi Germany and that both were the faces of death: that of the killer and that of the victim.

The Jewish community was shrinking. Jewish business owners sold to non-Jews as best they could. Sometimes the work of many years brought ridiculously little under the great pressure of having to leave. With their departure, my father's clientele also dwindled. The new owners went elsewhere with their printing jobs. The end of my father's income and our possibility to live was clearly visible for the second time. Around the dinner table, my parents talked with friends and acquaintances into the night. I remember that I, who had learned shorthand in school, wrote the words "Spain" and "Palestine" in my secret book, and I think the adults also talked about Shanghai and Cuba. Several Zionist parties in Palestine at that time had offices in Munich to recruit immigrants for kibbutz and moshav (cooperative agricultural villages). My parents did not want to go to Palestine, but I took an evening course in Iwrit, today's Hebrew language. Behind every thought lurked the question, "What do we do? Where do we go? Where can we go? What will become of us?"

For many years, Aunt Babette, sister of my mother's mother,[21] who had raised the niece who had been orphaned at an early age, had lived in the Jewish old people's home in Würzburg, old and mentally frail, but physically healthy. My parents and a distant cousin of my mother in America,[22] of whom little was known except his name, made possible a peaceful retirement for the old woman there by jointly paying the expenses. In early 1938, my father wrote this cousin a long letter, which I translated with my school English. The content was very careful and yet clear: it is getting difficult for us here, we need help to emigrate. Could he please help us with the magic affidavit—the guarantee—that would make it possible for us to come to America? We are five . . .

My mother and I carried the letter to the post office and we began to wait. Time passed slowly, but the answer came quickly, not a letter, but a telegram in English, something like, "You don't need to explain anything, we know. The necessary papers are waiting for you at the American Consulate in Stuttgart." When I translated it to my mother, she said excitedly, "Erich, are you sure, are you absolutely sure? You mustn't get it wrong! If we tell Dad wrong, he won't get over it." I was sure, and we were safe, we were saved. It was only much later that I realized that without my father's foresight, without my mother's diligence and both of their courage and energy, none of the five of us would have escaped the camps.

Saying goodbye to Munich was easier for me than saying goodbye to Passau. Perhaps it is not so difficult the second time, perhaps it was easier because I was five years older. My youth in Munich was necessarily short because I quickly had to think and act not like a schoolboy but as an adult. We were on our way to an unknown country and an unpredictable life that would demand (and did demand) a lot from us, but we also knew that we could leave the great threat in Germany. Uncle Max and Aunt Regina accompanied us to the station and waved as the train departed—two dear, prematurely old and frail people who could not (or would not) understand what lay ahead of them. A few years later, they perished in Theresienstadt (when I was there in 1993, I looked for their grave and found none). We stopped briefly in Berlin to say goodbye to relatives, then went on to Hamburg and an American ship to New York.[23]

A few months later, we read in the newspapers about Kristallnacht and that the hunt for Jews and their deportation to the beginning extermination camps became more and more systematic and draconian. From letters from relatives who had stayed behind, which soon stopped coming, we learned of the Star of David,[24] of blackmail, of the now total lawlessness for the Jews and other enemies of the state. Only then did I know that, without our being able to know it, at the last moment a strong hand had led us out of the land of death into a free country.

Then came the war. I volunteered for the American Army, and after D-Day I served in England and France, then Belgium and Germany. Shortly after the war ended and the last camps were liberated, I was stationed in Augsburg and drove over to the former Dachau concentration camp. The many bodies found by the Allied liberation forces had been buried, most of the barracks emptied and demolished to stop the further spread of disease. In the temporary exhibition set up for visitors in a barrack that was still standing, a prisoner's uniform hung right at the entrance with a sign around its neck: "ICH BIN WIEDER DA" ("I'm back"). It was reminiscent of the prisoners who had tried to escape, had been seized again and brought back, had to stand in the roll call square with the sign around their necks, and then were slowly and methodically beaten to death in front of the assembled camp. I can still feel the terror that went through me today. I believed the sign was meant for me, too—I was back from my new home, back in the land of my birth, surrounded by the soul-crushing echo of the long and relentless inhumanity during the twelve long Nazi years. I saw before my eyes the fate of countless people just like me. I knew now that the fear that went through my limbs when I saw the SS man and the prisoner in the clinic was an accurate prediction of what could have happened to me.

NOTES

1. The St. Crispin's Day speech is a part of William Shakespeare's history play *Henry V*, Act IV, Scene iii (3), 18–67. William Shakespeare, *Henry V: The Oxford Shakespeare*, ed. Gary Taylor (New York: Oxford Univ. Press, 2008).

2. At the time of writing, the world's population was about six billion people.

3. Passau is a German city, located in Bavaria, on the border with Austria, where the Danube, Inn, and Ilz rivers meet.

4. Max Simon Hartmann (1887–1952) was married to Irma Hartmann, née Blättner (1898–1982).

5. This probably refers to Max Hofmann (1875–1940), a merchant, and his wife Regina Hofmann, née Klein (1880–1941); she was deported on November 20, 1941, from Munich to Kovno (Kaunas), where she was murdered on November 25, 1941.

6. This refers to the Munich University Women's Clinic on Maistraße, which opened on December 18, 1916.

7. German, Austrian, and former Italian title for a senior physician, roughly translatable as medical officer or surgeon general.

8. Adolf Hitler was not elected, but appointed Reich Chancellor by Reich President Hindenburg and charged with forming a government.

9. German: "Death to the Jews." Antisemitic slur that was frequently uttered in Germany between 1933 and 1945 and is still used today, especially in right-wing and antisemitic circles.

10. The "boycott of the Jews" organized throughout the Reich on April 1, 1933, was directed primarily against Jewish businessmen, doctors, and lawyers. This aggressive harassment was the first massive step toward eliminating Jews from German economic life.

11. The company Hartl & Hartmann, Passau, retail sales and dispatch of textile goods, was owned by Alois Hartl and Max Hartmann, soldiers who became friends in 1916, while they were English prisoners-of-war in France. They founded and ran the company together in 1919 and thus earned a modest, good living for their two families.

12. In 1938, the Ludwigs-Realschule became an upper school for boys ("Oberschule für Jungen an der Damenstiftstraße").

13. Ernst Jakob Henne (1904–2005), legendary racing driver of the 1930s, who achieved spectacular victories and records, especially on BMW motorcycles.

14. The company Auto-Henne was located at Sonnenstraße 5. Nothing is known about SS barracks in this area.

15. In newspaper and letterpress printing, a cliché is a photo chemically or mechanically produced printing form for the letterpress process.

16. *Leberkäse* (German), literally means "liver cheese" and is a southern German specialty made from corned beef, pork, and bacon; the ingredients are ground very finely and baked as a loaf in a bread tin until they have a crispy brown crust.

17. The main synagogue, built in 1884/1887, was already demolished in June 1938 by the Munich construction company Leonhard Moll on Adolf Hitler's personal orders.

18. Dr. Siegfried Keßler (1883–1943) lived with his family in Munich from 1926, where he taught religion, Hebrew, and Jewish history at secondary schools as a senior teacher. In March 1943, he was deported to Auschwitz where he was murdered.

19. The Philo-Lexikon *Handbuch des jüdischen Wissens* was first published in 1935.

20. Presumably, this refers to the association "Werkleute, Bund deutsch-jüdischer Jugend," a 1932 spin-off of the "Deutsch-jüdischer Wanderbund," a youth association within the Jewish youth movement in Germany.

21. Irma Hartmann's mother was Fanni Blättner, née Hoffmann (1863–1911), wife of Maier Blättner (1852–1915). It seems that Aunt Babette is not the sister of the mother of Erich Hartmann's mother, but of her father, Babette Blättner (1855–1940).

22. Could not be identified.

23. The Hartmann family left Germany on the steamship *Washington*, which departed from the port of Hamburg on July 14, 1938, bound for New York, USA, where they arrived on July 20, 1938. See Passenger and Crew Lists of Vessels Arriving at New York, New York, 1897–1957. Microfilm Publication T715, 8892 rolls. Records of the Immigration and Naturalization Service; National Archives at Washington, DC, quoted from: Year: 1938; Arrival: New York, New York; Microfilm Serial: T715, 1897–1957; Microfilm Roll: Roll 6186; Line: 28; Page Number: 120,

in: *Ancestry.com.* [database online]. Provo, UT, USA: Ancestry.com Operations, Inc., 2010.

24. This refers to the compulsory indicator introduced by the National Socialist regime, the Jewish Star or Yellow Star; persons considered Jews under the Nuremberg Laws of 1935 had to wear it in the German Reich after September 1, 1941.

Chapter 3

A Student's Fate, 1933–1945

Christine Roth-Schurtman

Christine Elisabeth Roth-Schurtman was born in Munich on November 13, 1927, as the oldest child of Bruno Roth and his wife Else, née Walter. Christine and her two younger sisters, Gertraud (Traudi) Barbara and Elfriede (Elfi) Maria, were baptized and brought up as devout Catholics. Her childhood was ordinary, normal, protected, and happy, even after 1933. They attended the local elementary school and went to the Mass every morning under the strict eye of their maternal grandmother, who lived with them in their large apartment. Also living with them was their aunt Anna, their father's sister.

Christine's Jewish father, Bruno Roth, had a freelance textile business. He loved his family but was strict, serious, quite rigid, and a completely assimilated German Jew, who had formally resigned from the Jewish community in 1923. As a child, Christine Roth-Schurtman was not aware of her father's Jewishness, other than that he did not attend the Mass with the family on Sunday. After facing increasing persecution, most notably during Kristallnacht, *gradually losing all his work and fearing for his life, Bruno Roth seriously pursued his emigration and was able to escape Nazi Germany for the United States in August 1939. The plan was for the rest of the family to follow him a year later, yet this became impossible with the outbreak and expansion of World War II and Hitler's ever-growing grip on every detail of life. Those left behind faced financial worries and great insecurities, which they were only able to overcome due to faithful Catholic relatives. Once the United States entered the war in December 1941, there was little to no communication between the two parts of the family, and life for "half-Jews"—as the Nazis classified Christine and her two sisters—continued to grow more challenging and life-threatening until the liberation by American troops in 1945.*

After many complicated formalities and two stays in Displaced Persons camps (one in Munich, one in Bremerhaven), Christine Roth-Schurtman, her Catholic mother, and her two sisters were able to leave for the United States, where they arrived on December 22, 1946. The family was reunited shortly thereafter. Christine Roth-Schurtman became a teacher, got married to William Schurtman (1932–2020), a lawyer, in March 1959, and had two children, born in 1959 and 1962. Later in life, the couple split their time between New York City and a farm in upstate New York.

Christine Roth-Schurtman predeceased her husband of 55 years in 2015. The personal recollections shared here were written in response to a request from the magazine München Mosaik *and sent to the magazine in their original German version on March 14, 1984. In them, the author talks about her experiences during the Nazi era in Munich; her father's flight and the breaking off of all communication with him during the war; the difficult supply situation in Munich and the reality of air raids; and her experiences of exclusion and resistance. The text was supplemented in a few places with paragraphs from two other personal recollections deposited in the memoir collection of the Munich City Archives, in order to illuminate biographical information and to elaborate on the topics she addressed, such as her family's reunification in the United States.*

Figure 3.1   Christine Roth as a Little Girl Near Oberaudorf in Upper Bavaria, Undated.
Source: Stadtarchiv München.

[. . .] I am "only" half-Jewish, or "half-Aryan," as it was euphemistically called under Hitler. Still, my life was deeply shaken by the events of that time.

I was born in Munich, the daughter of a Catholic mother and a Jewish father.[1] The Catholic priest who had married my parents [. . .] baptized me in the church of St. Georg in Bogenhausen.[2] When I was 3 or 4, I entered the Bogenhausen nursery school. I have several very vivid recollections of that period: the glistening dewdrops on the nasturtium leaves in the garden of my beloved nursery school teacher "Aunt" Lisbeth; a white horse, which little "Ringlet Hansi" is allowed to ride in the schoolyard; I am chosen to play an angel in a Christmas play; and something called an "election" takes place in one of the nursery school buildings, with lots of people in and out. That was early in 1933.

Later, after we moved, I attended the elementary school on Versailles Street.[3] By then, of course, every classroom had a picture of Hitler and a swastika flag. We worked on "Four-Year-Plan" programs,[4] we collected industriously for "Winter-Aid,"[5] and had air raid drills. I remember clearly, during the Saarland plebiscite in 1935,[6] writing on my slate: "If I could already vote, I would vote 'yes'!" My mother told me (only much later, since politics were then never discussed in front of us children), that my third-grade teacher, whose favorite I was, took her aside one day and said to her: "Dear lady, you really don't need to worry; the Jewish problem is solved." That was in 1936.

One day, my younger sister came home from school dissolved in tears. "Mami," she cried, "Erika called me 'Jew girl'! What does that mean?" My mother explained to her as briefly as possible that her father happened to be Jewish, that Hitler and his Nazis didn't like Jews, and that Erika's parents must be Nazis. That was that, and my sister had lost her best friend.

My father, himself born in Munich, had had Jewish religious instructions as a child but had never practiced his religion. He officially called himself "without denomination." He was always the one to play the "Christchild"[7] at our house, and his uncle Ignaz[8] was our "St. Nikolaus." With serious devotion, my father photographed my first communion, Corpus Christi processions, the ordination of priests in our St. Gabriel's church, and sold many of his pictures to the Munich Catholic church paper. But all that meant nothing—he was officially classified a Jew and the Nazi "laws" took their course of horror relentlessly.

My father was a textile salesman. He represented textile firms in the Rhineland, whose products he sold wholesale and retail. Before long, he lost all his accounts, because "Aryans" weren't allowed to employ Jews any more. [. . .] Now, my father seriously studied photography, in the hope that at least he could earn some money free-lancing. [. . .]

In April of 1938, I entered the "Girls' High School am Anger," then directed by Sister Laurentine Bloessner,[9] who, knowing about our family situation, particularly took me under her wings. The following year, when the school was taken over by the city (i.e. it was taken away from the nuns), Sister Laurentine gave my parents permission to skip me from grade one of the high school to grade three of the Humanistic Gymnasium.[10] Grade three was the lowest grade available, since the nuns had been given the promise that they could finish out already existing classes of the Gymnasium, but not accept new ones. That promise, as so many others, was not kept and, in 1940, the city took over the Gymnasium also.

In the meantime, during "Crystal Night," November 9, 1938, the first public mass terror against the Jews in Germany had taken place. I still remember it well: my father's sudden mysterious disappearance; my mother's extreme nervousness, especially when I came across her the next evening in the kitchen digging in boxes full of letters and photographs, some of which she was burning over the gas flame (one picture, I know, was a photo of my actor uncle Ludwig,[11] my father's brother, in the role of Kurt Eisner[12]), and I remember the horrible fear in my mother's face when the doorbell rang. [. . .]

Later, I discovered that my father had fled into the mountains on his light-weight motorcycle, tried without success to cross the Swiss border, and had found refuge in a convent. Ten days later, he returned home. During that period, my uncle (my mother's younger brother)[13] had had the courage to meet my father three times in small villages to bring him money, clothes, and news . . . In the meantime, all Jewish men in Munich had been taken to Dachau. Their heads were shaved, and after a short time, most of them were released.

Now, finally, my father pursued his emigration to America in earnest. But that was not easy—one had to register with the American consulate in Stuttgart and was assigned a number; then one waited until the number was called. In the meantime, one had to find a sponsor, an American citizen who declared himself willing to accept financial responsibility for the immigrant until the latter was able to support himself. After much fruitless searching, my father found, through our loyal family friend Lotte W., who was my music teacher, a Quaker family in Boston, who offered an affidavit for my father. The plan was that my mother, my two sisters, and I should follow him a year later.

The summer of 1939 was full of uncertainty and tension. I still did not know exactly what was happening. My parents spoke as little as possible about external events, as well as about their feelings—out of the great fear that we children might, sometime, say something politically risky in public. My sisters and I (we were 11, 9, and 7)[14] were sent to a Catholic children's home in Schäftlarn[15] (paid for by Caritas[16]), where we suffered the most agonizing home sickness.

Shortly after our return, my father left Munich. The weight and content of his luggage had to have official approval, and he was not allowed to take more than $10.00 (perhaps it was 10 marks?). His ship landed in New York on the day war was declared in Germany.[17]

The next few years were truly hellish for me. My mother, who had always led a rather protected life, suddenly had sole responsibility for three little girls. She had no income and only small savings. Germany's situation was horrifying domestically as well as in its foreign relations. And so my poor mother suffered a terrible depression, which also had physical effects—she had constant stomach cramps and was as if paralyzed.

By skipping a grade and changing to the Gymnasium, I was forced to catch up on three years of Latin, as well as lots of math and history. Although I'd always been a good student till then, my grades got worse and worse—I simply couldn't cope with so much at once, academically as well as psychologically.

My grandmother,[18] who had lived with us for many years, became ill with stomach cancer and died in 1940. My beloved Aunt Hanna,[19] my father's sister, who also lived with us and who had never (I don't know why) registered for emigration, moved into the only remaining Jewish children's home in Schwabing,[20] where she helped to take care of orphans.

We had to give up our nice large apartment and move into a tiny one, where the four of us shared a small bedroom.

Slowly, my mother became stronger again in body and soul. She found work as a seamstress (earlier, she had sewn all our dolls' clothes!) and so earned herself a little money. Her two brothers, one a chemist, the other a government tax official,[21] gave us incredibly loyal assistance, morally as well as financially. Both of them had refused to join the Nazi party and were therefore denied any promotions.

Several of my father's relatives still lived in Munich, all of them under the most difficult circumstances: they had to wear the hated yellow star, officially had to use Sara or Israel as middle names, were not allowed to use public transportation, or to visit theaters, movies, museums, restaurants, or parks. Almost all stores were forbidden to them. We helped them as much as we could.

In the fall of 1941, they were ordered to make preparations for their deportation to a "labor camp": work clothes, warm things, trade equipment where applicable . . . Thus, a cousin of my father's who was an elegant fashion designer packed a small sewing machine . . .

Once more, I visited my Aunt Hanna in the children's home: the little children sat or stood in their white cribs and watched us with large, dark, sad eyes—without a whisper—as we said good-bye to each other, crying . . .

Together with Aunt Hanna, my great-aunt Regina was also deported, as well as her two daughters [Johanna and Marianne] and her 7-year-old granddaughter Ilse, and several other distant relatives, and friends.[22] A week later, we received a postcard from Aunt Hanna, from "under way": "We are fine. We'll write as soon as we arrive."

They never arrived. We were told after the war that the whole transport was gassed outside of Riga, still in the cattle cars in which it had traveled.

When America entered the war in December 1941, we could correspond with my father only through the Red Cross: 25 words once a month censored. And so, my mother wrote: "Relatives left . . ."

Jews living in mixed marriages were soon taken to the camp at Theresienstadt. Among them was my great-uncle Ignaz—at the age of 78. Miraculously, he returned in 1945.

In 1943, a ruling was passed that all "half-Aryans" over 14 must leave high school. That applied to my middle sister and me. [So that was it: the Nuremberg Laws were kicking in for us. I didn't know a lot about these laws then beyond their name, though they had been on the Hitler government books since 1935. In icily bureaucratic language, they regulated every aspect of the lives of Jewish Germans: how they would lose their government positions, their teaching jobs, their professions, and when they had to dissolve their businesses, give up real estate, turn in jewelry and silver, give up their Aryan maids, and whom they could marry (only other Jews). Starting in 1936, Jewish kids could no longer attend public schools and had to switch to all-Jewish schools. Every prescribed action was bound to a timetable. And now, the time had come for us "half-Aryans."][23] I therefore had to leave the Gymnasium at the end of 6th grade.[24] It was very hard for me to give up daily contact with my classmates.

My possibilities for work were also very limited. But as soon as I turned 16 [in November], I found work as a "Chemical Laboratory Young Worker," as it was called in "pure" German Nazi jargon.[25] In a hospital lab, my main job was the washing of test tubes; but my wonderful boss [. . .] allowed me to assist him during his lectures for lab technicians, and so I learned a lot of interesting things. Later on, we were all required to help carry patients into an air raid shelter during the alarms [which was in a never-finished subway tunnel underneath our building. The patients were strapped into stretchers, and I was truly petrified that one might slide off and fall down the stairs. The tunnel floors were usually flooded, though they were covered with wooden planks. We would stay with the patients till the all-clear sounded and then carry them back upstairs].[26]

All schools were now evacuated to the country because of the air raids, and my former classmates were sent along to take care of the younger children. My youngest sister (she was 12) was not permitted to join her evacuated class because she was not a member of the BDM[27] (which she was not allowed to be, of course!).

[Food was always a big concern. With everything so strictly rationed, we often had to wait in long lines for bread, some margarine, a little meat, or even water, when pipes had been damaged. We also scrounged around for fuel: wood, a little coal, both for heating and cooking. Our apartment had no central heating system, and the winter of 1943/44 was brutally cold. We also spent many hours helping friends and relatives whose apartments had been damaged in air raids: nailing broken windows shut with plywood, removing debris, even re-shingling roofs.][28]

1944 brought increasingly worse air raids both day and night, a horrendously cold winter, hunger, and then, in July, the unsuccessful assassination attempt on Hitler. Afterwards, many people, some probably involved, were arrested and executed. Among them was Father Alfred Delp, the incomparably intelligent, understanding, kind Jesuit, to whose youth group in Bogenhausen I belonged. He was shot on February 2, 1945 (I think of "high treason").[29]

During the last few months of the war, rumors circulated continuously that "persons of mixed blood" were to be deported to labor camps—for street cleaning, rubbish removal, etc. Whether my mother would have been involved, too, we luckily never had to find out. American troops liberated Munich at the end of April 1945.[30]

My father, who didn't even know if we were still alive, was now finally able to make contact with us again—at first through an American soldier stationed in Munich. He had become an American citizen in the meantime and could therefore very soon request our emigration. But it took a while till the American consulate functioned in Munich, and till all the necessary formalities were taken care of.

People in Munich, or at least we young ones, tried to normalize life again as quickly as possible. My former classmates and I went hiking into the countryside (on foot or by hitch-hiking, since public transportation was nonexistent); we made parties, took dancing lessons; all that surrounded by ruins and plagued by hunger. But we celebrated life . . .

A very good family friend, [. . .] an English teacher who was "quarter-Jewish" and had therefore been unable to teach under Hitler, made it possible for me to attend an interpreter school in Schwabing to learn English intensively.

Finally, in the summer of 1946, everything was ready: for a short time, we still had to live at the Funk barracks in Milbertshofen,[31] where we, together with several hundred survivors of concentration and labor camps, waited for a departure date to Bremen. These were amazing, admirable people! After unimaginable horrors, they were determined courageously to start a new life, like the Polish family with whom we shared a room: a mother, her daughter and her son-in-law, who had been concentration camp inmates, and now the young couple had two-month-old twins! Never again have I seen such deeply radiating joy.

It was not easy for me to say good-bye to Munich. Munich was, after all, my home town. And our specific circle of relatives, acquaintances and friends had stood by us in unconditional loyalty through terrible, dangerous times. We had been very lucky.

In August of 1946, we were transported (ironically, in cattle cars, since all normal trains were destroyed) to Bremen, where we, again housed in barracks, had to wait for a ship till December because of a maritime strike.

Finally, two days before Christmas, after a separation of 7½ years, we were reunited with my father in America.[32] [. . .] My mother, my sisters, and I arrived in New York on a troop transport on December 22, 1946. My father had not been notified of our arrival. After a very bewildering train journey at night from New York to Hartford, Connecticut, where my father lived, we were reunited very early the next morning in a snow storm.

As it turned out, it was not easy living together again after our long separation—not for my mother, who still loved her relatives and friends in Germany, not for my father, who understandably was totally embittered over the murder of his beloved relatives, not for me and my sisters, who had turned into young women from the children we had been in 1939. All of us, except my youngest sister, had to go to work within two weeks of our arrival, since my father had not become financially successful in the United States.

We never discussed the fate of our Jewish family. No one even tried. In retrospect, I can imagine how hurtful it must have been for my father not to receive any expression of sympathy from us, no condolences. Information about what happened to the people on this first Jewish transport from Munich was slow to emerge, and false for many years. It was thought that they had been taken to Riga and murdered there on arrival. It was not until 1999 that their true story was discovered through newly found archival material. So it continued on to Kovno (Kaunas) in Lithuania. Again, no room could be found there for 1,000 people. They were put up in decaying old Russian fortresses, and after 2 or 3 days they were ordered to go on a "morning run." As they reached ditches which had been dug earlier, they were all shot down into these ditches, layer upon layer. All this is recorded in cold bureaucratese in SS records now available.

[During an earlier visit in Munich,] I spoke of my father's—and some of my relatives'—loss of jobs and professions, all results of Hitler's "Aryanization." I spoke of my own loss of schooling. And I spoke of the ultimate Aryanization of Munich—making Munich, like the rest of Germany, "judenrein"—Jew-free, accomplished by forced emigration, and by murder. It was a challenge for me to dig up old facts again, to refresh my memory about these long-past times, and then to speak and answer questions from the moderator and the audience. My emotions were in turmoil, my body tense. But I needed to do this for the memory of my murdered relatives. I needed to do this for my father. I needed to do this for the new generation of young people [. . .].

NOTES

1. Bruno Roth (1896–1984) married Else Walter (1894–1968) in 1924.

2. St. Georg, a Catholic filial church, is the former village church of Bogenhausen, a district in the north-eastern part of Munich.

3. This probably refers to the Versaillerschule München-Haidhausen (primary school at Versailler Straße 4), now the primary school at Ernst-Reuter-Straße 4.

4. The Four-Year-Plan (German: Vierjahresplan) was a series of economic measures initiated by Adolf Hitler in Nazi Germany in 1936.

5. During the National Socialist era, the *Winterhilfswerk des Deutschen Volkes* (Winter Relief Organization of the German People) was a foundation that carried out relief campaigns ("Winterhilfe") and fundraising in the winter months to benefit needy sections of the population.

6. From 1919 to 1935, the Saar region had been separated from the German Reich and was a mandated territory of the League of Nations; on January 13, 1935, the scheduled referendum (the population had to decide whether the region belonged to the German Reich, to France or whether the status quo should be maintained) took place, in which 90.7 percent of those voting declared their allegiance to Germany.

7. In Germany, the "Christkind" brings presents and trims the tree at Christmas. "St. Nicolaus" visits little children on his name day, December 6, to lecture them about their conduct, and to dispense nuts, fruits, and candy out of his sack if they've been good.

8. Ignatz Georg Stiefel (1865–1951), Bruno Roth's maternal uncle, survived Theresienstadt (1943–1945).

9. This probably refers to Sr. Maria Laurentine (Gabriele) Blößner (1905–1972), who was a nun with the Arme Schulschwestern (Poor School Sisters).

10. In Germany, when Christine Roth-Schurtman was a pupil, high school started with grade 1 (after four years of elementary school). High school, or Lyceum, emphasizes modern languages and contemporary studies, Gymnasium ancient languages and history.

11. Ludwig Roth (1890–1968), actor, arrived to the United States in November 1939.

12. Kurt Eisner (1867–1919) was a Jewish Social Democrat, born in Berlin, who had set up a "People's State" in Munich in November 1918. Three months later, he was assassinated by a right-wing officer.

13. Eugen Walter (1901–1989), chemist.

14. Her two sisters Gertraud (Trudi) Barbara (b. 1929; owner of a sewing service; married Alexander Arzoumanian in 1953; mother to two daughters; divorced 1966; Lawrence Salzman (b. 1930) became her life companion in 1980) and Elfriede (Elfi) Maria (b. 1931; architect and landscape architect; married Robert Poirier in 1954; mother to five children; divorced 1976) experienced the years of persecution with Christine and their mother in Munich. Together, they emigrated to the United States in 1946.

15. A small town near Munich.

16. Similar to Catholic charities in the United States.

17. Bruno Roth left Germany from Hamburg (on the *George Washington*) and arrived in New York on August 31, 1939.

18. Elisabeth (called Luise) Walter, née Bareiter (1862–1940), had been married to Hans Walter (1862–1923).

19. Johanna (Hanna) Roth (1891–1941), an unmarried kindergarten teacher, moved to the Jewish orphanage in Antonienstraße 7 on May 21, 1941; she was deported on November 20, 1941, from Munich to Kovno (Kaunas), where she was murdered on November 25, 1941.

20. A district of Munich.

21. Eduard Walter (1886–1962), government finance official; Eugen Walter (1901–1989), chemist.

22. Regina Rödelheimer, née Stiefel (1872–1942), had married textile salesman Julius Rödelheimer (1893–1925) in 1893. Together with her daughters Marianne (b. 1897) and Johanna (b. 1898) and granddaughter Ilse (b. 1936), she was deported on November 20, 1941, from Munich to Kovno (Kaunas), where they were murdered on November 25, 1941. Her son Hans (1895–1975) and his wife emigrated to Spain in 1923, later they lived in Morocco. Since 1945, they lived in Brazil with their two children.

23. Taken from Christine Roth-Schurtman, "Sweet Sixteen," 1.

24. Corresponding to 10th grade in the United States.

25. Christine Roth-Schurtman's uncle Eugen knew the head of a hospital lab and arranged for her to get a job there as an apprentice.

26. After the hospital was damaged in an air raid, the decision was made to evacuate many of the lab's chemicals and instruments, such as microscopes, to the country. Sometime in the summer or fall of 1944, the hospital was completely destroyed by bombs in a night raid, which ended Christine Roth-Schurtman's work at the lab. Christine Roth-Schurtmann, "Sweet Sixteen," 3.

27. The female branch of the Hitler Youth.

28. Taken from Christine Roth-Schurtman, "Sweet Sixteen," 3f.

29. Alfred Delp (1907–1945) was a German Jesuit priest and philosopher of the German Resistance.

30. On April 30, 1945, Munich was liberated by US soldiers.

31. A district of Munich.

32. The following passage up to the end of the excerpt is taken from Christine Roth-Schurtman's manuscript "I live my Life in Widening Circles" (2004).

Chapter 4

The Jaws of the Swastika Tighten

Fred Bissinger

Fred (Fritz Albert) Bissinger was born in Munich on June 14, 1928, the son of Otto Bissinger, a merchant, and his wife Luzia Rivka, née Schloß. He had one sister, Ellen, and grew up in a liberal Jewish home. He initially attended the Simmernschule, an elementary school which was in the immediate vicinity of his parents' home in Munich-Schwabing. When he was excluded from classes there in 1935, he had to transfer to the Jewish elementary school in Herzog-Rudolf-Strasse.

Since 1919, Bissinger's father was employed as a business partner in the renowned company Weinberger & Bissinger, located at Rindermarkt 7, which engaged in wholesale and retail trade in cotton goods and tailor's articles. Otto Bissinger was arrested on the morning of November 10, 1938, and imprisoned in the Dachau concentration camp. After his release and the forced abandonment of the business, the entire family emigrated to the United States via Zurich on December 4, 1938. The voyage took place on the USS Manhattan. *Fred Bissinger, who dropped his first name Fritz Albert in the United States, became an officer in the US Air Force. He received numerous decorations and was stationed in Wiesbaden and Ramstein from 1970 to 1975.*

Fred Bissinger passed away on March 5, 2003, in Sacramento, California (USA). He wrote his memoirs of the rise of National Socialism in Munich in English in 1997, after a visit to the Munich City Archives.

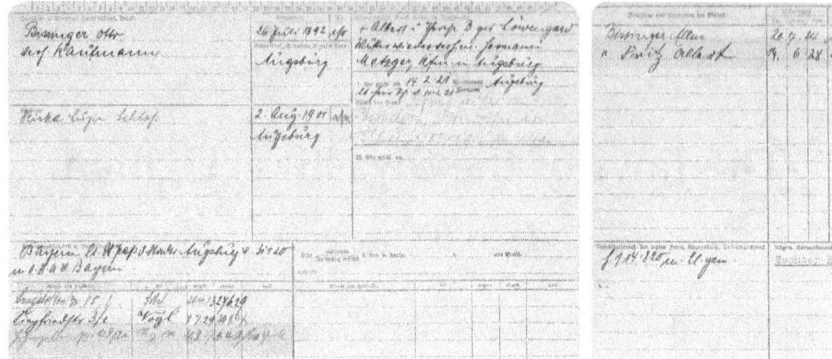

Figure 4.1   City of Munich Registration Card for the Bissinger Family, Created in the 1920–1930s. *Source*: Stadtarchiv München.

In retrospect, the turmoil that I remember of the year 1938 even now brings shudders to my memory. I was not quite ten, when in the spring of that year, I believe, it was in March, that Hitler marched into Austria, under the pretext of bringing "Oesterreich zurueck in die Heimat."[1] Officially he called it "Der Anschluss" as if Austria was a caboose to be coupled to the train of what was to be Greater-Germany (Gross-Deutschland).[2]

Traditionally, we always celebrated Passover at my maternal grandparents' home. The first home of theirs I remember was the apartment on the Wiedenmeir Strasse,[3] adjacent to the Isar River in Munich. By 1938, they had moved to Franz-Josef-Strasse 41 in Munich's Schwabing section.

There was an ominous and somber note to that Passover celebration. Just before the Seder, Oma Flora and Opa Adolf[4] gave Ellen[5] and me our Passover gifts. These presents were different from previous years. Ellen received the sheets, pillowcases, tablecloths, and towels, engraved with her initials (ERB), which in those years were the traditional bridal gifts (Die Ausstattung) from grandparents to the Granddaughter-Bride. Ellen was 14. I received a suitcase, a matching leather fitted toilet kit and a sum of money (2000DM) "for things I would need."

I did not know it then, but the decision had been made that we would leave Germany and emigrate to the United States. I was not told then, but both grandparents explained their uncertainty that they could attend Ellen's eventual marriage or even my Bar-Miztvah. I was then not yet ten years old; I only understood the solemnity and meaning of my grandparents' explanation later that year.

For Easter recess in 1938, Opa Herman,[6] from Augsburg, took my sister Ellen and me to Mittenwald. [. . .] Mittenwald is one of the most charming, scenic villages in southern Bavaria. Long the center for violin construction, it is world famous for quality, hand-crafted violins. Mittenwald is on the Austrian border. I vividly remember, from previous visits, Austrian border patrol manning the crossover points just outside the village. On the occasion of this Easter vacation, I remember German Wehrmacht now patrolling the former border, and grandfather Herman explaining to us, because we were Jewish we could not cross into the former Austria.

Grandmother Theresa died on August 30, 1935; my memories of her are vivid, warm, and loving. What I do recall is that grandfather, as a recent widower, was very brave to take a 14-year-old granddaughter and a 10-year-old grandson on a week-long trip. I have very loving and fond memories of my paternal grandfather, who with his long white beard and aristocratic bearing, stature, and appearance commanded immediate respect. Ellen and I called him OPA Herman. [. . .]

On another trip with Opa Herman, likely in 1937, he took Ellen and me to our first visit to Bechhoven, the birthplace of my maternal grandfather Adolf Schloss. [. . .] None of the family knew it then, that this was to be our last summer in Germany. [. . .]

In reading my maternal grandfather's (Opa Adolf) memoirs I became aware that the parents[7] and grandparents made the decision in 1937 that we had lost any security or future in Germany, and they applied for an American visa. By then, Richard Schloss (Sloane),[8] my uncle, and Ernst Metzger,[9] my uncle on the paternal side, had already left for the United States. The Jewish class I attended continued to lose students, as they emigrated with their parents to places like England, United States, South America, and Palestine (Israel).

Two history shaping events occurred in the late spring and fall of 1938. In June, Hitler visited Munich and while he attended a function at the Kuenstler Haus (Museum of Art)[10] on the Herzog-Max-Strasse, he asked, "What is the tall, red structure, across the street." When he was told this was the main Jewish Synagogue, he ordered its immediate destruction. The tall, multi-cupola iron-red brick, expansive building was an architectural favorite of the Munich scene. It was in direct line of sight, between the baroque style House of Art and the dual domed Frauenkirche [Cathedral of Our Dear Lady], the famous landmark of the city.

The Jewish community (*Die Juedische Kultusgemeinde*) was notified that same day that the demolition would commence the following day.[11] That very evening, the leadership of the congregation assembled and removed the Torahs from the Arc and the Sanctuary. Demolition started the next day and when complete left a large, empty lot, a parking lot, for which there was no requirement; cars were a luxury and scarce. None of us knew on Yom Kippur 1937 that this would be the last High Holiday of the main Munich synagogue. Our Rabbi was Dr. Leo Baerwald[12] and the Cantor, a young, talented, ashkenazik named Hohenemser,[13] with a booming operatic voice.

The second synagogue in Munich was and still is (reconstructed) on the Reichenbach Strasse.[14] This was a sephardic house of worship, a smaller congregation which sponsored a children's choir. Some of my classmates were in that choir I joined—a little to the dismay of my parents, who had wanted me to worship with them. Although the sephardic service was some-what strange, more orthodox and the men wore top hats, I was very proud of my long sleeved, black velvet choir gown and large black felt cap. I went to services there, singing in the choir. The fact that we children were given fruit and candy snacks MAY have influenced that decision. After the main synagogue had been demolished, all services were held at the sephardic synagogue. Events moved quickly. What started out as an anti-Jewish policy of hate, harassment, and exclusion now escalated to official state-sanctioned persecution. The die was being cast.

Only a handful of survivors will recall that the fifth grade of Munich's Jewish public school met for the last time on November 9, 1938. Neither teachers, parents, nor students knew on that day the sanctuary and classrooms would be set afire and torched that night and the student body would never see each other again.

It was only a few weeks before that fateful day that Prime Minister Neville Chamberlain (Great Britain),[15] President Eduard Daladier (France),[16] Benito Mussolini (Italy),[17] President Benes (Czechoslovakia),[18] and Hitler met at the Hotel Vier Jahreszeiten, within perhaps two city blocks, a pebble's throw away from the Jewish Public School, to carve up Czechoslovakia and incor-porate the Sudeten territory and eventually the entire country.[19] Some of us were witnesses as these world leaders entered and left the hotel. The stage for World War II was nearly complete.

In retrospect, my childhood ended in the early morning hours of November 10th, 1938. I was ten years and four months [old]. At 4:45 AM we all awoke to a loud banging of the front door to our very comfortable three-bedroom apartment on the second floor on Hohenzollernplatz 128.[20] The door bang-ing was accompanied by the dreaded announcement, "This is the Gestapo (*Geheime Staat's Polizei*)." The banging was also accompanied by the shrill sounds of the high pitched ringing doorbell. From that moment on, till the end of her days, Mother[21] would shudder whenever she heard a doorbell ring. It was a conditioned reflex caused in the early morning—November 10, 1938.

I immediately awoke to the commotion. Two Gestapo agents, dressed in civilian attire, stood in our large entrance lobby, a quadrangle, off which the main rooms were situated. They announced they were there to arrest my father. No reasons were given, nor would they answer any questions. They spoke relatively quietly and did not assault us. Dad was permitted to go to the bathroom to wash, but the door had to remain open. This was the early morning of November 10; Munich was headed for an early winter. Mother had the presence of mind to get one of Dad's warmer suits, hat, and overcoat. I believe they permitted him one small suitcase, for personal items. None of us knew why they had come for Dad. Mother was frightened, but composed. Of course they did not allow him to have breakfast and in a very short time Dad left with the two agents. There was a tearful goodbye. Dad was stoic and I remember him saying this was a mistake and he would return shortly.

Mother and Ellen and I went to the living room window, and I will always remember that sight. He is walking, flanked by the two Gestapo escorts, carrying that small suitcase. Even today, nearly 60 years later, time has inexorably inscribed this scene in my mind. I still see the scene in the dark of night.

Our living room windows overlooked the Hohenzollernplatz and we watched as they crossed the street to the Teng Strasse, which was on the street car line going to downtown Munich. In the early morning, wintery mist, the entire scene was a dark, silent grey; the only activity in sight was Dad and his Gestapo guards. The only sound was the threesome, in near-military gate, on the wet pavement. Mother made numerous phone calls to my grandparents who lived nearby, to business associates in vain effort to determine why Dad was taken. Up to this point, the discrimination and harassment was directed at a specific section of the population. This now escalated to personal confrontation. Within a few hours, the circumstances became evident. The single remaining Munich synagogue and the Jewish public school (*Die Juedische Volk Schule*) had been torched, set aflame, and the fire department stood by to ensure there was no collateral damage to adjacent buildings. Many of the retail stores now displayed printed flyers, "Business with Jews is not desired." ("*Geschaeft mit Juden ist Unerwuenscht.*") [. . .]

Mother called my grandparents, Oma Flora and Opa Adolf Schloss, whose apartment at Franz-Joseph-Strasse 41 was within 15 minutes walking distance. Mom prevailed on them to leave their home and come to us. She was certain that the Gestapo would also pick up Opa Adolf, who was then 67 years old. They left immediately and moved in with us. We became aware later that day, that indeed the Gestapo had attempted to pick him up. (German law required that every resident register the domicile with the local police. This information made the arrest sweeps possible.)

Additional information was piecemeal. The radio reported that "numerous, independent actions against Jewish institutions had broken out in the Reich, as reprisal for the assassination of a German diplomat in Paris and that thousands of adult Jewish males had been taken into protective custody." Eyewitnesses informed Mom that the Munich Jews who had been arrested were assembled at Gestapo Headquarters, on the Wittlesbacher Platz[22] in downtown Munich. In those days, the very name Wittlesbacher Platz was a sinister pseudonym for the dreaded Gestapo headquarter in Munich.

Within the next few hours, we became aware that Dad had been taken to Dachau, under a provision euphemistically named by the Nazis as protective custody. Who was under protection was never made clear. The news received via the state-controlled radio announced that "spontaneous" actions all over the Reich were directed at all houses of Jewish worship, known Jewish business establishments, and that thousands of Jewish males had been arrested and sent to concentrations camps. The names most often mentioned were Dachau, 25 minutes from Munich, Buchenwald in eastern Germany, and Sachsenhausen, near Berlin.

The reason given was this was a reprisal for the assassination of a second secretary at the German embassy in France. The accused was a French Jew by the name of Gryngspan,[23] I was told that three of my Jewish teachers had also been arrested. Our school had been torched; I was not [to] see the site again, until 1955, when as an American Air Force Officer I was to return, for the first time, to Munich. [. . .]

The next three weeks passed ever so slowly and my recollections are a little vague. Opa Adolf and Oma Flora had moved into the master bedroom and Mother would visit their apartment periodically for very short times. Most days, Mother spent the entire day at Gestapo Headquarters talking to whomever would listen to get Dad released. She was energetic and unrelenting. She wrote letters to the Gestapo informing them that we had a quota number for emigration to the United States. We received two postal cards from Dad in Dachau, the front of each was a pre-printed message outlining the rules of mail to inmates. Of the two cards, one survived. When we dissolved the parents' apartment in 1969, I reasoned that Dad would not want to be remembered for his Dachau experience and destroyed it. I regret doing that. The other card is dated November 16, and Dad requested a postal deposit of 15 marks to be spent at the Dachau canteen. This was the maximum allowed. Ironically, he wrote, this is a onetime request, as everything was furnished. I suspect this was a Gestapo dictated message.

One significant event of this time is firmly in mind. Mother, Ellen, and I were walking on the Odeonsplatz, across from the Feldherrnhalle[24] in downtown Munich. I remember having bread to feed the pigeons I believe it was a Saturday afternoon. I can still see the big black Mercedes convertible screeching to a hold, within feet of where we were standing. An SS officer, in black SS death-head uniform, wearing spectacles, approached us. He took my mother's hand, came to attention, clicked his heels and looked her straight in the eye and congratulated her on being "a fine Aryan women, with two good-looking Aryan children." He patted Ellen and me on the head. I can still feel that pudgy, soft, wet hand. Mother stammered something and he disappeared, back to his car. Mother blushed and said to us, "Do you know who that was?" Of course I had no idea. Mother explained, "That was Heinrich Himmler."[25]

Here is Dad in the concentration camp in Dachau and my blond, blue-eyed Jewish mother is mistakenly congratulated for her Aryan appearance. This episode, a postscript to Mom's most trying days has a message of its very own. Mother would say years after, "I wish I could have disappeared into a sinkhole in the pavement."

Dad had been confined in Dachau for three weeks. Now that school was closed for me I have little recollection of how we passed the time. On the afternoon of the 30th of November, I had a music lesson at a private music school. The woman who was my teacher continued to provide private lessons, even after they were told to drop their Jewish students. I was learning to play the block flute, also known as the recorder. I used to bike to the school on a used, reconditioned bike I was given on my eighth birthday. That bike was my joy. We used to take our bikes to Oberammergau and the four of us biked all over the Bavarian Alps. The bikes then had one speed and on those mountainous roads we pushed as much as we rode. Great Memories.

On returning form my music session, I came home in the later afternoon and to my great joy I was greeted by my Dad, Mom, Ellen, and Grandparents. Dad looked very strained, his hair had been cut to a stubble and he had lost some weight. It was a tearful, joyous reunion. Dad did not say one word of his experiences as a prisoner in the concentration camp Dachau, and that silence would continue for the rest of his life. He did tell me that my teachers were killed, and the manner of his telling made me think he was a witness to those and other murders.

A condition of his release was that he was to leave Germany, within 72 hours and was under sentence of death if he ever returned. He never returned. Dad was released in the first group of what the Nazis called Haeftlingsjude (Jewish inmate). The reasons for his "early" release is a combination of circumstances. My parents had a quota number for emigration to the United States and permission from the Swiss government to temporarily stay in Switzerland as transients. We only became aware after the war that it was the Swiss who requested Nazi Germany to mark the passports so that German Jews could be identified. The Nazis stamped Jewish passports with a large J and every female was given the obligatory first name of Sara and all males received the name Israel [since 1938]. This was the precursor to the yellow stars all Jews were obligated to wear as of 1941. The names Sara and Israel were entered as appropriate in the German passports. [. . .]

Dad was a decorated combat officer in World War I. He served at the front for the entire war as an artillery officer, was wounded and decorated with the Iron Cross.[26] He remained active in the reserves and assembled with other Jewish war veterans on annual reunions and parades. [. . .]

I believe that Dad's release with the first group was also influenced by Mom's tireless efforts and energetic knocking on and opening traditional closed doors. I also believe that Mom's activism could easily have placed her in danger. Dad was a highly respected business owner in Munich, employment at Weinberger & Bissinger was considered a plumb. [. . .] Dad became partner in 1919 with Weinberger & Bissinger at 7 Rindermarkt, two long blocks off the Marienplatz, near a Munich landmark, Der Alte Peter, a well-known church. Weinberger & Bissinger had offered employment to many, was respected for its quality business practices and support of communal service efforts. In very seldom conversations as to what transpired in Dachau I do recall he mentioned that it was common knowledge that guards and administrative personnel had been customers.[27] The business was involuntarily liquidated by Opa Adolf and Dad in 1938. [. . .]

I have few specific memories of the early days, of December 1938, after Dad's release from Dachau. My main recollection is the large wooden crate, in German it was called (ein Lift) into which our furniture was taken, sitting on a flatbed, parked in front of our apartment house on the Hohenzollern Platz. This was the container to be shipped by sea to the United States. We were size and weight limited. Books were carefully segregated; some of my favorites did not make it. My bike was too big and was left behind. I do recall that the Gestapo agent took inventory of my parents' belongings and checked off each piece as it was loaded. I was not aware of it at the time, but Mom told us later that she hid her diamonds into the spindle and rolls of thread into the treadmill Singer sewing machine, which had a checker board surface, to the underside of which was affixed the sewing machine. It was one of the last pieces to be loaded and to her dismay there was no apparent room. After some consternation and re-shuffling, the sewing machine was the last piece to [be] loaded unto the crate.

The Gestapo agent's final job was to wax seal the crate to be certain no "contraband" could be added.

As a child I frequently played with Dad's Prussian dress helmet, which had the round artillery ball on the top, rather than the spike, his dress belt and sword. It is not surprising that none of his uniform or military equipment was taken. Of his military mementos, his artillery field glasses, decorations, and WWI German dog tags remain with us.

We said goodbye to Opa Adolf and Oma Flora, with the full expectation that they would follow us [to] the Switzerland. The Bissinger's were on a 72-hour escape schedule. [. . .]

The next day, we left the apartment and for our last night moved into the Hotel Bayerischer Hof, then as now a four-star hotel, not far from the site of the former synagogue. Dad was not allowed to take any money out of the country. He treated Mom and Ellen to a hair coiffure at the hotel. The trip to Switzerland and the cabins on the USS Manhattan[28] were pre-paid. Dad spent his last marks on two four-colored mechanical pencils, one for Ellen and one for me, which I treasured for a long time.

Our train was to leave early the next day. We took a taxi to the Munich train station. The early morning was cold, frosty, and very quiet. All of us very quiet. We had our individual thoughts. I was very aware that a significant chapter in my young life was about to end. Grateful, that the four of us were together, but a sadness for leaving friends and familiar places. Leaving for places unknown, for a future that was also unknown and much different from what we were about to leave.

My last memory of Germany was when the train stopped on the Swiss-German border, the last stop in Germany. Uniformed SS and Gestapo boarded the train, checked every passport and every passenger. They were particularly slow in checking the papers of male adults, whose close cropped hair was the telltale sign that they had just been released from confinement. That last stop on the way to freedom seemed to take forever. As the train pulled out of that border town, Mom and Dad exchanged a very intimate look and their sigh of relief was louder than the clacking of the wheels on the tracks.

Mother would say in the following years, "It was five minutes before midnight." When that train made its first stop on the Swiss side, the four of [us] got off, stood on the platform adjacent to the train, and Dad said, "Let's all breathe some free air."

We arrived in Zurich on December 3, 1938. We were free. Mother would say later, "It was five minutes before the gates were closed" ("Fuenf Minuten vor Torschluss"). The jaws of the swastika closed in September 1939.

NOTES

1. German phrase, meaning: "Austria back to the Homeland."

2. Austria had been part of the German Reich under international law since the signing of the Law on the Reunification of Austria with the German Reich on March 13, 1938.

3. This refers to the Widenmayerstrasse, an inner city street located on the eastern edge of Munich's Lehel district.

4. Oma and Opa—grandma and grandpa—refers to merchant Adolf Schloss (1871–1963) and his wife Flora, née Jandorf (1877–1949), maternal grandparents of Fred Bissinger, emigrated to the United States via England in 1938. They were passengers on the *SS Lanastria*, which left Southampton for New York on December 18, 1939.

5. Ellen Ruth Anker, née Bissinger (1924–2004), sister of Fred Bissinger, emigrated from Munich to the United States with her parents and brother in 1938.

6. This refers to Fred Bissinger's grandfather Hermann (Herman) Metzger (1863–1954), second husband of Therese Bissinger, née Loewengard (1870–1935), whom she married a few years after the death of her first husband, Augsburg merchant Albert Bissinger (1858–1895), with whom she had two sons, Fritz (1890–1914) and Otto (1892–1961).

7. Otto Bissinger (1892–1961) and his wife Luzia Rivka (Lucy) Bissinger, née Schloß (1901–1969) arrived in the United States with their two children in March 1939.

8. Richard Schloß (1904–1957), uncle of Fred Bissinger, emigrated to the United States in February 1936, where he called himself Richard Sloane and married Lore Levy (1913–1982).

9. Ernst (Ernest) Adolph Metzger (1900–1970), son of Herman Metzger, and Therese Bissinger, brother of Siegfried Metzger (1899–1917) and half-brother of Fred Bissinger's father Otto Bissinger arrived in New York on June 5, 1938.

10. This refers to the Künstlerhaus, which opened in 1900 and was built according to plans by the German architect Gabriel von Seidl (1848–1913).

11. The main synagogue, built in 1884/87 in the neo-Romanesque style by Albert Schmidt, was demolished in June 1938 by the Munich construction company Leonhard Moll on Hitler's personal orders.

12. Dr. Leo Baerwald (1883–1970), rabbi of the Jewish Community of Munich since 1918, emigrated to the United States in 1940.

13. Jacob Hohenemser (1911–1964), cantor in Munich from 1936 to 1938, was incarcerated in Dachau in the fall of 1938 and, after his release in 1939, fled to the United States, where he served as cantor of the Temple Emanu-El congregation in Providence, Rhode Island, until his unexpected death in 1964.

14. The "Reichenbach School," founded in 1931 by Jews of Eastern European origin, was desecrated during *Kristallnacht* and the interior was completely destroyed; after 1945, the synagogue at Reichenbachstraße 27 was restored and officially reopened on May 20, 1947. For 60 years, until the moment of the inauguration of the new main synagogue Ohel Jakob (Tent of Jacob) at St.-Jakobs-Platz in November 2006, it served as the main synagogue and community center of the Jewish Community of Munich.

15. Arthur Neville Chamberlain (1869–1940), British Conservative Party politician; prime minister of the United Kingdom from 1937 to 1940.

16. Éduard Daladier (1884–1970), French politician and prime minister during January–October 1933, nine days in January and February 1934, and from April 1938 to March 1940.

17. Benito Mussolini (1883–1945), Italian politician; prime minister of the Kingdom of Italy from 1922 to 1943, dictator of the fascist regime from 1925.

18. Edvard Beneš (1884–1948), Czechoslovak politician; he was foreign minister from 1918 to 1935, prime minister from 1921 to 1922, president of the state from 1935 to 1938 and from 1945 to 1948, and president in exile from 1940 to 1945. Beneš was not invited to the meeting in Munich.

19. This refers to the Munich Conference, which took place on September 29, 1938, in the Munich Führerbau on Königsplatz. The "Munich Agreement" signed by the aforementioned heads of state on the night of September 30 stipulated the cession of the Sudeten region, sections of northern and western Bohemia, and northern Moravia to the German Reich.

20. This refers to Hohenzollernstraße.

21. Luzia Rivka (Lucy) Bissinger, née Schloß (1901–1961), had married Otto Bissinger in Augsburg on February 14, 1921.

22. This probably refers to the Wittelsbacher Palais on Brienner Straße, the Munich police headquarters at the time.

23. Herschel (Hermann) Feibel Grynszpan (1821–1942/1945), a Polish citizen of Jewish faith, had emigrated from Germany to France in 1935, where he shot and fatally wounded the German diplomat Ernst vom Rath (1909–1938) in Paris on November 7, 1938.

24. The Feldherrnhalle, whose architectural model is the "Loggia dei Lanzi" in Florence, was built between 1841 and 1844 by order of King Ludwig I of Bavaria to commemorate the Bavarian army and its victorious commanders. In 1923, the battle that ended Hitler's beer hall putsch took place here.

25. Heinrich Himmler (1900–1945), German Nazi politician; Reichsführer-SS (from 1929) and Chief of the German Police (from 1934), also Reich Minister of the Interior from 1943, Commander of the Reserve Army from 1944. He committed suicide after being captured by the Allies in 1945.

26. The Iron Cross (*Eisernes Kreuz*, EK), an original Prussian, later German war award. From 1813 to 1918, the upper class of the Iron Cross was one of the highest Prussian war awards.

27. Author's footnote: When in 1972–1973 I met with *Bundesnachrichtendienst* (BND) personnel in Munich on USAFE exchange visits, the name Weinberger & Bissinger was still well remembered and respected.

28. The *Manhattan* launched on December 5, 1931, and was renamed *Wakefield* in 1941. The Bissinger family arrived in New York on March 3, 1939 (Departure Port: Le Havre, France).

Chapter 5

An Emotional Handicap

Hugo Holzmann

Hugo Holzmann was born in Munich on March 27, 1929. His mother, Anna Holzmann, née Reiter, had been raised Catholic but converted to Judaism before her marriage to Martin Leopold Holzmann in 1924. He was a merchant and proud World War I veteran soldier who had received several decorations, including the Iron Cross, First Class. After he died of illness a decade later, Hugo, his older sister Herta Jeanette, and their mother endured poverty in Munich.

In 1935, Hugo was expelled to the all-Jewish school in Herzog-Rudolf-Strasse. On November 20, 1941, he had only 16 classmates left, all of whom— except for Hugo—were among the almost 1,000 Munich Jews "sent to the East" on that day. They were shot dead upon arrival in Kovno (Kaunas), Lithuania. In the eyes of the Nazis, his birth made Hugo Holzmann a "half-Jew," a fact that defined his life during the "Third Reich" but kept him safe from the danger of deportation until shortly before the end of the war.

In April 1942, the Gestapo assigned Hugo to a garden company for forced labor. For the following three years, he served as a decorating assistant at a garden nursery belonging to a Nazi party and SA (Stormtrooper) member. During this time, his mother, who refused to renounce her Jewish conversion, was in a Nazi work program. On January 8, 1945, their two-room apartment (without bathroom and kitchen) was destroyed in an air raid, and so Hugo and his mother decided rather spontaneously to go into hiding. With the help of neighbors, Hugo was taken in by a family in the countryside while his mother found shelter with her sister in Vilshofen, a German town in the district of Passau. Due to this decision, Hugo escaped capture by the Nazis and deportation to Theresienstadt after the Nazis removed all protections from the so-called Mischlinge in February 1945. He remained hidden until the liberation by American troops on April 29, 1945.

In December 1946, Hugo emigrated with his mother to Philadelphia to join his sister Herta, who had successfully emigrated to the United States in 1938. Hugo joined the Army in 1947, became a sergeant, and served for 20 years, including tours in Korea and Vietnam. After retiring from the service, he worked for the University of Colorado in a supervisory capacity before moving to Solana Beach, California, with his wife Isabella, a Ukrainian Jewish survivor of World War II.

Hugo Holzmann passed away on October 22, 2019, and has been laid to rest at Miramar National Cemetery, located approximately 15 miles north of downtown San Diego, California. The short essay included here provides an insight to the experiences of a "half-Jew" during the Nazi period. It was first published in "The Hidden Child 25th Anniversary Issue: Infant Survivors of the Holocaust—The Last Witnesses. A Publication of Hidden Child Foundation" in 2016.

Figure 5.1 Hugo Holzmann, Passport Photo c. 1938/1939 (Kennkarten-Doppel).
Source: Stadtarchiv München.

I believe my handicap first appeared on the day of my bar mitzvah, Saturday, February 28, 1942. By then, there were only a couple dozen schoolchildren left in Munich, my hometown. Most of them were now living in the Jewish orphanage.[1]

My father[2] had died in 1934, due to seared lungs, which he'd contracted as a German soldier in 1918 during a British gas attack. In 1938, my mother, Anna,[3] had managed to get my sister, Herta,[4] then 14 years old, to a Jewish couple in Philadelphia who adopted her. Mother had tried to get me adopted by an American couple too, but by 1940, when my papers were ready, the ship that would have brought me to America could not leave because of U-Boat danger.

We were forbidden to use public transportation, so Martin Sandbank[5] and I[6] walked every day to the only remaining synagogue, in the Lindwurmstrasse,[7] to meet Cantor Lachmann[8] who taught us our Torah portions. Martin had his bar mitzvah a week before mine, and he and his sister, Bertel, left for Nuremberg to join relatives. Their father[9] had been killed in Dachau. Scheduled to take the Kovno transport[10] in November 1941, their mother[11] and the children had taken poison. She died, the children survived. But in the end, in April 1942, Bertel,[12] Martin, and their Nuremberg relatives were sent to Izbeka[13] and then to Chelmno.

On the day of my bar mitzvah, my mother and I walked the one-and-a-half hour to the synagogue. In the courtyard, our names were checked off a list held by two Gestapo men, who also examined our yellow stars to make sure they were sewn on properly. As we entered the synagogue, Dr. Kessler,[14] the only teacher we had left, told us that the Gestapo had arrested Cantor Lachmann, and that he would conduct the service and my bar mitzvah. Terrible news on my day of confirmation!

When the men to be called to the Torah gathered in front, I did too. When Dr. Kessler called my name, I went to the *bimah* where the Torah lay open and sang the *broches* [blessing]. Before chanting from the Torah, I glanced down and there sat the Gestapo men, staring at me. Out of extreme fear, my voice trembled, my body shook. Could I continue in such a moment of panic? Emotionally overwrought, I willed myself to go on and finish. Upon returning to my seat, a man said "the Gestapo left when they saw you in a panic, but you did well."

From this time on, into adulthood and old age, I have not been able to speak in front of a group or audience, not even to state my name. There was the time when I was in the army in Honolulu. My wife and I were in a large group of military men, some with families, going over to a rest camp in Hilo. The MC had a list and said he would call everyone by name, asking each person to state his name and unit. When he reached my name, I was in a dreadful state. My voice quivered as I knew it would. This was but one of many incidents when I succumbed to panic. Only now in my old age, am I able to overcome this emotional handicap.

NOTES

1. This refers to the Antonienheim of the Jewish Youth Welfare Association (Israelitische Jugendhilfe e. V.), which was located at Antonienstraße 7.

2. Martin Leopold Holzmann (1884–1934), a textile tradesman, moved to Munich on November 1, 1912.

3. Anna Holzmann, née Reiter (1895–1982), was born Catholic, converted to Judaism before her marriage in 1924, and remained Jewish even during the period of persecution. In 1941–1942, she had to wear the yellow Star, she was obligated to do forced labor, and she received only the inferior Jewish ration cards (about 700 calories daily). After the end of the war, Anna Holzmann emigrated to Philadelphia in 1946 where she died in 1982.

4. Herta Thomas, née Holzmann (b. 1924), was brought to safety in the United States as a 14 year old where she was adopted by an American family in Philadelphia.

5. Martin Hans Sandbank (1929–1942) was sent to the Antonienstraße children's home together with his sister Berta after their mother's suicide in November 1941; moved to relatives in Nuremberg on March 21, 1942; was deported on March 24, 1942 from Nuremberg to Izbica Ghetto; murdered there on April 10, 1942.

6. Although a person with only two Jewish grandparents, Hugo Holzmann was legally considered a "Jew" (so-called *Geltungsjude*) because he met the first of the additional categorical conditions set by the Nazis for defining a person with two Jewish grandparents as a Jew, namely, he was enrolled as a member of a Jewish community when the Nuremberg Laws were passed in 1935.

7. In October 1938, only a few months after the demolition of the main synagogue, the Jewish community had to vacate the administrative buildings in Herzog-Max-Straße 3–5 directly next to the former main synagogue, which it had first moved into in 1888. As a substitute, the community was allocated premises in the former tobacco factory Abeles GmbH at Lindwurmstraße 125. The former machine room on the first floor was converted into a prayer room that could accommodate about 500 people. During *Kristallnacht*, these rooms were destroyed, and the property temporarily seized. It was not until November 22, 1938, that the Gestapo released the rooms. A little later, on December 14, the new *Betsaal* (prayer space) was opened. In June 1942, the *Betsaal* was closed by order of the authorities.

8. Julius Lachmann (b. 1887), married to Meta Lachmann, née Sachs (b. 1891), worked as a cantor and religion teacher for the Jewish community in Munich since 1923. They were deported from Munich to Piaski on April 4, 1942, where they were murdered.

9. Moritz Lasar Sandbank (1894–1941), businessman and engineer, was married to Luise Regina Sandbank, née Bergner (1905–1941).

10. On November 20, 1941, the first deportation train with almost 1,000 Munich Jews departed from Munich. It arrived on November 24 or 25, 1941, in Kovno (Kaunas) in German-occupied Lithuania, where all were murdered.

11. Luise Regina Sandbank, née Bergner (1905–1941), died by suicide on November 12, 1941.

12. Berta Cäcilie Sandbank (1928–1942) suffered the same fate as her brother Martin Hans Sandbank (1929–1942).

13. Izbica, located 36 miles south-east of Lublin, was declared a ghetto after the occupation by the Nazi Germany in 1939. Until its dissolution, about 26,000 people passed through the ghetto.

14. Dr. phil. Siegfried Keßler (1883–1943) married Selma Keßler, née Weinberg (1881–1943), in 1910. Since June 1926, he taught religious education, Hebrew, and Jewish history at secondary schools as a senior teacher in Munich. Together with his wife, he was deported on March 13, 1943, from Munich to Auschwitz, where they were murdered.

Chapter 6

A Jewish Child Growing Up in Nazi Germany

Pesach Schindler

Rabbi Dr. Pesach Schindler, Rosh HaYeshiva, was born in Munich on April 11, 1931, to Alexander Moshe Schindler and his wife Esther, née Zwickler-Stiel. His grandparents had moved from Eastern Europe to the Bavarian capital at the turn of the century, where the family ran a small grocery store. By the time their first child was born, the family business established by the Schindler couple had evolved into a mail-order company that also employed non-Jewish staff.

Together with his brother Ruben, who was two years younger, Pesach Schindler grew up in an Orthodox home and followed the rise of the National Socialists in the "capital of the movement." He attended the Jewish kindergarten and, from 1937, the Jewish elementary school in Munich. To escape the threat of arrest by those in power, his father fled in the spring of 1938 via Poland and Italy to New York. His wife, a Polish citizen, was able to follow him to New York in 1939. It was not until the end of 1939, however, that the two stateless sons, who had been temporarily housed in a Jewish orphanage, received their long-awaited entry permits to the United States, where the family was reunited in 1940.

Pesach became Peter after arriving in New York. During his first months on the Lower East Side, he attended a public school and then transferred to an Eastern European yeshiva. As a violinist and violist, he developed a passion for music, was a member of several symphony orchestras, and graduated from Brooklyn College in New York with a BA in music in the mid-1950s. In 1956, after years of study, he was also ordained as a rabbi. In 1964, he received a Master of Science degree from Yeshiva University and, another eight years later, earned his Doctor of Philosophy degree from New York University. From 1959 to 1972, he held various administrative positions in

*Toronto, Canada, and New York, USA, before he moved to Israel in 1972.
For more than 25 years, he was chairman of the United Synagogues of
America in Israel and director of the Center for Conservative Judaism in
Jerusalem, the city where he finally settled with his wife, Shulamit Feldman,
and their five children, and where he taught Talmud and rabbinic studies for
decades at the Rothberg International School of the Hebrew University and
at the International School of Yad Vashem.*

*Rabbi Dr. Pesach Schindler passed away on August 2, 2017, in Jerusalem,
Israel. He wrote his memoirs addressing his childhood in Nazi Germany in
September 2004. They are dedicated to his parents.*

Figure 6.1   Pesach Schindler, November 2008. *Source*: Photo property of Daniel
Kalman Epstein, ©2021.

[. . .] The Jewish community in Munich has a history stretching over 700
or 800 years. It was one of the smaller Jewish communities in Germany
and Western Europe, never reaching more than between 6,000 and 10,000
Jews. My family were defined as "Ost-Juden," Eastern European Jews,
who migrated from Poland. German Jewry was composed of two groups:
German Jews, sometimes referred to as "Yekes," who had been living in
Germany during many generations; and the newly-become Germans, such as
my grandfather,[1] who came from Galicia, from the shtetl of Tuczyn, next to

Rajcza (Rzeszow), where the Schindler family had lived during their formative years. [. . .]

Why would my grandfather decide, in the year 1888, to leave the seeming pastoral scenes of the shtetl in Eastern Europe? At "home" within his familiar Hasidic and Yiddish speaking surroundings? The reason was, of course, parnosoh, livelihood. As his family grew to include four boys and three girls, he immigrated to Germany in search of better economic conditions. Armed with a Hasidic lifestyle and incredibly unrealistic expectations, he settled in an alien and hostile environment. In Munich, my grandfather opened a little grocery store.[2] Since he sold kosher goods, I remember it being especially busy during Pesach time and prior to The High Holy Days.

Owing to the Nuremberg Laws and the open hostility to Jewish children enrolled in German schools, I never attended the public school system. The Jewish community was compelled to create its own schools. This is where I received my initial education. [. . .]

Outside of life at school and within the family circle, we learned early to appreciate the spiritual and cultural shelter provided within our modest Jewish community. My family had been very active within the community, helping build a small Hasidic synagogue, a shtiebel. The Schindler family from my father's side was Belzer Hasidim.[3] Any time that the Rebbe in Belz, Poland, would send emissaries to make contact with relatively wealthy Eastern European Jews who were now in Munich, they would stay at my grandparents' home. Our shtiebel in Munich was named Mahzike Ha'dat ["those who strengthen Faith"], the very name that Belzer shtieblech have to this very day everywhere, including one in Jerusalem. [. . .]

GROWING UP IN MUNICH

While I grew to the ages of four to six, Hitler rose to power in Germany. My memories were of Munich streets and plazas frequently serving as stage settings for grandiose Nazi party demonstrations, with shouting and lauding, trumpets and drums. Children of my age were often dressed in the uniform of the Hitler Youth. Street extravaganzas were staged in order to transform ordinary citizens into obedient masses—to encourage them, among other things, to join the antisemitic campaigns promoted by the Nazi government in Germany. Huge street banners written in Gothic German letters screamed: "The Jews Are Our Misfortune."[4] Why would I and my family and my people be the misfortune of the German people? I could not arrive at any answers. When I attempted to discuss it with my parents,[5] inevitably I would be told that there are bad people and there are righteous people in this world. We would have to be able to learn to live in such a world of black-and-white contrasts.

I also remember torch parades when Hitler came to Munich. Mussolini[6] visited him there in 1937, and once again in 1938. It was mandatory that every apartment in Munich have a metal torch affixed to its windows facing the streets. Masses, hundreds of thousands of people responded to this hysteria in the form of torch parades. People were excited. I myself was swept into these mysterious and powerful emotional experiences. If you were not part of this mass psychosis, you simply did not belong. The situation was tense and very uncomfortable for Jews.

I clearly recall one occasion, when I was in grade one in the Jewish school, that my friend Kupfer[7] and I saw anti-Jewish posters plastered on bill-boards. Although my reading level had not achieved the sophistication of deciphering "Do not Visit Jewish Physicians" and "Do not Buy in Jewish Stores," we felt that these public instructions concerned our people. The proper thing to do was to tear them down.

And so we did. As we were busy with our childish and foolish act, a man in a raincoat asked for our names which he jotted down in a small notebook. A few days later, I was asked to leave my classroom. In the corridor, I met my friend Kupfer, who was in a higher grade.

Accompanied by the synagogue and school caretaker, a gentile, we were taken to the Munich police for interrogation. Kupfer was asked to enter a room with other men. After what seemed like a moment, he came out crying. I realized that this was more than an interrogation concerning our childish prank. They seemed to look at this seriously. An apology would not have sufficed. I was then called in. They asked who was it who had sent us to tear down the posters. Were we part of a larger gang? Who were our parents? Who were our teachers? I was told in a threatening voice: "If this happens again, not only will you be sent away, but your parents will be sent away as well!"

MY FATHER'S ESCAPE: SPRING 1938

Working in our family's business "A. & S. Schindler," a catalogue mail-order house, was a German who was a member of the Nazi party. He was now torn between two loyalties. On the one hand, he was able to support his family as a result of working for the Schindlers, the Jews.

On the other hand, he was committed to Nazi ideology. This man, evidently having some influence in the local Nazi party, noticed that my father's name and my aunt's name—my father's sister-in-law, my aunt Sally Schindler[8]— were on a list of Jewish business people who were to be sent either to Dachau or to Sachsenhausen, the earliest of the concentration camps. This was part of a Nazi campaign, by which Jews who had businesses would be sent there for a week or two of "education." When they came back, they usually sold their businesses to the Nazis for a fraction of the price of their actual value. This "good" Nazi shared this critical information with my father and aunt. That very night, they decided to flee Germany. Their families would follow.

My father made his way to Milan, Italy. There he awaited the elusive visa being sponsored by the Klaristenfeld family,[9] our cousins who were residents in New York City. This process compelled him to remain in Milan for a number of months attempting to reduce the tortuous delays of seemingly endless impediments. In contrast, my aunt's efforts went relatively smooth. After checking into a hospital in order to blur any evidence of her whereabouts, she made plans to bring her family to Switzerland where she had contacts, and from there they would emigrate to the United States.[10] She would eventually see her son Rabbi Alexander Schindler lead the Reform Movement in Judaism in America.

Incidentally, I failed to note that prior to their respective escape to Italy and Switzerland, they exited Germany via the Polish border in order to bid farewell to the Hasidic Master, the Belzer Rebbe, Rabbi Aaron Rokeach,[11] and to receive his blessings as they embarked upon their fateful journeys. They received his special blessings.

KRISTAL[L]NACHT: NOVEMBER 1938, MUNICH

In August 1938, my father arrived in New York City.[12] Given the deteriorating situation, he immediately set out to bring out my mother, myself—at the time seven years old—and my brother Ruben, a year and a half younger.[13]

But time was working against Jews in Germany. The government under the totalitarian rule of Adolf Hitler integrated into their legal system draconian laws which aimed at expelling Jews from every aspect of a normal life. Among these was a decision to expel Jews of Polish origin and citizenship from Germany. On October 28 and 29, 1938, trains began to move from north to south collecting Jews rounded up by local police. Entire families were caught in this web of expulsion and literally dumped on the Polish side of the border. They came to our home as well.

By then, my father was no longer there. We told the police that our father had left and had abandoned us. But they would not believe us: "Jewish fathers never abandon their families." We were told to get our packages together. We would be expelled to Poland on the next train. My mother and brother took refuge in the Polish Consulate. I somehow managed to remain inconspicuous until my mother returned to our apartment before Shabbat. To this day, I have difficulty reconstructing these events. We literally "missed" our train. On the Polish side of this international drama, the Polish government refused to accept the Jews. Thus, approximately 10,000 Jews were stranded without shelter or food in no-man's land near a Polish village Szponzin. My grandparents, uncles, aunts, and cousins were among this forlorn community on this cold October. Polish Jewry quickly rallied to ease their plight. The Polish government protested, and the international community expressed their revolt in the media. The Germans were taken aback by all this fuss made over some alien Jews and they, for the moment, canceled the expulsion. After a harrowing experience, the trains transported the Jews back to their communities in Germany.[14]

One of the families who survived the ordeal was the Greenspan family from Hanover. When they were able to return home, they sent a postcard to their 17-year-old son Herschel,[15] who was living in Paris, describing their misfortunes. Herschel Greenspan decided to take vengeance. He obtained a gun and went to the German Embassy in Paris. He asked for the Ambassador of Germany, who happened not to be there at the time. He was then shown in to see the third consul, whom he shot, was critically wounded, and died shortly after.

Herschel Greenspan's actions set off the events of the night of November 9–10, 1938, known as Kristal[l]nacht. That night, our synagogue, the Kanalstrasse Schule, adjacent to our school went up in flames.[16] Jews who were attempting to rescue Sifrei Torah[17] were kept away by police. Firefighters were on the scene. Their job was to make sure that the flames did not spread to Aryan property. I remember seeing scores of Jewish shops on the morning of November 10; they were burned and plundered. While my brother and I were on the way to our classes, the main streets were littered with glass, hence, Kristal[l]nacht. Although German insurance companies suffered heavy losses for the huge damage, eventually it was the Munich Jewish community and all other German Jewish communities who actually had to pay a tremendous tax to pay for the cost of the damage that took place on Nov. 9–10, 1938.

My Mother's Decision

Kristal[l]nacht set off a panic among German Jews. There were enormous lines outside the travel agencies as people attempted to get out. Every week my class diminished in size.

My mother was also caught up in the panic. Wearing her best clothing, she dressed us up as well and took us to the American Consulate in Stuttgart. We encountered a frenzied scene at the Consulate. Applicants for visas had at most 10 to 15 minutes to state their case before the local US consul. When she finally got her turn, my mother told our story to the consul. She told him that her husband was already in the United States and that the family would like to receive permission to reunite as a family in the United States. It was a matter of utmost urgency in view of all that was happening in Germany. The consul responded that she could obtain a visa immediately. As a Polish citizen there was a place for her within the Polish quota to rejoin her husband. However, he added matter-of-factly, according to the Nuremberg Laws, the children were "stateless" and would not qualify for a visa.

Alone in a hostile and increasingly dangerous environment, without the relatively safe and instant international communication systems of today, my mother faced a terrible dilemma, which she had to solve immediately, before leaving the consul's office. He kept looking at his watch. Many others were outside waiting their turn. My mother began to cry. He began consulting his manuals looking for some relief from his own dilemma. He then recommended that my mother first take her own visa. She should get out of Germany while she still could. In the interim, she should place her children in a local orphanage. Once in US territory, she could then send a cable to the Stuttgart Consulate requesting visas for the children. He explained to her that according to US regulations once a mother and a father are united in the United States, they would be able to apply for entry visas for their children, including stateless children. She agreed to follow this course of action.

I cannot imagine what it must have been for my mother to make this kind of decision. Yet, she did. She enrolled us in the Jewish orphanage known as Antonienheim, located on Antonienstrasse in the Munich suburb of Schwabing.[18] At the beginning of December 1939, she came to say farewell to us. It was snowing outside, and we were about to go on a ski trip. Munich is situated on the edge of the Bavarian Alps. We were now in a children's community trying to live normal lives within an abnormal world. A child learns to shut out the traumatic and to absorb the experiences with which they feel comfortable and secure. It is likely a form of mental defense to protect one's sanity.

My mother in this quick farewell comforted us with: "We will see each other very soon." And, she was gone.

She departed by ship and arrived in the United States on the fourth candle of Hanukah, in December 1939.[19] World War II had already formally erupted on September 1, 1939.

The orphanage where my brother and I lived had a skeleton staff of adults, taking care of 140 children, from infancy till the age of 17. It was then modeled along the lines of Dr. Janos Korczak[20] who founded the famous Jewish orphanage in Warsaw. Seventeen-year-old youngsters would take care of a 15-year-old; a 15-year-old's responsibility was to work with 12-year-old children, and so down the line. The youngest, as I indicated, were infants no more than 6 months old.

How can one forget the lovely Hanukah party that was organized at the close of 1939, with the war now in its fourth furious month. Looking back, and now aware of the terrible fate of our people being slowly massacred in Eastern Europe, our children's Hanukah in Munich was a form of kedusha [an experience of sanctity][21] within that of tum'ah [defilement and desecration].[22] These were rare moments where Jewish tradition provided us with a sense of sacred memory and a moment of sanity as well.

Each child had its own story: those with parents who were inexplicably missing, and others whose parents were still somewhere in Europe but no longer in Munich. Yet, others who were actual, normal orphans.

The last time that I saw my grandfather was during our stay in the orphanage. A Hasidic Jew with beard and traditional Eastern European dress prior to the Hitler regime now came to visit us. His face was drawn, his beard a shadow of his former hadrat panim [elegant aristocratic appearance],[23] he came to visit perhaps to say goodbye. He was eventually transported to Theresienstadt. There, he met Rabbi Leo Baeck,[24] one of the great Jews of that tragic period, who was elected head of the Jewish community prior to being sent to the Terezin camp. My grandfather Avraham Yitzhak Schindler died in that deceptively conceived "Paradise ghetto." He was trapped within a hopeless population which reached 41,500 prisoners, with a daily death toll averaging 125.

OUR ESCAPE

What I did not know at the time is that plans were being made to smuggle the two of us under false pretenses out of Munich. On a cold winter day in February 1940, my brother and I were woken up at about 4 o'clock in the morning. We were taken out of our room by our supervisor and advised to remove our regular clothes. We were dressed in typical Tyrolean clothes, which were worn by many of the non-Jewish children in Bavaria, southern Germany.

One of our roommates, also a classmate, by the name of Werner Grube,[25] came down to see what all the commotion was about. He visited me in Jerusalem four years ago and reminded me of this farewell scene that I had completely forgotten. Somehow, he remembered. The kitchen staff had prepared packages of food for our unknown journey. It included a Bavarian-sized salami. I had asked innocently if the salami was kosher. This annoyed the adult, who was preparing the package. Noting my discomfort with the non-kosher food, she relented and substituted bars of chocolates. To this day, I have a warm weak spot for chocolates, which were my secure companions on the critical trip which would begin momentarily. Werner Grube and his brother [Ernst][26] were subsequently sent as children to the Terezin camp. The fact that he had a non-Jewish father may have saved his life. He still lives in Munich and is active in local civic affairs.[27] His efforts to remember this children's home eventually proved successful when the municipality built a memorial on the site where The Antonien Kinderheim once stood.

My brother and I were provided with name tags, as children traveling alone usually are. We were to be on our way to visit our "relatives" in Holland. We boarded the train, alone, without any supervision. The train at first appeared as a normal passenger train. It was crowded, however, with Wehrmacht soldiers being discreetly transported to the Belgian and Dutch borders. The troop buildup for the German invasion of the Lowlands which would materialize four months later in May 1940 was taking place before our very eyes. Whoever concocted this scenario for our flight probably felt that this may actually have been the safest route out of Germany. There were a few civilians on board. The soldiers, some who smelled of alcohol, were in a joyous mood, singing songs. We were "adopted" by some of them as a kind of a mascot.

Perhaps we reminded them of their own children. When I recall this ironic counterpoint, and contrasts of states of mind—two young children traveling alone on an uncertain journey in close proximity to self-assured, merry men-of-war, confident in their cause—I cannot help but recall a similar scenario portrayed in our ancient tradition: "The king and Haman sat down to drink, but the city of Shushan was bewildered."[Esther 3:15]

At every station, there was a civilian or two who came up to the train and sought us out. They quietly and discreetly said "Shalom Aleichem"[28] to us. Later on, I learned that these were possibly members of a Jewish underground, who were moving children out of Germany in any way possible since the Kindertransport projects to England were already coming to a climax. About one thousand of those children eventually reached the United States. We were to be among them. These unsung heroes to whom we owe our lives were members of Jewish communities who organized escape routes for children in February 1940. Time was precious as options for flight to safety diminished by the day. We subsequently were told that most of these anonymous people never made it out themselves. They delayed their own departure in order to get as many children out as possible.

The train was uncoupled in Germany and a new locomotive was attached for those who went on into Holland. We were welcomed at the station by a Jewish family in Rotterdam. To this day, I have been trying to locate who these people were. My father thinks he remembers the name "Fischer" in Rotterdam. It is very likely that none of those people survived, following the terrible bombing of Rotterdam and the subsequent transportation of Dutch Jews to Bergen-Belsen or Auschwitz.

ARRIVAL IN THE UNITED STATES

We spent a few days in Rotterdam. Dutch children were playing on huge ice blocks in the wintry North Sea. Much of the daily routine escapes me. Was it the anxiety of the unknown? The feeling that we were not in control over own routines—the lack of "normal" daily activities of children our age?

We boarded the SS Volendam[29] of the Holland-America Line and were given a room with a bunk-bed for two. I am still puzzled, more accurately upset, that we never maintained contact with the good people in Rotterdam. Were they not a critical link in our exit to life?

We began our voyage to the United States. Once again we traveled unaccompanied. The ship picked up passengers in Southampton, England, and continued to the United States. Among those on board, we subsequently learned, was a future editor of *The New York Times*. Max Frankel[30] was 12 years old on this fortunate voyage. He was somehow able to leave Berlin despite the late date, six months into World War II.

Despite the constant surveillance of British navy sea planes, it was a pleasant voyage—an island of fragile tranquility in seas of storm. This sense of optimistic anticipation which was prevalent among the adult passengers was caught by the young people aboard as well. We were "adopted" by kind people for various leisure-type activities. I learned how to play the challenging game of chess. Another gentleman taught us English . . . in a broken German accent.

We arrived in New York City harbor. The excitement reached its peak as the legendary Statue of Liberty passed before us. Needless to say, the entire passenger community was on deck. As our assigned peer in the port of Hoboken, New Jersey, was temporarily unavailable to receive us, our ship had to make its way up the Hudson River and u-turn back. While on this sight-seeing maneuver, we saw a magnificent bridge in full view bedecked with American flags. I asked an older person: "Why is the bridge flying these flags?" He replied: "Young man, America is welcoming you!" Actually, this was the George Washington Bridge and it was February 22, 1940, Washington's birthday!

And then a jovial adult, evidently in a state of euphoria, realized that he too was now free from the fears which had accompanied him and his family during his recent past, was in a frame of mind to play a harmless prank on my brother and I. He asked if we could speak English. I said that we knew no English. With a concerned look he indicated that we had about ten minutes to learn the numbers from "one" to "ten." Without passing this test we would not be permitted to disembark. Hence, we had our first crash course in an English "ulpan" right on that deck: "Van, Tu, Tri, For, Fife, . . . !"

As we came off the boat, we noticed that my mother was not there. My father came alone. We later learned that the reason for my mother's puzzling absence was a disturbing telegram from Geneva, Switzerland, received a few days prior to our arrival. The cable informed my parents to be prepared to meet "their son" on the SS Volendam upon arrival.

Fearing the worst for the other son, my mother could not bear meeting the boat. When we docked, my anguished father had no clue as to the son who was on board, and . . . who, God forbid, was left behind.

One cannot imagine the feelings of thanksgiving and joy when we were all reunited.

IN RETROSPECT

I have never spoken to my mother, ever, about her decision back in 1939 in Germany, as to why she traveled and left us there. In retrospect, this very unmotherly decision saved our lives. Many years later, we learned that of the 140 children who were in the orphanage, only 4 survived, including me and my brother and Werner Gruber and his brother.[31] The Gruber brothers survived Theresienstadt. All the others perished in Auschwitz. [. . .]

NOTES

1. Avraham Yitzhak Schindler (1872–1943), merchant in Munich, was married to Necha (or Nehama), née Tenzer (1869–1940), with whom he had seven children; he was deported on July 23, 1942, from Munich to Theresienstadt, and murdered there on May 11, 1943.

2. Since 1907, Avraham Schindler operated a ritual grocery store under rabbinical supervision and a retail shop with bottled wines and liqueurs in three rooms at Buttermelcherstraße 14/0.

3. Belz is a Hasidic movement within Orthodox Judaism founded in the early 19th century by Rabbi Shalom Rokeach (1781–1855) in the former eastern Polish, Galician small town Belz (since 1951 Ukraine).

4. The phrase "The Jews are our misfortune," which was made into a catchphrase by the National Socialist rabble-rousing newspaper *Der Stürmer* can be traced back to Heinrich von Treitschke's (1834–1896) essay "Unsere Aussichten" (1879), which triggered the Berlin Antisemitism Controversy (1879–1881).

5. Alexander Moshe Schindler (1904–2000) was married to Esther, née Zwickler-Stiel (1904–1995).

6. Benito Mussolini (1883–1945), Italian politician; prime minister of the Kingdom of Italy from 1922 to 1943, dictator of the fascist regime from 1925.

7. This is probably Erich Kupfer (b. 1929). He was deported on November 20, 1941, from Munich to Kovno (Kaunas), where he was murdered on November 25, 1941.

8. Sally (Sali) Schindler, née Hojda (1899–1992), was married to Eliezer (Lazar) Schindler (1892–1957). The couple had two children, Eva Oles, née Schindler (1924–2012) and Alexander (1925–2000).

9. Could not be identified.

10. The family of four emigrated from Switzerland via France to the United States; they left Le Havre on July 27, 1938, and disembarked in New York on August 1, 1938.

11. Aaron Rokeach (1880–1957) was the fourth rabbi in the tradition of the Belzer Rebbe and led the community from 1926 until his death in 1957.

12. According to the New York, US State and Federal Naturalization Records, 1794–1943, Alexander Moshe Schindler arrived in the United States on November 24, 1938.

13. Ruben Schindler (b. 1932) married Rachel L. Bornstein in 1960.

14. "Polenaktion" or "Polish Action" was the term Nazis used to describe the arrest of at least 17,000 Jews living in the German Reich, who had immigrated from Poland, and their deportation and transfer to the Polish border, which was carried out by the Nazis at short notice and by force at the end of October 1938.

15. Herschel (Hermann) Feibel Grynszpan (1821–1942/1945) was a Polish citizen of Jewish faith who, after emigrating from Germany to France in 1935, assassinated the German diplomat Ernst vom Rath in Paris on November 7, 1938.

16. This refers to the Ohel Jakob synagogue in Herzog-Rudolf-Straße—formerly Kanalstraße—and the Jewish elementary school in Herzog-Rudolf-Straße.

17. *Sifrei Torah* (Hebrew), "Books of Torah," handwritten copy of the Torah, meaning: of the Pentateuch, or the five books of Moses (the first books of the Hebrew Bible).

18. The Antonienheim (Children's home of the Israelitische Jugendhilfe e. V., Antonienstraße 7) was originally home to parentless and illegitimate children as well as children from socially weak families. Since 1933, there were also children there who were waiting to be brought home by their parents who had already emigrated.

19. Esther Schindler escaped Nazi Germany via Genoa, Italy, and arrived in New York on December 6, 1939. Passenger Lists of Vessels Arriving at New York, New York, 1820–1897, Microfilm Publication M237, 675 rolls. NAI: 6256867. Records of the US Customs Service, Record Group 36. National Archives at Washington, DC, quoted from: Year: 1939; Arrival: New York, New York, USA; Microfilm Serial: T715, 1897–1957; Line: 15; Page Number: 152, in: *Ancestry.com.* New York, U.S., Arriving Passenger and Crew Lists (including Castle Garden and Ellis Island), 1820–1957 [database online]. Provo, UT, USA: Ancestry.com Operations, Inc., 2010.

20. The Polish physician and important educator Janusz Korczak, born Henryk Goldszmit (1878/1879–1942), distinguished himself by his selfless commitment to children. In order to take over the management of a new orphanage in Warsaw built according to his plans, he gave up the medical profession and decided to accompany "his" children to the Warsaw Ghetto and—despite an opportunity to emigrate—to the extermination camp Treblinka, which meant certain death.

21. *Kedusha* (Hebrew), experience of holiness.

22. *Tum'ah* (Hebrew), desecration and profanation.

23. *Hadrat Panim* (Hebrew), elegant noble appearance.

24. Leo Baeck (1873–1956), rabbi and in his time the most important representative of German liberal Judaism.

25. Werner Grube (1929–2013), Theresienstadt survivor.

26. Ernst Grube (b. 1932) survived the Theresienstadt concentration camp with his brother.

27. Pesach Schindler wrote his memoirs during the lifetime of Werner Grube (1929–2013).

28. *Shalom Aleichem* (Hebrew), peace be upon you.

29. The brothers arrived in New York on February 22, 1940. Passenger and Crew Lists of Vessels Arriving at New York, New York, 1897–1957. Microfilm Publication T715, 8892 rolls. Records of the Immigration and Naturalization Service; National Archives at Washington, DC, quoted from: Year: 1940; Arrival: New York, New York; Microfilm Serial: T715, 1897–1957; Microfilm Roll: Roll 6445; Line: 5–6; Page Number: 88, in: *Ancestry.com*. New York, Passenger Lists, 1820–1957 [database online]. Provo, UT, USA: Ancestry.com Operations, Inc., 2010.

30. This is the US journalist Max Frankel, who was born Max Fränkel in Gera on April 3, 1930. He was editor-in-chief of the *New York Times* from 1986 to 1994 and is a recipient of the Pulizer Prize. Together with his mother, he emigrated to New York on the steamship *Volendam* in February 1940.

31. This assessment by Pesach Schindler is not entirely correct. For example, Ruth Grube (b. 1938), the sister of Werner and Ernst Grube, also survived.

Chapter 7

"... What One Leaves Behind"

Schwager Family Letters

Leopold Schwager (1884–1941), born the son of a leather goods merchant in Kötzting in the Upper Palatinate, came to Munich around 1900, where he attended business school for three years. In 1911, he married Sabine (Bini) Teller (1885–1941), daughter of a merchant in Unterhaid, Bohemia, with whom he had two sons: their first son Erwin was born in 1913, followed by their second son Karl in 1921. Their daughter Charlotte, born in 1912, died in infancy.

The family's life was interrupted in 1914 when Leopold Schwager became a soldier and took part in World War I, becoming an English prisoner of war in 1917. He was released in 1919. In Munich, he successfully ran a leather und shoemaker's supplies shop at Fliegenstrasse 3 with a branch in Burgstrasse. However, due to the radical anti-Jewish economic policy of the Nazi regime, he had to give up his company in 1938/39. The profiteer of the "Aryanization" was Gerhard Fiehler (1893–1950), brother of the Nazi party official and then Lord Mayor of Munich from 1933 until 1945, Karl Fiehler (1895–1969).

In 1938, Leopold and Sabine Schwager helped their sons emigrate. Karl, the younger son, left for a kibbutz in Palestine in August as part of a youth Aliyah. Erwin wanted to go to the United States but the search for an American citizen, willing to act as a sponsor for the potential immigrant and assume financial risks, was challenging. Fortunately, an aunt living in New York was willing to help, allowing Erwin to leave for the United States in October of 1938. He last lived in Pittsburgh, where he died in 1992. His brother, Karl, had followed him from Palestine to the United States in 1947, where he died in 1975 in New York City.

The parents, who had stayed behind in Nazi Germany, made desperate attempts to get out of the country. In 1939, Leopold and Sabine pursued immigration to England and by late July had secured jobs as housekeepers in London through Bloomsbury House. However, war broke out between Germany and England in September 1939, and this opportunity was lost. They continued pursuing other avenues for emigration, including to Cuba, Chile, Palestine, and the United States. In February 1941, for example, Leopold Schwager applied for a visa for Cuba for himself and Sabine, which was received at the beginning of November 1941. By then, however, it was too late to leave Germany, not least because of the war. A few days after obtaining their visas, Leopold and Sabine Schwager were deported to Kovno (Kaunas) in Lithuania together with about 1,000 children, women, and men and murdered there on November 25, 1941.

The letters published in excerpts here are merely a small selection of more than 500 family letters translated in the 1980s by Erwin Schwager. This lively and heartfelt correspondence during the years 1938–1941 shows a close-knit family that was torn apart by the aggressive antisemitic policies of the Nazi regime. They give an impression of the countless small and large problems that had to be solved—and in many cases could not be solved—before emigrating abroad. These letters also document that even if the escape across the borders was successful, this step was a traumatizing caesura for many, because the family members who remained behind were left to an uncertain fate.

Figure 7.1 Karl (Left) and Erwin Schwager, 1938. This photograph may have been the last professional photo of the brothers before they emigrated. (Photographer: Herm. Plappert, Sendlingtorblock 11). *Source:* Private Collection.

Letter from Leopold Schwager to Leo Apple, Baltimore
Munich, March 23, 1938

Dear Relatives,

This is my first letter that I address to you and I know no excuse for this, only that we are living far apart. I introduce myself to you as the oldest son of my mother Anna,[1] my name—as yours, Leo,[2] is Leopold, after our grandfather of blessed memory.

Since we are close relatives, permit me to use the "du" ("thou") usual among family members. . . . About myself I want to report, I am 54 years old, married since 1891 to my wife Bini, nee Teller;[3] I have two sons age 24 and 17.[4] I have run until now here in Germany a respectable business, wholesale and manufacturing, in which my oldest son, Erwin, helped me diligently. Perhaps Siegfried and Thea[5] told you about us. I also would like to hear about your 3 families and cousins unknown to me.

My first letter to you already contains a request and asking you for your help. I hope that your Jewish readiness for help, dear relatives, will show you ways that could fulfill my following request. Our oldest son, Erwin, wants to leave Germany to build a new life for himself in America. For this I need your help. I ask you to give an Affidavit of Support to make his immigration into the USA possible. I understand it is asking a lot to request this much in a first letter. However, you have to understand the conditions here in Germany. You are three families...surely one of the cousins is in a good financial position and can take on the responsibility of an Affidavit or part of one.

The risk you'll take is not great. Erwin is a very healthy young man (picture enclosed). He is industrious and experienced in business matters; he reads, speaks, and writes fairly good English. He would soon get ahead in America because of this. He will always thank you for your assistance. You will get to know him as a person who was worth the sacrifice. My wife was born in Bohemia and has a well-situated brother in Italy and three brothers in Bohemia, one of them in very good financial circumstances. All four brothers like my son very much and would be ready at any time to assist Erwin if he—against my expectations—would not be successful in the USA.

Please write to me whether you will be able to help me in this important step. We would be grateful to you for this family assistance. From the Jewish situation alone you will understand my request and I hope, assist us. My second son Karl we want to send to a carpentry school. He is already a carpenter and plans to go to Erez Israel after finishing his education.[6]

I look forward to your response and greet you, even without knowing you,

Your nephew and cousin
Leopold

> Letter from Leo Apple to Leopold Schwager, Munich
> Baltimore, MD, USA, April 11, 1938

Dear Relatives,

I received your registered letter and was glad to hear from my new relatives.

In reference to your coming to the United States, my mother and I went to the Hamburg-American Steamship Line,[7] where we had to inquire about coming to this country. We found out the person who signs for someone coming to this country must receive a very large income so as to be responsible for the person coming over, so as not to be an expense on the US government.

I regret to advise that I, or none of the relations here have large enough income to do anything. We all just make a fair living.

I would suggest that you make a tourist trip to this country and find out for yourself. There are thousands of people out of work.

Best of love from my mother and me, to all the relatives.

Yours very truly,
Leo Apple

> Letter from Leopold Schwager to Emilia Holub, Bronx
> Munich, April 26, 1938

My dear Ones,

You will still remember me, dear Aunt Milka,[8] and be surprised that after such a long time I am contacting you again. I hope this letter finds you in best of health; I can say the same thing about myself, my wife, and both my sons.

I don't want to make a secret of it here that this missive includes a request to you, dear Aunt. As my mother said, long ago many relatives by the name of FLEISCHER went to America. I would ask you if you have addresses for them or their descendants. Please write them to me, especially the ones that do well. The reason for this letter is that my oldest son, Erwin, wants to emigrate to the USA but he needs an Affidavit. I understand that in America there are well-situated Jewish people who would like to have a chance to help young people go to America.

It is very important to us that our children find a future away from here. We don't want to miss an opportunity to interest our relatives in the USA to help. Please don't be upset when I ask you and write for this purpose. My younger son expects to go in a few months to Palestine. My oldest son Erwin, who wants to go to America, is 25 years old, Karl 17. After 27 years of marriage, we have grown children and we'll have our children away from here and shall be alone!

I look forward to your answer, dear Aunt, and greet you most cordially and remain your Nephew,

Leopold

Letter from Emilia Holub to Leopold Schwager, Munich
New York, May 9, 1938

Dear Nephew Leopold,

I received your letter and was happy to hear from you! I still remember you very well when you took me to the train station on my trip to America. It was in Cham;[9] it is now 33 years back.

I shall now respond right away to your request in your letter. I surely feel with you when you say that both your sons want to emigrate. I found nobody here in New York of our family FLEISCHER, only an old uncle who was a German teacher and died long ago. There are relatives of ours in San Francisco. But I have never heard from them.

However, as far as an Affidavit for your son Erwin is concerned, we can make one for him. You don't have to be a millionaire for this, only a businessman or a house owner, for which we might have somebody. But we would like to know whether Erwin speaks some English and whether he worked in your factory which is very important here. You can imagine that there are a lot of immigrants here and they have only the hope for luck. It is also important whether Erwin wants to work hard. In that case everything may work out for the best. Perhaps you also will be able to come and you and your family will be together once more. This is how many German families do it. It therefore depends only on the capabilities of Erwin, and we shall try to help as much as we can!

There is not much to report about us here. Thank G'd,[10] we are quite healthy; of course, we are rather old and worked out. I am always happy when I receive some lines from my sister, also your mother. It has been rare, I hope she is well. [. . .]

Now we look forward to your further letters with the greatest of pleasure. Best regards to you and your wife Bini and your sons,

Aunt Milka

N.B. I would like to mention that Erwin should learn the sewing and gluing of shoes. It might be good for him here. With knowledge of working by hand, things here are often easier.[11]

Letter from Leopold Schwager to Emilia Holub, Bronx
May 27, 1938

Dear Aunt,

Your dear letter brought to us an extraordinary amount of joy.

That you and your family will give an Affidavit to Erwin I learned with many thanks and you took a great worry from our shoulders with your information. Your letter, which by the way was sweet and good, the way I remembered you always, gave me once more the assurance that one has friends and relatives in many places who are willing to sacrifice and who—without many big words—feel what is urgently needed!

I did not want to ask you yourself for the Affidavit and put a burden on you; but since you offered it on your own, I am doubly pleased that you and your dear ones are so helpful to us relatives in Germany. Erwin also will thank you for this always.

First of all, I want to assure you that you will not incur great risks with the guarantee for Erwin. He is a very healthy, capable, young man, happy to work, industrious, and has been my right hand here all the years—six years—that we worked together in my business, at home, or on the road. He is a good sportsman, quick, ready for all work, and experienced in many things. He will easily find his way in America without trouble and—G'd willing—get ahead. You probably know I have for many years owned a well-managed and important business here; it was my great hope that my sons one of these days would enter this business. But fate wanted it that they themselves have to build their own futures.

A picture of Erwin is enclosed, also a testimonial from his former boss where he apprenticed. Both shall prove to you what I mentioned before. I might say Erwin is quite advanced in the English language. He has been practicing for years intensively, has conversation one evening a week with an American student, has been subscribed to the LONDON TIMES WEEKLY EDITION for three years which he reads fluently and quickly. Also, I want to mention that for five years he has been a careful and experienced driver of a car and took business trips winter and summer in any kind of weather. He traveled everywhere by himself, an experience that is acknowledged nowadays in the world. A few days ago, he also passed a test for driving heavy trucks. He already has many friends in the USA who surely are ready to help him with advice and deeds.

Erwin has worked little in my shoe-manufacturing business and I shall try to teach him yet as much as possible from my own extensive knowledge in shoe designing. I myself shall try to reduce the risk as much as possible. As much as foreign exchange laws permit, I shall give Erwin a small amount of money for his emigrating so that he possibly can help himself. Also, a well-situated, unmarried brother of Bini who has been living for years in Italy will possibly help Erwin.

Now permit me to ask you, dear Aunt, by what time we may count to receive the Affidavit so that we may take further steps with the American Consulate in Stuttgart. Erwin shall report to you regarding necessary data. My dear mother[12] is well and thank G'd in good condition. Only writing is hard for her now in her—thank G'd—eighty years. I am enclosing a letter from her and my sister Mina.[13] I went yesterday evening with your letter to the Liebigstrasse to Mother, who was very happy with the news and read your letter repeatedly.

Many thanks once more for your offer and receive many regards from us all, also to Uncle and Gretl,[14]

Your true-loving Nephew
Leopold

Letter from Erwin Schwager to Emilia Holub, Bronx
Munich, May 27, 1938

Dear Aunt,

It is hard to express really how much joy your letter brought to us. This, the more so, because you offered us your help in obtaining an Affidavit. Already here I want to thank you very much for this and I just wish that your and my own endeavors shall lead to a good ending!

We have tried here with all our strength to maintain our existence for the last few years. Today, however, it has become an absolute necessity that I myself should try to find a new homeland and a place to build a future. It has been my intention for a long time to make my immigration to America possible, the more nowadays since I already have quite a few friends and acquaintances in fairly good jobs.

First of all, I shall improve my knowledge of English to the point where I may be able to go job hunting from the first day after my arrival.

From the local agency of the UNITED STATES LINES, I obtained a form for the Affidavit necessary for my immigration, which I include. The UNITED STATES LINES, New York, Broadway 1, they tell me, will be available at any time to help with the proper execution of the papers and to give any necessary advice.

To question #7, I speak German, English, and Latin.

To question #19, my address is: Munich 5, Gaertnerplatz 4/111

MY NAME: Erwin Schwager

Day of Birth: July 24, 1913

Land of Birth: Germany

Town of Birth: Munich

Profession: Merchant

Let me add to the letter of my dear Father that I am very healthy, physically and mentally. Before obtaining the permit for the immigration to the USA, I'll have to pass a medical examination at the American Consulate in Stuttgart that has to confirm the above.

Finally, let me add that I shall undertake everything possible after my arrival in the states to become independent and to avoid anything that might be to you, dear Aunt, or to the person giving the Affidavit, any cost or financial burden. I do not doubt in the least that my efforts shall soon lead to success.—Many thanks once more for your letter and the help offered.

With many cordial regards to you and dear Uncle, I remain,

Erwin

Letter from Emilia Holub to the Schwager Family, Munich
New York, June 5, 1938

My dear ones,

Yesterday, I received your letter, written by all of you and I was very happy with it, especially to learn that you are all well. Also, that my dear sister is well. Certainly, your dear children and grandchildren give you much pleasure and I wish you from my heart that you, dear sister, may enjoy this for a long time and many good things in the circle of your family.

I was very happy to receive your photograph, dear Leopold and Erwin, and we shall try to get the Affidavit for you as quickly as possible. Dear Gretl and her husband shall give the required guarantee and it will take a few days since these papers also have to be signed by a notary! I also was glad to hear that you, dear Erwin, are able to read and write English, this will help a lot! You will soon be an American citizen!—The main thing I want to report to you today [is] that I shall go this week with Gretl and Sylvia[15] to the country. They took a little house on the beach at the Ocean and we shall stay a couple of months over the summer. Please use the following address the next time: A. Holub. c/o M. Katz, 179 Beach 56 Place, Avenue, L.1., N.Y. [. . .]

Furthermore, I want to say that we don't require any thanks for the Affidavit, we are glad to do this. We hope that you, dear Erwin, will have luck and we shall try here to help you with this here as much as we can. If you should arrive before we are back from the beach, we shall still get you from the boat and we shall have shelter for you. [. . .]

Now many regards and kisses from all of us. Just stay all well. This wishes you and yours the best. Your sister and aunt

Milka

N.B. I would like to add that I am glad to read that Erwin will work in the shoe manufacturing so that he can learn leather cutting and anything he can learn will be of help. By accident, we know here such an enterprise!

Letter from Erwin Schwager to Emilia Holub, Bronx

Munich, July 22, 1938

Dear Aunt,

To our great joy the Affidavit arrived here yesterday. You can imagine the first thing I did was to mail it right away to Stuttgart.[16] Indeed, the entire immigration, all purchases now and also steps to be taken with the authorities depend on when I'll be called to the American Consulate. As soon as I'll have an answer from there, I'll report this to you because I'll be able to make the date for my immigration to the USA.

I thank you also for the information you wrote to me to purchase a photo camera which of course I'll gladly do![17] [. . .] As my dear Dad wrote to you, I am trying to get some experience in our shoe-uppers manufacturing place in leather cutting and design. I hope I can manage to learn enough in this short time that I may be able over there to find at least a starting position, until I'll know my way around!—You can imagine that we have a lot of shopping to do right now also because of the emigration of my brother Karl.

Now I wish you, dear Aunt, also your dear ones [. . .] a good summer recreation and beautiful days.

I am looking very much forward to get to know all of you soon personally and greet you in the meantime most cordially,

Erwin

Letter from Erwin Schwager to Emilia Holub, Bronx
September 29, 1938

Dear Aunt,

All of us here again were delighted to receive your letter of September 14. You can imagine that we expected it with real desire. We nearly thought your letter may have got lost. We hope your cold has improved. And we hope that you in New York will have the same outstanding fall weather that we are experiencing here. We forwarded the greetings to dear grandmother. All of us here once more got together with grandmother at the Jewish New Year's holidays as always in previous years. A few days ago, Uncle Fritz went with his family to Zurich to continue from there to Palestine.[18] Just about every day, one has to take best friends and family members to the railway station. Regretfully, there are still a lot of people here for whom it would be very important to emigrate who have a bitter financial battle.

[. . .] I thank you especially for your fine words that our family one day will be together once more. It is naturally important now that I shall get ahead in the USA which I really expect to do! Then, we shall be able to find practical possibilities. One always has to hope!

My own travel preparations still are not completely finished. I still am working to improve my knowledge of English. I also have tried to put my luggage together as simply and practical as possible so that there won't be any difficulties on arrival. The sea travel, as reported before, will start October 26 on the SS President Roosevelt.[19] I hope there won't be any changes. The boat is nearly full. It is impossible to get any more tickets for that date.

Here, we are always kept very busy, and our business demands a steady pace. As you can imagine the last few days were exceedingly exciting. We just hope that the get-together of Hitler, Mussolini, Chamberlain, and Daladier has prevented the most important difficulties![20]

Karli[21] has written very special and satisfactory letters from Palestine. He is satisfied with the climate and scenery. When you know the beauty of Munich and the Bavarian mountains, which Karli loved, it is hard to imagine how he could befriend himself so quickly with life and surroundings of Erez. He already is able, as he writes, to work there in a carpentry shop and to improve his knowledge in his profession.

Should there be any changes concerning my departure from here, I shall inform you of this right away. I am already counting the days to my emigration. And I can only repeat I am really looking forward to meeting you all, hopefully in the best of health, and to get to know you. And if I shall only have a bit of luck with my plans, I can assure you, dear Aunt, and everybody that has done so much for me that you shall not have much trouble with me for sure! For today the most cordial regards,

From your
Erwin

Letter Written by Erwin Schwager to Emilia Holub, Bronx
Munich, October 17, 1938

Dear Aunt,

This morning we received your dear letter of October 7, for which we thank you very much. I would have written to you today so that you would have received mail from me before my departure. You may imagine that we had a lot to accomplish the last days and weeks. There is still a lot to be done in the days ahead and to finalize many details. Up until today, we had with all this work a lot of luck, thank G'd, and it feels good to see the preparations come to their end.

I shall spend the next days saying my good-byes to many friends and relatives that are still here. There are still a lot of trifles in our business that, also, have to be discussed. My luggage is already on its way since last Friday to the ship in Hamburg. I hope I'll find it there in good condition. All pieces shall go to New York in the baggage room of THE PRESIDENT ROOSEVELT, and they can stay in the warehouse there at no cost for 2 weeks. Up to that time, we may decide then without haste and talk about how best to store everything.

I regret to have to add that the moving camera which I would have liked to bring, was not permitted for me to take. You only can export new items when required professionally, which I could not fulfill. On the other hand, I bought a very beautiful typewriter, which I enjoy a lot, which I need urgently as a merchant.—Before departure, dear Aunt, I shall send you a telegram yet with paid return answer. Please leave this unused so that we can wire my parents of my arrival.

I am looking forward to the trip very much. I took ocean trips previously and had no trouble on the ocean even in bad weather. A good friend of mine will accompany me on the boat so that I'll have excellent company. I hear there will also be Americans on the trip. I look forward to that I shall depart here a week from this Monday. Tuesday will be the embarkation and Wednesday morning we shall leave Hamburg at 2 a.m.; in Le Havre where the boat will remain a while, a good friend of mine will come to the ship, and then in Southampton a cousin of mine will see me, who is married in Birmingham. We are enclosing a letter from dear grandmother which she wrote today for you. [. . .]

I look very much forward to my arrival in America to meet you all there! I am convinced that it won't take me long to find a job. I have tried all these weeks to improve my knowledge of English. Until today, I have kept my lessons going. I hope you will all be satisfied with me!

Once more my cordial and best thanks to you, dear Aunt, and to everybody. And for the last time: "To a beautiful and healthy Wiedersehen!"

Yours,
Erwin

Letter from Leopold Schwager to Erwin Schwager, New York
Munich, October 31, 1938

My dear Erwin,

Your letter plus 4 postcards, 2 from Hamburg, 1 from Le Havre and from Southampton was received here. Even though there was sadness mixed into your good reports, the contents gave us much joy; they speak of your courage and readiness for battle.

Now that I am writing this letter, you are destined to your journey towards life. I can no longer advise you, we can no longer complete each other, which we have done so often for many years.

When this letter reaches you, you'll be already in New York and have the struggle ahead of you. Keep your head up, my boy. You will win this battle. Your youth, your diligence, and your fitness will help your forward.

Quick and agile as you are, you will learn to master all difficulties and be polished by them and grow to be a real man after all the difficulties. Be always undaunted, trust in G'd, and you will reach your goal. You will experience disappointments and often you will have to postpone your wishes. But if you possess the hard, definitive will, everything will just be minor matters, to enrich your experiences and to steel your determination.

And now with G'd, my boy, be without hesitation, and time will be on your side and my side.

Together with your letter from Southampton came one also from Karli. He writes so cleverly and reasonably that you cannot believe that he is only 17 years old. You can see that living in a foreign country already has reshaped him. I just hope it will become more quiet in Erez so that we could have pleasure to know he is there.

I am enclosing a letter from the "Jewish Women's Organization."[22] You will learn from it that the relatives in Baltimore were really not in a position to give an Affidavit. [. . .] We sent a return-telegram Friday and expect to receive the confirmation of your arrival.

Regards to all our loved ones from me, especially to Aunt Milka. And be many times most cordially greeted and kissed by your always concerned for you

and True-loving
Father

Letter from Sabine Schwager to Erwin Schwager, New York
Munich, November 7, 1938

My dear Erwin,

I waited with this letter to you until the customers and employees were gone to write to you in a quiet surrounding. I have a lot to tell you and shall try to start at the beginning, what has happened since your departure. Let me mention right here, nothing unpleasant occurred. The days roll by like programmed, without pleasure, connected with a lot of work. But we like it that way because otherwise one has too much time to think of oneself.

Yesterday, we received in the morning the telegram, telling us of your good arrival. This improved our Sunday, knowing you did land all right. In our minds we were with you the entire trip. I nearly believed in my sleep I felt the ship roll and when I once woke up in the morning, I believed I heard the horn of your OPEL.[23] Mr. Wallach[24] was ahead of me with his phone call. I had his number before me in our office when he phoned. He also mentioned that Iche[25] already had a job. This I felt was great. I hope from my heart that you too will be successful. Anyway, at first, look around you a bit because once you will be working, you won't get away from it! I am SOOO curious for your first letter and am confident it will be detailed. Today already all relatives and friends asked whether there was news from you. [. . .]

Now I wrote a lot of all kinds of things. [. . .] Yesterday, Mr. Kammerer[26] was here again (= re. buying the store). The men plan to go to Dr. Reis[27] next week. Perhaps we'll be successful sooner than we think. Whatever will be—it is a pity... Now I have to change typewriters and would need you urgently for repairs. Dear Father will need a while and finally we still shall need a repairman. I finish for today with cordial regards for all dear ones. I embrace you most cordially,

Your true-loving
Bini

Letter from Erwin Schwager to His Parents in Munich, Letter #5
New York, December 1, 1938

Dear Family All, especially Dear Parents,

Although I am regretfully without mail from Munich, I am going to write today again. The last news I received was a postcard of November 13 with an attached postage-paid card which was returned yesterday. Let me repeat; I wrote since my arrival here five letters and two postcards. Please let me know how long it took this mail to reach you.[28]

It is now 9 p.m. I just washed myself well, shaved, and look forward to talk to you a bit by mail. I sincerely hope (and I cannot express HOW MUCH) that this letter finds you all well and that you will feel with me when I state and speak egotistically and contentedly of my fate here. Since there is no mail to answer, I'll talk now about myself, hoping however urgently to obtain missives so that I may have a chance somehow to help you!—First of all, dear mother, I hope to learn where to mail the Affidavit. Morris Katz[29] was unbelievably helpful. He will do everything possible to obtain all papers quickest to mail them to you the beginning of next week. Please write to me as clearly as possible how you plan to manage your emigration from Munich.[30]

We receive over here a lot of news from all quarters, newspapers, and private letters. However, it is important to be informed about your individual position.

Now, about myself. First of all, I can write to you the good news that my endeavors to find a job were rewarded. And, as it seems to me, I did not find a bad one. Today already, I started and worked the first eight hours. I shall write to you details later some time. I am now "Shipping Clerk"—and an all-around girl in a "Slipper Factory," a manufacturer of slippers and casual shoes in Jersey City, N.J. As wages [are concerned], the boss told me yesterday, I shall receive $11 for a start—which surely is not much, but satisfactory at this time. When you see how tough it is here to find employment, you will be content. Initially it is important for me that it is in my branch of work, also with nice Jewish people who showed great personal interest in me. It is a factory with about 70 to 80 workers, mainly Italians.

Before informing you about my working day, I'd like to let you know shortly the pre-history of how I found the job. At the beginning, I was running around from early till late, calling on people recommended to me. Although I tried hard to get a job 100 to 150 miles away from New York, I was not successful in this. In three weeks, I called on approximately 150 companies and private persons. I wrote about forty job offers and requests in English. I received ten answers by mail from leather manufacturers, telling me I'd have to wait for "the season," which of course mostly was a polite "NO." I also had a chance to get into a department store in Elizabeth, N.J. Again, this was not immediately and questionable. The pay also would only have been $12 to start. There was also a possibility for a leather clothing factory and another shoe manufacturer as cutter. I believe I might have obtained one or the other job, applying repeatedly. The pay for a beginning would have been the same. However, these opportunities would have had one disadvantage that I would have had to rent a room. This meant I'd get into more personal expenses than I have now staying with Aunt Milka practically free, surely without making any trouble for her. How I'll settle with Aunt Milka financially, I'll report in my next epistle. –

My present job can easily be reached by local transportation and for New York the distance seems to be normal. "As the crow flies," the job is about 30 miles from the Bronx. I have to use two subways and then the Hudson Tunnel train. The return trip I do by ferry since this is one of the most beautiful rides across the Hudson River from Jersey City to Manhattan. I also can save a few cents yet. The boat leaves every 20 minutes. The ride tonight was absolutely "grandiose" and something special for me since I love water so much. The boat crosses the Hudson towards the Manhattan skyscraper center which the immigrants see first when arriving. This is supposed to be one of the most exciting sight of the world. You see nothing of the individual buildings, only millions of lights suggesting the building outlines.—At a distance you can see the Statue of Liberty with her torch also lit up.—Across the river go daily hundreds of ferries, also the big ocean steam ships.

The building where I work is a huge complex situated directly at the water. It has its own pier where freight boats can land and load. Inside the building are about ten big manufacturers, each one renting a big space. This place is about ten stories high, has streets inside big enough for many trucks. It has two railroad stations and the subway from New York, etc. etc... As far as my job is concerned, I like it a lot. You have to adjust to the great speed, but I was not at all tired at quitting time. I found this place the day before yesterday about 3 pm. At first, I received the usual responses. But then it seems that one of the three bosses liked me. He asked what I could do. I told him exactly and showed him several recommendations. He told me to take off my coat. Then he requested a handwriting sample which seemed to please him. He wanted to know whether I was well physically or whether I would mind doing some floor sweeping. When I told him, "Of course not." He said that I am his man and I should start tomorrow morning. With that, I was hired.

Workers here seem also very nice. Some asked me today how I like being here. One of the workers offered me chocolate, which I accepted of course. One fellow told me in the evening I'll soon be a good worker. I also feel that some people are sympathetic with me, but I am not taking anything too seriously. We'll see. . . . I'll work daily eight hours, have one hour for lunch. I'll leave home at 6:45 a.m. and return at 6:15 p.m. After I have adjusted to this, I'll start taking courses to improve my language and try other studies. [. . .]

I receive all kinds of mail, but nothing from my parents! I am doing well here beyond expectations. I weighed myself already and still have the same weight as at home . . . I have a bad conscience knowing how well I am doing and how little I can do to help you!

With the most cordial regards and kisses, especially to Dad,

Your
Erwin

Letter of Sabine Schwager to Erwin Schwager, New York
Munich, Sunday, December 11, 1938

My dear Erwin,

Your dear letter that we received yesterday gave us much pleasure. We sent an NLT [Telegram] right away which surely reached you today, Sunday. It told you, first of all that Dad returned healthy.[31] Thank G'd, he looks well and he had a lot of joy with your mail. Of course, he is occupied now reading all the correspondence. Only a letter from Karli is missing this week. We hope there is no reason to worry.

I would like to make this letter interesting but I really do not have the patience for this. The 1,000 questions that I would like to address to you shall remain unspoken. I'll postpone all details from here from one letter to the next although I know that everything is of great interest to you. I hope, however, that things shall improve now that Dad will help me again. Besides, I took endless walks and went around restlessly. [. . .] Aunt Gustl and Mina[32] are awaiting impatiently their visitors.[33] One of these days, they shall be surprised.

Uncle Pepi[34] is touchingly worried about us. He writes nearly daily. Yesterday we received even a shipment of fruit. Naturally, we are occupied with hundreds of plans. However, as long as we don't know what will develop with our business, we are unable to make arrangements. Regretfully, Mr. Krammerer did not get the clearance. Perhaps, I may be able to name the successor in my next letter. [. . .]

Please thank everybody in the family most cordially for the help and goodwill they extended to us! I still cannot imagine how things will turn out one of these days but I ask G'd for one thing only that we should not become a burden to anybody! I'll be happy to work and produce and be modest.

Hopefully, we shall be successful to obtain what one needs for a livelihood! Now the most cordial greetings and kisses from

Your true-loving
Mother

NOTES

1. Anna Schwager, née Steindler (1858–1888), was married to Isidor Isaak Schwager (1860–1927).

2. Leo Apple was a cousin of Leopold Schwager, son of Katharina (Kathi) Apple, née Steindler, sister of Leopold Schwager's first wife Anna Schwager, née Steindler (1858–1888); no further information known.

3. Sabine (Bini) Schwager, née Teller (b. 1885), born in Unterhaid, Bohemia (today: Dolní Dvorište, Czech Republic), married Leopold Schwager on August 31, 1911, in Munich; she was deported from Munich to Kovno (Kaunas) on November 20, 1941, murdered there on November 25, 1941. For more information on the fate of Leopold and Sabine Schwager, see the biographical information provided by Dianne Schwager in Stadtarchiv München, "Leopold Schwager," accessed July 12, 2021, file: ///C:/Users/A/Downloads/SchwagerLeopold_Erinnerungszeichen_engl.pdf.

4. Both sons, Erwin (b. 1913) and Karl (b. 1921), were born in Munich and emigrated via different routes to the United States.

5. Siegfried Schwager (1878–1943), bank clerk, was the son of Bernhard Schwager (1848–1913) and Elisabeth (Elise) Schwager, née Steindler (1855–1931), sister of Leopold's mother Anna; he died in Theresienstadt; his daughter, Thea Schwager (1916–1944), was murdered in Auschwitz.

6. According to information from the Munich City Archives (registration documents), Karl made it to Palestine in 1937 and later moved to New York, where he died in 1975. However, this letter from 1938 describes Karl's emigration as a future event.

7. Hamburg-Amerikanische Packetfahrt-Aktien-Gesellschaft (HAPAG), often referred to as Hamburg-American Line, was a transatlantic shipping company founded in Hamburg in 1847 that soon became the largest German shipping company, serving the market created by German immigration to the United States and later immigration from Eastern Europe.

8. Emilia Holub, née Fleischer (1864–1960), called "Aunt Milka," aunt of Leopold Schwager, was the sister of the second wife of Leopold's father Isidor Isaak Schwager, Karolina Karla Schwager, née Fleischer (1858–1940).

9. This refers to Cham (Upper Palatinate), which is located about 60 km northeast of Regensburg.

10. Religious Jews do not write out the word God so as not to dishonor the word. They either use a Hebrew designation (e.g., Adonaj = my Lord) or express reverence by omitting a letter, here: G'd.

11. Retrospective comment by Erwin Schwager: "This letter that gave me hope for an Affidavit and emigration from NAZI Germany hit us like a bomb. It has become by

this time very dangerous for Jews in Munich. Trying to assist my parents in their still flourishing business has become a nearly insurmountable threat to my emigration!"

12. This probably refers to Leopold's step-mother Karolina Karla Schwager, née Fleischer (1858–1940).

13. Hermine ("Mina") Gunz, née Schwager (1898–1941), was deported and murdered in Kovno (Kaunas).

14. Emilia (Aunt Milka, Emily) Holub was married to Adolf Holub (b. 1870); their daughter Margaret (Gretl) Katz, née Holub (b. 1905), married Morris Katz (b. 1904) in New York in 1934; exact life data unknown.

15. Sylvia Katz, daughter of Morris Katz and his wife Margaret, née Holub; exact life data unknown.

16. Stuttgart was the seat of the US consulate responsible for Munich.

17. Erwin Schwager was a passionate amateur photographer.

18. Fritz Schwager (1885–1973), a brother of Leopold Schwager, emigrated from Munich to Palestine in September 1938; he was married to Meta Schwager, née Sommer (1893–1978).

19. Erwin Schwager boarded the *SS President Roosevelt* in Hamburg and arrived in New York on November 5, 1938. New York, USA, Arriving Passenger and Crew Lists (including Castle Garden and Ellis Island), 1820–1957, Year: 1938; Arrival: New York, USA; Microfilm Serial: T715, 1897–1957; Line: 8; Page Number: 10, in *Ancestry.com* [database online]. Provo, UT, USA: Ancestry.com Operations, Inc., 2010.

20. This refers to the infamous "Munich Agreement" of September 1938; the Anglo-French appeasement policy did, for the time being, prevent the war sought by Hitler. However, a lasting peace in the center of Europe could not be achieved, since the Nazi aggression was given new impetus by the diplomatic restraint of England and France.

21. Karli = Karl Schwager.

22. National Council of Jewish Women (NCJW), oldest volunteer Jewish women's organization in the United States, founded in 1893.

23. German car brand.

24. This probably refers to Moritz Wallach (1879–1964), the owner of the famous "Firma Wallach. Haus für Volkskunst und Tracht" in Munich's Residenzstraße 3 and father of Anneliese (Iche) Rosenberg, née Wallach (b. 1919).

25. Anneliese (Iche) Rosenberg, née Wallach (b. 1919), a good friend of Erwin Schwager, also traveled with the *SS President Roosevelt* from Hamburg to New York.

26. Could not be identified. Presumably it was an interested party who wanted to take over the company of the brothers-in-law in the course of the "Aryanization."

27. Probably Dr. Fritz Reis (1892–1971), a lawyer who had a law office at Karlsplatz 7; he emigrated to the United States via England in June 1939 and returned to Munich in 1952.

28. Retrospective comment by Erwin Schwager: "I have to add here that I did not know my Dad was in Concentration Camp Dachau at that time."

29. Morris Katz, husband of Aunt Milka's daughter Margaret Katz, née Holub.

30. Shortly after *Kristallnacht*, Sabine Schwager telegraphed her son Erwin asking for Affidavits for the United States. Erwin asked Morris Katz to obtain the Affidavits again and telegraphed his parents the same day that the Affidavits would be obtained. Sabine and Leopold applied for emigration to the United States, and in December 1938, they received a waiting number of 39,000 from the US consulate, which meant that they would have to wait for years to leave the country.

31. Retrospective comment by Erwin Schwager: "From Concentration Camp." Leopold Schwager was arrested on *Kristallnacht* and sent to a concentration camp at Dachau for about a month. This was the turning point when Leopold and Sabine decided to leave Germany.

32. This probably refers to two half-sisters of Leopold Schwager, Auguste Schnurmann, née Schwager (1892–1941), and Hermine ("Mina") Gunz, née Schwager (1898–1941); both were deported and murdered in Kovno (Kaunas).

33. Retrospective comment by Erwin Schwager: "meaning their husbands returning from concentration camp."

34. Josef (Pepi) Teller (b. 1881), Sabine Schwager's older brother, lived in Meran, where he was a member of the board of the local religious community; he fled to Switzerland on September 22, 1943.

Chapter 8

"I'm Alive: It's a Miracle!"

Blechner Family Letters

The Blechner family in Munich was undoubtedly a "normal" Jewish family. But they were also a special Jewish family in that the fate of the individual family members reflects many of the various facets and dramatic courses of Jewish biographies after 1933.

The merchant Markus Blechner (1879–1939), born in Cergowa, Galicia, and his wife Mina, née Schaffer (1888–1941), came to Munich in October 1913. The two elder sons, Jakob and Oskar, were born in Dukla, Poland; the younger sons, Salo and Leon, were born in Munich, Germany. The family lived at Klenzestrasse 65 in Isarvorstadt. Here, Markus Blechner built a flourishing wholesale business in footwear. His four sons also later became successful businessmen.

Despite repression by right-wing conservative and antisemitic Bavarian authorities at the beginning of the 1920s, the Blechners remained in Munich. In this city, they had found a new home and were firmly established in the everyday life of the Isar suburb, which was dominated by Eastern European Jews. However, the steadily intensifying anti-Jewish measures of the Nazi regime after 1933 fundamentally changed the family's living situation. After the expulsion of Polish Jews from Germany in October 1938 and the terror of Kristallnacht in November of the same year, the Blechners decided to emigrate, but were confronted with unexpected difficulties.

Leon Blechner (1916–2002), the youngest of the four sons, was the first to escape. He left Germany in March 1938 and reached New York on April 1, 1938. There, he waited for his wife Regina (Gina), née Spatz (1916–1979), whose arrival was delayed because heavily pregnant, she had been arrested in the course of the "Polish Action" but, fortunately, was released after a night in prison. However, it was another year before she was able to join him in the United States (in October 1939) with their son Gerson (Jerry), who had been born in Germany in November 1938. Leon died on January 31, 2002, in Palm Beach, Florida.

Oskar Blechner (1911–1976) experienced and suffered the notorious odyssey of the "St. Louis"; after Cuba's refusal to allow the passengers to enter the country and the United States' refusal to accept the refugees, he managed to enter England on June 21, 1939, where he remained for the rest of his life. He died on October 25, 1976, in London.

Jakob Blechner (1909–1978) and his wife Frieda, née Rosenzweig (1911–1969), managed to escape to Switzerland in August 1939. From there, they wanted to travel via France to Great Britain and ultimately to the United States but the outbreak of war prevented the realization of their plans. Although life in Switzerland was not easy for Jewish refugees, Jakob was able to correspond with all his family members from neutral Switzerland and pass messages between them. He died in Zurich on April 15, 1978.

After a failed attempt to emigrate to Switzerland in August 1939, Mina, Markus, and Salo Blechner returned to their empty flat in Munich. A few days later, the "Inschutzhaftnahme" or "protective custody" of Polish Jews was ordered. As a result, the Gestapo arrested Markus Blechner in Munich on September 9, 1939, later taking him to Buchenwald concentration camp, where he was killed on November 14, 1939. His widow, Mina Blechner, was deported from Munich to Kovno (Kaunas) in Lithuania on November 20, 1941, with about 1,000 children, women, and men and murdered there a few days later in the course of a mass shooting.

Salo Blechner (1914–2007), who was unable to leave the country, fled to Berlin, where he was arrested on September 13, 1939. After six years of life-threatening concentration camp imprisonment and forced labor, he returned to Munich in 1945 and emigrated to New York in May 1946. He died in Boston on May 28, 2007.

The correspondence between individual members of the Blechner family, excerpts of which are printed here in English translation, gives an impression of the extraordinary and life-threatening situation in which Jews living in Germany found themselves, especially after 1938. The letters written mostly in German but partly in Yiddish and code to get around the Nazi censors are also an impressive testimony of the desperate hopes and often futile efforts to save family members who stayed behind. They also tell of the bureaucratic and economic difficulties and emotional burdens of making a new start abroad.

Figure 8.1   Photo of the Blechner Family, 1938 (from the back left: Leon, Oskar, Friedl, and Jakob; front: Mina and Markus). *Source:* Stadtarchiv München.

Letter from Salo Blechner, Munich, to Jakob
and Frieda Blechner, Zurich (No. 6)
Munich, August 30, 1939

Dear Friedl, dear Jacl!

This morning we received your card to Damitts[1] and also heard about your telephone conversation yesterday. Well, we were unlucky again, it's just terrible. But for your information, a married couple (German passports with J.)[2] with permits [for immigration] for England and flight tickets were also turned back. So, as already written, at the Swiss border in St. Margarethen, the passports were checked. We had to get out, and he kept the passports with him and told us he had to call Bern[3] on Monday morning. Monday at 11 am, we were told at the hotel that our luggage would be taken to the 12 pm train. All our interventions were of no use. Among other things, I made the suggestion to let us go to Basel (possibly under escort), where we could cross the French border since the border is right in the middle of the city. This was not allowed either, despite our visa to France [and] Holland and also the onward travel tickets, which he also took away. Incidentally, in Rorschach,[4] one couple traveling to Erez[5] (as capitalists, I have seen a certificate [. . .])

and ship leaving Italy in Sept. was also refused, and it was noted in the passport "refused due to lack of means." He wrote in the passport for each of us "rejected by decision of the federal authorities Bern." Here, we were welcomed in a very nice and friendly way, and we were really amazed at what the Swiss did with us. Yes, flying would have been the right thing to do. But who would have thought of it? I got my Swiss visa on Friday at 5 pm.

Yesterday, I also received mail from Oskar, saying that the Home Office[6] is not issuing anything and is locked. Am I not the unlucky one. With this Swiss visa, there is nothing we can do now, and there is only one thing to do: wait and see. I had the luggage returned yesterday. We need something to wear. You don't know how long it will take, and you can't get anything here. But I hope that everything will be settled in a few days. You were really lucky just in time! The flat is completely empty and looks desolate. Sleeping is quite primitive. The main thing is that it turned out that way, and we must be grateful for that.

Is the Ventimiglia-Nice border[7] actually open? Should we try via Italy? [. . .] Can't you go any further? The Zurich flight route is working. But on Saturday, we were told that everything had been shut down since 12 noon; otherwise, we would have flown already. For the time being, we'll stay in the old flat.

That is all for today. Many warm greetings and kisses and all the best.

Your Salo

Spatz'[8] ship leaves tonight from Le Havre already, were not able to get there either! [. . .]

Dearest children!

I can't begin to describe my hurt. We are both back to the beginning. May dear G-d help that everything will be all right. Greetings and kisses

also from your mother

Letter from Leon Blechner, Lowell/USA, to Jakob
and Frieda Blechner, Zurich (No. 9)
Lowell, September 25, 1939

Dear Jak and Frieda,

Was I delighted to receive a letter from Switzerland! In the midst of all the Zores,[9] at least it's one bit of good news. I haven't heard from anywhere else anything like what has happened to our dear family. Now, I am glad, dear Jakl, that at least you were clever and left in time. How often have I written about it. How often have I written home that our dear parents should stay in Switzerland or leave immediately for a foreign country. How many times I wrote to Zurich about the last time our dear parents were in Italy and

Switzerland. Stay in Switzerland or in Nice. But I think our dear parents, especially our dear Mama,[10] have been so indecisive, always because of money or something else. Saving lives is the most important thing today, so we hope to G-d[11] that they all stay well, and we can all meet again soon. It was a blow for me that dear Regina[12] has such bad luck. She has the visa and can't go. I only hope that both of them[13] stay healthy. Oh, dear Jakl, my nerves are shattered. You know that you have to work hard to live here, and on top of that, you have such terrible news from Europe. But I am glad that I am here. I only hope that the USA doesn't go to war. Who knows what will come. I think the bill will pass that America will send war material to England and France. Then, it is economically better for America. But there is then the danger that [the] USA will be involved in the war. But America will help to bring about the end of the dog of Germany, or as America says, "the Madman from Germany," more quickly.[14] The population hates the dog so much that they want to tear it to pieces.

So, the war is on,[15] and Poland is finished for now. We don't know what will happen later. There is so much to write about it, but there is no point. [. . .]

I haven't heard from dear Oskar for a long time. I don't know what's going on. I sent him a telegram but got no answer about Rosh ha shono.[16] Hope he is ok. Now, for New Year and Yom Kippur, I wish you all the best and [that] all our wishes shall come true. The day should come soon when we can all meet again in joy. What a stupid thing to do with the furniture. I don't understand why Oskar said you should leave it in Germany. I hope you can see it all again.

My dear Jak, do you have money to live in Switzerland? [. . .] Sad [about] our dear parents and Salo—where will they get money to live in Germany? Please answer! I hope that [they] will not get into trouble because they have a Polish passport [. . .] there is a danger that they will be interned. I hope to G-d that everything turns out well. How can you stay in Switzerland? Don't leave here. Otherwise they'll take you into the army. Who would have thought it would come to a war? But now it has happened. Tell me, dear Jak, what about the 1,000 [Dollars] that are [waiting] for you in London? I have not yet received the 500 [Dollars]. I will get it when Oskar proves that he does not receive any support from the Com.[17] Oh, they're villains. They also would have taken your money if you had asked the committee for support. If they have the money in their hands, it's an uphill battle. Should I do something about the 1,000 Dollars? I'm not done with them yet because of the 500 [Dollars]. I'm all right so far. Nobody should feel badly, but I'm very worried about my dear family. So, I ask you, my dear brother, that you write [to] me every week [about] what is going on, good or bad news, you understand. I will answer immediately. We have to stay in contact with each other.

Let our dear parents and Salo know that I wish them all the best for the Jomteff,[18] and let dear Regina know that I have received your letter and am waiting for her to come and write to me. Salo should try everything to get her out, after all. How is my dear child?[19] I hope alright. Dear Jak, I would like to thank you for all the good deeds that have helped a lot. Hopefully, the day will come when I can repay you with joy. Please keep me informed about everything. So, my dear brother, with this I close my lines and remain with best wishes for you and dear Friedl.

Best wishes and kisses,
Your brother Leon

Dear Friedl,

Thank you for your letter, and I wish you all the best for the Jomteff. May G-d grant you both that life will still bring good times for you both.
    I remain with best regards and kisses,
    Your Leon
    How is your family?
    P.S. I think there is still 50 Dollars at the bank in Amsterdam that I sent for Salo. Do you know about it?

Letter from Leon Blechner, New York, to Jakob
and Frieda Blechner, Zurich (No. 14)
New York City, October 22, 1939

My Dear Ones,

I have received your dear letter, and you can imagine how I am affected by all these Zores. It is terrible, and it looks like our family has no luck at all. Dear Jak, has our dear Mama written to you again? Where is our dear Papa[20] and Salo? Did you get a message again? Today, I am here in New York, and I am trying to do something. How do you imagine I will get 1,400 D[ollars]? If I had, [I] would do everything to get our dear parents and dear Salo out of Germany. Now, I was at the local Com, and the first thing I demanded was that the money that was paid for you [should] be returned. There is no point in leaving the money frozen there. Even if we lose [something] in the process, it is worth receiving the money. However, the money is paid out in Dollars only in America. It cannot be transferred to other countries from England. So, I think the best way is how I do it. [. . .] The 500 [Dollars] for Oskar, [I'm] still trying to get. But as long as [Oskar] gets support from the Com. in England, I don't get anything back. So that's the way I'm going now. When the money is free, I can send it to you. Because of the 50 Dollars from Amsterdam, [I] have already taken care of that, too. And this money can only be paid out here. It takes about four weeks. Dear Jak, I can't understand. How many times I asked you to leave, but you always didn't believe [me]. Who knows, because of a stupid thing, you have waited so long. It is no use to reproach [yourself] about it now. Maybe there is a way that I can request the lift?[21] If you don't have any money and the Com. doesn't want to give anything, write to Oskar—he has some money. Dear Jak, believe me, if I had a Dollar to spare, I would send it immediately. Dear Regina is coming on Wednesday, and I have to use the 80–100 Dollars I have for that. I hope you understand? [. . .] What do you think [concerning] Chile—how can we get our family out of Germany? That is not so simple, even with money. Is this a sure thing from you or just an assumption? If I have the money, I can do it immediately. I may be able to get some of the ship's tickets from the committee. Where is poor, dear Salo? G-d should help him so that everything turns out well.

[. . .] Dear Jak, you are not going to France, out of the question. I beg you to do everything possible to stay in Switzerland. Maybe now you can get your visa to America sooner. I will take care of your ship ticket here when the time comes. I think that maybe you can get it sooner because of the current situation (Polish quota). So, you see how it stands. Concerning the money in London, [I'll] do that by telegraph. This is the only way to save our dear parents and dear Salo. Poor beloved Mama, such a trouble. G-d should help and have mercy on us so that everything will turn out well.

Dear Jak, let me know everything new immediately and write to our dear Mama that I have written. [. . .] Cheer up, my dear ones! It will turn out well with G-d's help, and [they] will also be helped. Remain with best greetings and kisses,

Your Leon
Staying in N.Y. one week. Trying everything.

> Letter from Frieda Blechner, Zurich, to
> Oskar Blechner, London (No. 20)
> Zurich, November 21, 1939

Dear, dear Oskar!

I cannot tell you how difficult these lines are for me. Be strong, our dear, good father has gone from us forever. On November 14, early at 8 a.m., as a result of cardiac paralysis, he fell asleep quietly and gently, just as his whole life had been.[22]

I cannot send you any consolation, dear Oskar, as much as I would like to. It was G-d's inscrutable will. Let us grant the departed his rest. On Thursday, November 16, was the funeral. He was laid to rest in the cemetery at Ungererstr.[23]

Our dear father z"l[24] had been out of sorts since the summer; he had a heart attack once, but it passed quickly. We did not want to write about it to you, you know, he was never able to show his troubles; all the circumstances and commotion hastened his death. It is very bitter that we were all torn apart in such a way and cannot bear the sorrow together in this difficult time. One must resign oneself to the unchangeable, even if one sometimes believes life cannot go on any longer. May the dear G-d give our dear mother the strength and courage to bear her fate, and she has also so bravely and calmly told me about it. [. . .]; she is strong now and still wants to live for her children.

My dear Jakl has not yet been able to get a grip on himself from the first pain; he will write to you again himself after the Schiwe.[25] He tried everything possible to bring our dear parents here, went to the head of the foreign police in Bern, obtained a Spanish transit visa [and] a letter from the Geneva Committee, [and] on the 15th, as you know, he submitted [everything] for Chile. Nothing was missed, it was a chain of tragic circumstances, or it was the will from above. Our dear father z"l would not have lived much longer. He was tired and worn out. He is resting well, and in spirit he will always be with his family. He would have liked to have gone to Poland, but there it would have been even more terrible for him, the way everything turned out. A pious, good, and noble man has suffered, dear Oskar, and I have really lost a friend and father in him—take hold of yourself, as hard as it may be, pray to our dear G-d that he will accept the sacrifice and that the living will be saved. May he be a good intercessor for all of us with the Almighty.

With the warmest greetings always,
Friedl

Jackl sends you his warmest greetings and asks you to be calm, as it was certainly the wish of our late father.

> Letter from Leon Blechner, New York, to Jakob
> and Frieda Blechner, Zurich (No. 21)
> New York, November 23, 1939

My Dear Ones!

Today, I get to write to you. Please excuse me if you had to wait a little longer. How are you? I hope that you are able to cope with the circumstances and that you are at least healthy. From me, I can tell you that I and the dear Regina as well as the sweet boy is well. Unfortunately, I have no work now until the beginning of December. I have not worked for 4 weeks. Can you imagine, now where I urgently need it, [it] is bad with the work. At the moment, I am in New York and have rented a room with use of a kitchen. Until in two weeks, [when I] will move to Boston should I find nothing suitable in N.Y. The dear Regina and our dear child[26] were on Ellis Island,[27] after four days I got them out. There were two reasons: (1) because of the ship's ticket that the Hilfsverein ["Aid Organization"][28] paid, and (2) that we were not legally married. With the first one, I had to commit myself to pay the money back to the HIAS,[29] and I had to pay 30 Dollars right away. With the 2nd reason, I had to get married legally right away, which I did on Nov. 16. Thus, she got out. Lucky. Now, my dears, what do you hear from home? What does our dear Papa and Salo write about our dear Mama? Why don't you tell me about it? Of course, I know that it is terrible, and I would send something immediately if I only had something to help. You have to see that you bring our dear Papa and dear Salo out.

I have written twice to London to get the 1,000 back, but so far nothing. There are thousands who demand the[ir] money back, and the English Com., it takes time. Once the money is back, [I] can immediately do something. Dear Jak, if you think I have saved a lot since I have been in [Lowell],[30] you are unfortunately wrong. You do not know the conditions here, otherwise you would not assume so much. The money I had is now all gone. Of course, if I had [something] I would send it immediately. Well, our dear Oskar has about 400 Dollars in England; maybe he can do something for our dear father? What can I do from here if I have nothing myself and have to fight so that I can live? Even more so now that I have no work at the moment. But with G-d's help everything will be all right. What does our dear Mama write? It is all so terrible that I am completely exhausted when I think of our fate, but what can you do? This week, I spoke with Dr. Hirschberg[31] from Munich, who is here, and he told me that if our dear Papa and Salo can get a visa, there is a possibility that they will get out, but we cannot be sure because our dear Papa and Salo are imprisoned as Poles. But we should try everything. What does dear Oskar write to you? Can't our dear Mama ask for your lift back? It is possible to send food parcels to Germany from here—shall I do it? I am waiting for your advice on what to do. Can I perhaps write directly to our dear Papa as well as dear Salo?[32] Here people say yes, but I must have [the] exact address. At the same time, I will write to our dear Mama. Dear Friedl, what do you hear from your family? Can you stay in Switzerland for a long time? Dear Jak, I am very anxious to hear from you, so please write me everything that happens. I can't tell you much from here—it's always the same life. What about your number at the consulate?[33] Do you have a chance to get it sooner? So, please give me an answer soon and stay healthy and sincerely greeted and kissed.

Your Leon

[. . .] Concerning the 500 Dollars for Oskar, I need confirmation that Oskar is working and does not receive support from the Com. Then I will get money back. Have written the same to Oskar but have not received anything yet. I have heard that many are working in England.

> Letter from Regina Blechner (née Spatz) to Jakob
> and Frieda Blechner, Zurich (No. 22)
> Undated, probably enclosure to her hus-
> band's letter of November 23, 1939

Dear Friedl and Jackl!

As I could see from your letter, you are—thank G-d—healthy. You must not be angry with me for my silence. I had a lot to do in Munich during the final period, so that I did not have time to write. I sent you a card from the ship, which you will have received by now. Thank G-d, I have been here for three weeks now. As far as I could see and hear so far, earning money is actually very difficult. Well, it will be alright, because in two weeks Leo[34] can work again for sure, but unfortunately, we have to leave N.Y. then. As soon as it will be possible for Leo, it is of course in his interest, as well as in mine, that he does something for our dear Papa and Salo. But without money, [there] is just nothing to do. Leo has done until now what he could do, otherwise he would still have some money and would have done something immediately, but unfortunately! From my mother[35] and brother,[36] I have no news at all. I wonder what will happen to them. The first impression of the USA was not nice for me. I felt like a prisoner in Ellis Island. Stay healthy and keep your head high. Heartfelt Greetings,

Regina

> Letter from Leon Blechner, New York, to Jakob
> and Frieda Blechner, Zurich (No. 29)
> New York, December 19, 1939

My dear Jakl and Friedl,

I received your sad letter and with deep pain I heard the news of the passing of our dear Papa z"l. All this time, I have felt that something has happened, so

I called Else Damitt,[37] and at my insistence she told me the sad news on Dec. 14, 1939. I can't describe what a pain it was for me. My dearest, my good Papa z"l—a blow that hit me in the deepest way. I cannot believe it. My heart [is heavy]. In my mind, I see my dear Papa z"l standing at the station as I was leaving. I always hoped that the day would come soon when I could go to the pier and pick up our dear Papa from the ship. But unfortunately, our dear G-d wanted it differently. His life was a drudgery for his children, to raise us. A man who had no enemies and was satisfied with everything. Yes, losing such a good man and father is a deep wound in my body and soul. The departure of our dear father has broken me, and I have to hold myself together and be brave. And now, as a father myself, [I wish for] my child that he grows up big and strong. Little Jerry is my only comfort in these difficult days. It was our dear G-d's will and shall be granted to our dear Papa z"l the eternal peace in the other, better world. I will keep our dear Papa z"l in everlasting memory. Wherever I go and wherever I am, I think of my dear Papa z"l, and I pray to him in my Kadish,[38] that he should put in a good word to the dear G-d for all of us so that misfortune stays away from our family. May our dear G-d have mercy and show dear Salo and our dear Mama the way out of Germany. With a strong hand. Amen!

My dear ones, comfort yourselves and stay strong and brave. Life goes on, and it is a hard life struggle for which you need special strength. The day will come when we can be together, with G-d's help, in a free country. See to it, dear Jakl, that everything is done to save our dear Mama and dear Salo. You are the eldest son, my dear brother, and you now take the place of our dear father z"l. I pray to G-d that everything will work out with Chile. I have been in New York for five weeks and live here for the time being. In the factory in Lowell where I work, a general strike has broken out, demanding better pay (20 percent increase) for six weeks, and the company has stopped work completely and closed the factory. Now, they want to move to another city and hire new workers. As soon as they are in the new city, I start working there again. For the time being, things are not there yet. Now I'm here, looking for work, and [it] is hard to get something. For 1 ½ weeks, I have worked somewhere and already no more. My few Dollars that I have saved are already gone due to this week without work. In addition, there are still major expenses. Now, I am dependent on Com. and get $15 a week. Until I work again, then I have to pay back. Yes, so it goes here. But I hope to be back at work soon and set up a home. For now, I'm staying with people here in New York. That's how you have to start, until you get back on your feet. [. . .] So, what do you think to do? If you do not intend to go to England, let the English Com. know immediately and let me know immediately. Then, I get the money back and can send [it to] you immediately or do something else. Don't think I want to use it for myself; [we] need it for our dear Mama and dear Salo, when they are in Chile with G-d's help. So, what do you think? [. . .] The money from Holland came back. $45. [Five Dollars] are lost on it.

Dear Jakl, about the $45. I ask you to leave this with me until I have work again, because I need the amount for emergencies because of [the] child, etc. But if our dear Mama and dear Salo are out of Germany, I [will] send [it] immediately to the best address. Please, don't be angry with me; but this is the only cash I have at the moment, and I hope you understand my situation. I need to have the backing until I have work again. If you need anything, I can get it for you or anything else. What is Oskar doing with the $400 he has in England? Can't he send it out? For the photo,[39] you can get $130–140. [. . .]

About the $1,000 I deposited at the Com. [. . .] hope you are doing it right. I had no idea that Else Damitt still had a photo[40] of you. I asked her about it a couple of times, but she never said she had a photo of you. For the big Kontax [camera], you can get $140. For [the] Leica IIIa [camera], you get about $110, if sold privately. You still have the Leica in Switzerland? What happened to the photos[41] that are in Poland? Should I ask for the Kontax from Else Damitt? I am very surprised that she never mentioned anything about it. Does she also have something from you in her hands? [. . .] I have not yet received an answer to my last letter. Since I left New York, I am not so well informed about everything. I wrote to you that I also got a Jewish wedding, with Rabbi Wiesner[42] in Brooklyn. He wrote to you. Our aunt[43] does not know and must not know about our dear father's late departure. She also does not know about me. Please write [to] me how our dear Mama is doing. I hope to receive a personal letter from our dear Mama. With whom does our dear Mama live? I hope that the community supports [her]. Can you not send (food) from Switzerland to Germany? Please give exact information about it.

From America, the package allowed is only 1.5 kg content, and that costs $6.50 [for] customs. So, you can see how the dog in Germany comes up with everything. To send from here makes no sense. Now, dear Jakl and Friedl, I will close my lines and hope to get an answer from you soon.

Stay healthy and [be] warmly greeted and kissed by

Your Leon

Many kisses from Jerrylein,[44] and a picture is enclosed with the next letter.

Dear Friedl & Jakl!

As I can see from your dear lines, thank G-d you are healthy, which is the main thing today. Unfortunately, I have had no news from my loved ones for a long time; I do not know what is going on with my brother. My dear mother has not received any letter from me yet; she is so unhappy about it.

Would it perhaps be possible for you to write a card from Switzerland to say that I am well, etc.? The address is: Rosa Spatz, Biala-Bielitz, c/o Zehngut, Hoffmannstr. 1010. Perhaps this message will arrive. So, please be so good as to do me this favor. Leo is very upset about Salo and our dear mother. He is racking his brains as to what is best to do, but from here, one's hands are tied. With G-d's help, everything will be all right. Warmest greetings.

Yours,
Regina

NOTES

1. Maria, later Marie Damitt (1879–1944) emigrated from Munich via Italy to New York in 1940, where she died on July 11, 1944.

2. The so-called *Judenstempel* was a stamp in the form of a red "J" affixed to German passports by German authorities starting in 1938, identifying the passport holder as a Jew. The basis for this was the Ordinance on the Passports of Jews of October 5, 1938.

3. The city of Bern is the *de facto* capital of Switzerland.

4. Rorschach is a municipality in the canton of St. Gallen in Switzerland, on the southern side of Lake Constance.

5. What is meant here is Erez Israel.

6. The British Home Office (Ministry of the Interior), based in London, decided on residence and work permits for foreigners.

7. Ventimiglia is a city in Liguria, northern Italy, located 7 km from the French-Italian border; the port city of Nice, in southeastern France, is 32 km from the Italian border.

8. Regina Spatz (1916–1976), who was heavily pregnant in autumn 1938 and later became Leon Blechner's wife, was only able to emigrate to the United States in October 1939.

9. *Zores* (Yiddish) means trouble, inconvenience.

10. "Mama" was the affectionate name that the Blechner children used for their mother.

11. The original German reads "G'tt," translated here as "G-d." Religious Jews do not write out the word God, so as not to dishonor the word. They either use a Hebrew designation (e.g., Adonaj = my Lord) or express reverence by omitting a letter.

12. This refers to Regina Spatz (1916–1976), the future wife of Leon Blechner.

13. This refers to Regina and their son, Gerson (Jerry), who was born in November 1938.

14. With these phrases, Leon refers to Adolf Hitler.

15. This refers to the beginning of World War II, which was started by the invasion of Poland by the German Wehrmacht on September 1, 1939.

16. *Rosh ha shono* (Yiddish) means Rosh haShana (New Year).

17. This probably refers to the Jewish Refugees Committee (JRC), later the German Jewish Aid Committee, which was founded in the early months of 1933 under the aegis of the Central British Fund for the Relief of German Jewry. Its tasks were to arrange for the admission of refugees to Britain, their maintenance, training, employment, or remigration.

18. *Jomteff* (Yiddish) means holiday.

19. The son of Leon Blechner and Regina Spatz, Gerson (Jerry), was born in November 1938.

20. "Papa" was the affectionate name that the Blechner children used for their father.

21. A "lift" is a container in which emigrants stored and shipped their belongings abroad.

22. Markus Blechner, who had been arrested by the Gestapo in Munich on September 9, 1939, was taken to Buchenwald concentration camp, where he was killed on November 14, 1939.

23. This refers to the New Jewish Cemetery (German: Neuer Israelitischer Friedhof) in Munich, which is located in the Schwabing district.

24. The abbreviation z"l in this case stands for Iwrit Zichrono livracha (m.) and means "may his memory be a blessing." Z"L or z"l is traditionally added to the name of a deceased person in Judaism, especially for people to whom there is a personal connection of the speaker or the context being discussed.

25. Schiwe (Yiddish) means Shiva. Seven days of mourning after the death of a close relative.

26. Leon Blechner's son Gerson (Jerry) was born shortly after the arrest of Regina (Gina), née Spatz (1916–1979), in the fall of 1938 in Munich; it was not until a year later that Gina and Jerry reached New York.

27. With the onset of World War II in 1939, the facilities on Ellis Island, a federally owned island in New York Harbor that was once the busiest immigration inspection station in the United States, were used to detain enemy soldiers in addition to immigrants.

28. *Hilfsverein der Juden in Deutschland* was a Jewish aid organization founded in Berlin in 1901 for the purpose of supporting Jews abroad, especially in Eastern Europe. Later, it was an important aid organization for Jewish emigration from Germany.

29. HIAS (Hebrew Sheltering and Immigrant Society of America) was founded in 1898 in New York.

30. The word is illegible—possibly Lowell, a city in Massachusetts, in the United States.

31. Dr. jur. Max Hirschberg (1883–1964), lawyer, was admitted to the bar in 1911 and served as a defense counsel in political trials. In March 1933, he was taken into "protective custody," emigrated to Milan on November 1, 1934, and continued to New York in 1939.

32. After being turned back at the Swiss border, Salo Blechner returned to Munich, where he narrowly escaped arrest by the Gestapo. His subsequent flight to Berlin was also only a temporary rescue; he was arrested on September 13, 1939, and only

returned to Munich in 1945, after six years of life-threatening concentration camp imprisonment and forced labor.

33. With this question, Leon refers to the waiting numbers issued by the American consulate to applicants for an American visa. Between 1938 and 1941, US law allowed only 27,370 immigrant visas to be issued annually to persons born in Germany or Austria. Those who wanted to present their papers and be interviewed by the US consulate in hopes of obtaining a visa had to register and be placed on the (long) waiting list.

34. Regina, Leon Blechner's wife, refers to her husband as Leo.

35. Rosa Spatz, née Stark (1883–unknown), emigrated to Biala Krakowska (Poland) in July 1939 and became a victim of the Shoa.

36. Heinrich Spatz (1908–unknown) became a victim of the Shoa.

37. Else Damitt (1909–2004), daughter of Maria (Marie) Damitt, emigrated to the United States in January 1939. Since September 1947, name listed as Else Sichel.

38. Kadish (Hebrew), prayer for the dead with predominantly Aramaic text.

39. What is meant is a camera.

40. What is meant is a camera.

41. What is meant is a camera.

42. Rabbi Samuel Wiesner (1890–1961) emigrated to New York in April 1939.

43. This refers to Salo Blechner.

44. Jerry Blechner (b. Nov. 11, 1938), son of Leon and Regina Blechner, née Spatz.

Part II

EXILE—EMIGRATION AND NEW BEGINNINGS ABROAD

It was one of the largest and most dramatic mass migrations of the 20th century. Between 1933 and 1939, some 247,000 German Jews, almost half of the 1933 German Jewish population, left the country that had been their home. Far fewer, around 25,500, fled Nazi Germany between September 1939—the outbreak of World War II—and October 1941, when emigration was prohibited. The vast majority of those who emigrated were educated, wealthy middle- and upper-class citizens who would not have considered moving to a country with a language they did not speak and customs they did not understand before Hitler's appointment as Reich chancellor on January 30, 1933. While most of the Jewish emigrants from Nazi Germany initially fled to other European countries and Palestine, about 81,500 who self-identified as Jews by religion eventually made it to the United States, despite the strict immigration restrictions enacted by the US Congress after World War I. In contrast to earlier waves of immigration, this group of incoming refugees included a larger proportion of women, children, and adults aged 45 and older. The experiences of those trying to establish themselves in the United States differed, depending on whether the new immigrants were part of the German cultural elite (a minority) or came as refugees. The latter in particular were faced with many economic and cultural challenges while trying to find their place. Geographically, these Jewish immigrants settled primarily on the East Coast, especially in New York City. Los Angeles became a main center on the West Coast, but there were also many smaller settlements in other large and small communities throughout the United States.

The personal testimonies gathered in the second part of this book are all—except for two memoirs originating from the Leo Baeck Institute New York—part of the Judaica collection in the Munich City Archives. They represent an enormous diversity of fates and circumstances that shaped and defined the thousands of individual experiences of emigration and exile in the United States. They also feature many key issues that emigrants faced in different parts of the world and raise questions about the importance and dynamics of transmigration, migrant networks, and the complex relationships between national policies and migrant agencies. Compared to the rest of the German Reich, a particularly high number of emigrants fled from Munich to the United States. One possible explanation for this could be relatively higher rates of emigration from Bavaria to the United States in the 19th and the early 20th centuries. Immigrants who had family contacts in the country may have benefited in obtaining affidavits, which was crucial for entry to the United States.

The emigration process, including detours and experiences in other places, are the foci of the memoirs written by Charlotte Haas Schueller and Hanns Peter Merzbacher. These two young adults were just beginning their professional careers when they left Germany. After temporary stays in England and Brazil, respectively, they arrived in the United States shortly before the end of the war. Ilse E. Scholle and Lotte Bamberger, two young women who were baptized Christians but were persecuted as Jews by the Nazi regime, mention various problems they faced during their passage to the United States and after their arrival, as well as family matters and new encounters that defined their experiences in the United States. Inge Moss and Charlotte Stein-Pick—one young, unmarried, and inexperienced, and the other already professionally established, married, and deeply rooted in Munich—reported on their new lives in the United States and reflected in different ways on their return to and relationship with their former hometown after the end of the war. In addition, the collections of letters included here show how close success and failure were to each other in emigration. The letters of Carla Koppel, a wife and mother of six, and her husband Carlo speak with immediacy and anguish of the horrors that Jews faced while desperately trying to escape. In contrast, the letters of Hans Lamm, a bachelor in his early 20s, convey the hopes and worries of a Jewish refugee who had made his way to safety far away from Europe but still felt agonizing concern for the fate of family members and friends who remained behind or were scattered in all directions. In short, the memoirs and letters selected for this part reveal not only the social and physical upheavals of being a refugee but also personal traumas and emotional costs of fleeing one's homeland.

Chapter 9

My New Life in the United States

Inge Moss

Inge Moss was born Ingeborg Klara Marx on August 24, 1921, in Munich. She was the only child of Karl Marx, a representative for a textile firm, and his wife Else, née Zenner. The family lived very comfortably. Else had a maid to help with running the home and a governess (or "Fräulein") to care for Inge. Although Karl was frequently away on business trips, when he was home he would proudly take Inge on walks to meet his friends at the Beer Garden, and the family took frequent vacations to the mountains or the beach in Germany, Switzerland, and Italy. Inge's life was gradually more and more limited by the Nazi grip on Jewish life in Germany, and by 1938, the family had begun submitting the paperwork to leave Germany. Karl Marx had one brother, Bernhard (Uncle Hardy), who had already lived in the United States for several years, and another brother, Adolf (Uncle Ado), who arrived in the United States in 1939. Else's sister Trude and her brother Justin with their families had also recently emigrated and were living in Chicago. In the summer of 1938, when Inge was 16 years old, the fact that her father died of a brain tumor delayed Inge's efforts to leave the country as it necessitated reapplying for a visa to the United States because of the change in family relationships. At the urging of other family members, Inge submitted the necessary papers, and in May of 1940 at age 18, she left her mother and grandparents for her new life in the United States.

Upon arriving in the United States, Inge lived briefly with relatives in Brooklyn. She was soon hired as a live-in governess for a family in Brooklyn, where she cared for their young daughter. In early 1941, Inge met Herbert Mosheim, a German-Jewish emigrant, at the New America Club, a social club for new Americans in New York. After their marriage in 1942, the couple moved to Bellows Falls, a small town in Vermont, where their naturalization and name change from Mosheim to Moss took place and where their two daughters were born in 1944 and 1946. Jewish life was somewhat limited in Bellows Falls, so in 1957 the family moved to the nearby town of Claremont, New Hampshire, where there was a synagogue and a small but active Jewish community. For professional reasons, they moved to Palatka, Florida, in 1964, where Inge was active as a librarian at a school. Her husband Herbert Moss died there in 1978. A year later, Inge moved to a community in West Palm Beach, where many other German-Jewish survivors had already settled.

Inge Moss died on February 29, 2016. Contact with the Munich City Archives inspired her to write down her memories in 1999. The passage included here offers insights on the challenges of starting over abroad and

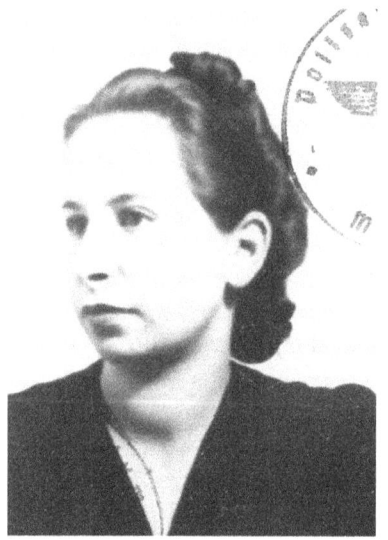

Figure 9.1   Inge Marx, Passport Photo c. 1938/1939 (Kennkarten-Doppel). *Source:* Stadtarchiv München.

the fears for those left behind, which constantly afflicted the vast majority of emigrants.

Though I grew up in Munich and had the best schooling, namely in Louisen Lyzeum,[1] I have to admit that the German language does not flow easily from my tongue anymore. Therefore I have difficulty sometimes expressing myself in correct German. The reason is this:

As soon as I arrived [in the United States] in 1940,[2] at 18 years of age, I did not want to give my relatives any reason to consider me a burden, and so I took the necessary steps immediately to find a job to become independent.

After two weeks in this country, I was able to find a job with a nice American family as live-in help, responsible for housework as well as the care of their only child. The little girl was a darling, but in my eyes, also a little spoiled. For an only child coming from a fine family, this was a great change for me, especially since I had to work hard from morning till evening. But I could cope with it since the family was very nice to me. I had absolutely no opportunity to speak German in this family and was able to better my learned school English. Most immigrants had settled in the same neighborhoods in New York, for instance Washington Heights, while I lived on the other end of N.Y. in Brooklyn. Only when I could take the long subway ride from Brooklyn to upper Manhattan on my one day off a week did I have an opportunity to meet with some of my old friends from home. Since we all were very young, and we all tried to fit in as much as possible, our conversation was more and more in English. Only my correspondence with my dear mother,[3] who unfortunately was still in Munich, was my only connection with the German language. At this time, my greatest interest was to save my beloved mother, and as I see it today, I had put too much trust in my relatives who had promised to work on the necessary papers for her. Timewise, I was also at a loss and couldn't go to the authorities so often as was necessary, and because I was at the tender age of 18, I could not see the seriousness of the situation until it was too late.

One day, on a rainy Sunday afternoon, I had a planned meeting with a few old friends in New York. Since the weather did not lend itself to walking around, and none of us had our own homes, our meeting place was in a popular hotel where monthly an afternoon social club was held for German-Jewish immigrants. The weather was bad, so the café was packed. With no tables available, it was meant to be that two nice gentlemen were looking for a seat. We were asked by the waiter if we would mind if these gentlemen joined us at our table. One of these gentlemen happened to be Herbert Mosheim, from Vlotho on the Weser. In our conversation, we discovered that we had similar interests. This was January 1941, and we were both focused on trying to get our families out of Germany by way of Cuba, since the war was now in full force and most of the borders were closed. And so, there was much to compare between dances. At the end of the afternoon, Herbert asked me for my telephone number and my permission to contact me. I was immediately drawn to him, and I had the very peculiar feeling that he was the man I'd be waiting for and who would be my future life's companion.[4]

From then on, we met whenever my free time permitted. Herbert worked in the office of Hudson Pulp and Paper in New York, but it was goal to work in the paper mill again to use his technical knowledge of manufacturing, which he had studied thoroughly in Germany. First he had studied in Cothen,[5] and when his father[6] died in 1936, he became copartner of two paper mills together with his uncles,[7] one in Wrexen[8] and one in Vlotho, which he managed until Kristallnacht. In September 1941, Herbert was successful in being sent to Hudson's paper mill in Vermont as assistant to the manager there. We corresponded almost daily, and whenever possible, Herbert hitched a free ride on the Mill Truck to N.Y. where he could spend the weekend with his relatives in Washington Heights. He was very lonely in Bellows Falls, a small place with a population of 3,000 residents, but he was happy to be working in his own field again. After December 1941, when America entered the war after Pearl Harbor, we were denied to give any more help to our loved ones. Even considering all the tragic happenings concerning deportations and destruction of our families in Germany, we had still not given up hope of reuniting with our dear ones, but our hands were tied. So we planned to get married in March 1942.

We had a small wedding in the home of my American relatives in Brooklyn,[9] and our former Rabbi, Doctor Baerwald[10] from Munich, performed the ceremony. We had no money for a wedding trip, but it was my first trip to Bellows Falls where we had a few days of honeymoon. We just were completely happy to be together, though we worried terribly about our loved ones. We did not know yet that my dear mother was already murdered in November 1941. Herbert's three sisters, two brothers-in-law, and his three-year-old nephew were deported that spring to the Warsaw Ghetto and lost their lives.[11]

We lived a very quiet and modest life in Bellows Falls. Before my daughter, Susan, was born, I worked at first as a salesgirl in a five and ten cent store and later in a factory where I could make more money. We both had the ambition to make something of our lives again. After our Susan in 1944, and two years later our Nancy arrived, I stayed at home and devoted my time to my family. [. . .] At that time, in 1946, due to his knowledge and efforts Herbert was made manager of the factory, and so we got ahead.[12]

[. . .] I wish to mention before I finish, that we never can forget the most sad memories of our youth. I don't even like to think anymore about how hard it was for me to be alone in a strange country, and to lose all family, mother, grandparents, as well as my father, and to have lost them in such a horrible way.[13] But in my heart, I am grateful, too, that America has given me the chance to build a new fine life for myself that I can look back on with contentment despite the usual ups and downs of life. Though I am now at an advanced age and widowed, I have no complaints. [. . .]

Before I close I wish to mention that in previous years I visited Munich three times for a few days mainly to visit the grave of my father, who had died in 1938 shortly before Kristallnacht. The first time I visited, I was there with my dear husband following an invitation from his former hometown, Vlotho, which he also wished to revisit. The second time, after I was widowed, I visited in 1988 with my two daughters [to show them where their father and

I grew up] and then again when I visited again with my boyfriend in 1997. In spite of all the horror associated with my later youth, I still have nice memories of my years before Hitler, and I still kept a little place in my heart for the city of my birth. Munich is still one of the most beautiful cities in the world, and is situated in one of the most scenic areas of the world. I am still proud to say I was born in the beautiful city of Munich.

NOTES

1. Since 1961: Städtisches Luisengymnasium München.

2. Inge Moss was able to emigrate on the *George Washington* from Genoa, Italy, to the United States, where she arrived on May 28, 1940.

3. Still in deep mourning after the death of her husband, Karl Marx (1885–1938), and under the false impression that nothing would happen to the women, Else Marx, nèe Zenner (1894–1941), was in no hurry to get a quota number necessary for emigration to the United States. Consequently, her number in the American consulate was so high that she did not receive a visa in time; she was deported from Munich to Kovno (Kaunas) on November 20, 1941, where she was murdered. Following Inge's emigration, letters remained the only connection between mother and daughter, all censored, until this also came to an end when America took an active role in the war and shortly before the Munich Jews were deported.

4. Herbert Loeb Mosheim, later Moss (1908–1978), was the second of five children, graduated from engineering school in 1931, and took over running the family's paper factory after his father's death in 1935. After spending six weeks in the Buchenwald concentration camp following his arrest during *Kristallnacht*, he managed to escape to the United States via Kitchener camp in England. He married Ingeborg Klara Marx on March 28, 1942 in Brooklyn.

5. Köthen, a German town in Saxony-Anhalt, about 30 km north of Halle.

6. Levi Mosheim (1863–1936) and his wife Sophie, née Loeb (1877–1941), raised their children in Vlotho, Germany, a small town in the rural Westphalia area.

7. Herbert Mosheim's father was particularly close to his brother Moses Mosheim (1861–1943), who shared the running of the paper mill; he was deported to Theresienstadt where he died in 1943.

8. Wrexen is a district of the German town of Diemelstadt in North Hesse.

9. Among the family in the United States were two brothers of Inge's father Karl Marx—Bernhard Marx (1884–1963) and Adolf Marx (1890–1991), as well as her mother's siblings—Gertrud (Trude) Bing, née Zenner (1905–1999) and Justin Zenner (1891–1959), and their families.

10. Dr. Leo Baerwald (1883–1970), rabbi of the Jewish community of Munich since 1918, emigrated to the United States in 1940.

11. Dr. jur. Julius Charig (b. 1897) and his wife Ilse, née Mosheim (b 1904), were deported to the Warsaw Ghetto on April 14, 1942 and later declared dead. Walter Kohlberg (b. 1905) and his wife Hildegard (Hilde), née Mosheim (b. 1910), with

their son Joel (b. 1939) and Gerda Friederike Mosheim (b. 1924) were deported to the Warsaw Ghetto on March 31, 1942, and later declared dead.

12. At that time, the family also became American citizens and exchanged the name Mosheim for Moss and "Inge" became "Ingrid."

13. Inge's elderly grandmother, Pauline Marx (1861–1943), over 80 and ill with cancer, was still deported to Theresienstadt as were also the parents of her mother, from Nuremberg, Josef Zenner (1860–1943) and his wife Carolina (Lina), née Fuld (1868–1943). They all died from starvation in 1943.

Chapter 10

Tossed by the Wind

A Proud Journey from 1920 to 1994

Ilse E. Scholle

Ilse Scholle was born Ilse Elisabeth Charlotte Franziska Wertheimer on May 16, 1920, in Munich. Her parents, Dr. jur. Simon Wertheimer and Katharina Wertheimer, née Krenn, had their daughter baptized and raised her as a Catholic. Since her mother, who came from the Passau area, was a Catholic, the parents' marriage was considered a "privileged mixed marriage," according to the National Socialist definition.

At the time of Ilse Scholle's birth, the family lived in Isabellastrasse 17, a solid conventional apartment house with a small grocery and notions store around the corner. Her father, Simon Wertheimer, was a non-practicing Jew and a director of the insurance company Bayerische Rückversicherungsbank AG. On November 10, 1938, he was arrested during the "protective custody action" and deported to the Dachau concentration camp. He was able to return home between Christmas and the New Year in 1938. From then on, Katharina and Simon Wertheimer made intensive efforts to find a way to emi-grate, initially to Uruguay. At the beginning of January 1939, Ilse was able to take a makeshift, emergency exit-school examination, or "Notabitur," at Munich's Luisengymnasium, before the family left the Bavarian capital for Zurich, Switzerland, on January 17, 1939. The next stop was the French city Nice. In September 1939, Simon Wertheimer, like other male foreigners, was temporarily interned in the Antibes camp. Finally, on November 18, 1940, the family received the longed-for entry papers for the United States. Their emi-gration route wound through France, Casablanca, Spain, and Cuba to New York, where Ilse, Katharina, and Simon Wertheimer set foot on American soil in mid-September 1941—more than a year and a half after they had left Munich. In November 1943, two years after her arrival in exile, Ilse married Dr. Julian Scholle (1897–1975), a doctor from Danzig, whom she had met on the ship passage from Spain to North Africa and who had also been on his way to the United States. The Scholle couple had two children, Peter and Karin, and five grandchildren.

Ilse Scholle passed away at Mount Kisco, Westchester, CO, on July 1, 1995. The year before, in 1994, she wrote her memoir, "Gone with the Wind: A Proud Journey from 1920 to 1994." The work is a powerful testimony, describing her long and arduous journey halfway around the world before she and her parents reached their emigration destination, the United States. Her descriptions of their first years in the new, still foreign homeland are revealing. She describes in detail, for example, how difficult it was to build a secure existence.

Figure 10.1   Sergeant Ilse and Corporal Katherine, Undated. *Source:* Private Collection.

[. . .] On the 7th of August, the Navemar[1] finally left Seville [Spain], went down the Guadalquivir River, and turned into a choppy sea on the way to Lisbon [Portugal]. The boat was a horror of a dilapidated relic. In their greed, they had stuffed far too many passengers into the hull and accommodated, at the last minute, a whole group of people saved from concentration camps, who had traveled like cattle in sealed trains. They arrived 3/4 dead. There were refugee doctors on board, but they had no medications nor the power to write prescriptions. Since I had volunteered to take care of some of the very sick passengers, the refugee doctors would send me to the Spanish ship doctor to get lifesaving help. The doctor looked me up and down and with a big grin said, "What beautiful legs!" Then he walked off. I was so furious that I literally turned him around and in my miserable Spanish told him what I thought of him. Then I repeated my request in the name of those wretched people. But he just walked away again. I knew then that the trip would be a miserable one.

On the aft deck were a herd of cattle. Every second or third night, one would be slaughtered. You could hear their bloodcurdling screams. On the second day of the voyage, we landed in Lisbon. The American visa had to be valid in the last European port. Ours expired that day in Lisbon. Since this calamity happened to other passengers too, negotiations started. Six days later, the American consul had been kind enough to arrange with the Portuguese authorities to hire a bus which would bring the refugees into the embassy's yard (American soil), renew everybody's visa, and bring the bus back to the lifeboats of the Navemar and then on board. We were very grateful for this show of compassion. The Joint, a Jewish charitable organization, handed out sandwiches, coffee, and cake.

In another two days, we sailed again. The Navemar lay at anchor, so it didn't cost them any berthing fees. It took from the 16th to the 29th of August to reach Bermuda.[2] By then, five passengers had already died of typhoid fever and were buried at sea. Those burials were a horrible sight to me. Everything on board was strange. In the ladies room, a Spanish sailor would sit, hand out tiny pieces of toilet paper and watch the ladies wash themselves. At breakfast, another sailor handed each person one roll, which was all the bread one would get for the day. I saved two of them and on the 24th of August, I gave them to Vati[3] as a birthday present. I also included Mutti,[4] who was already much too thin.

Claude[5] and I tried to find other young people to get together with in the evenings. It just so happened that we found a charming family from Vienna. The mother would sit down after supper and recite by heart lovely poetry, pieces out of plays, anything that would come to her mind. And young people would settle into the lifeboats around and listen in rapture under the starry sky. Those were the moments memories are made of. I still hear the lovely voice and I wish she were still alive to tell her how many people she saved from going insane.

The sea remained calm, it never rained, and then the rudder broke. But nevertheless, we made it into the harbor of Bermuda. I was completely unprepared for the beauty of the island. Green meadows in all directions. Lovely pink houses, scrubbed streets, and wonderful people. They brought food, toys for the children, and they played with them lovingly. They carried huge boxes of clothing for the refugees from the train who had nothing at all. They gave and gave and extended love and warmth to everyone aboard. The generosity was truly overwhelming. And we unloaded another "body" there for a more comforting land burial. It was a famous writer, but I can't recall who. His sister debarked with his body.

In Cuba, we anchored for only a few hours. Some passengers were taken by motor launch ashore. I thought of Julian[6] and hoped he was getting better. On the 10th or 11th, we reached via the Florida coastline, New York City. The authorities didn't let us land, because there had been by then 11 cases of fatal typhoid fever on board. Finally, they decided to let us dock in Brooklyn, and the Health Department inspected all passengers and continued to do so wherever they settled down. Once a week, they checked us all for quite a long time. On the return trip, the Navemar was sunk off the Portuguese coast. I couldn't feel sorry for the crew. Throughout the whole voyage, they were a dismal and unfeeling lot. [. . .]

Our friends, Fred and Ella Wertheimer,[7] were at the pier. They took one look at Mutti, and saw that she wasn't even able to walk unassisted. She had come down from 136 lbs. to less than 90. To look for an apartment was impossible. They took us to an apartment hotel on the West Side, where she would have full service and a tiny, tiny, improvised kitchenette in a closet, where I could prepare breakfast. I had to find a job quickly. America had come through the depression, and New York City was still coping with the arrival of large numbers of refugees. Most of them, who had arrived here, had no means to travel further. They needed work, like me, and they needed it right away. The competition was tough, and unless you knew somebody who knew somebody else, it was almost impossible to get your foot in. I felt like an octopus who tried, with all the tentacles available, to reach a large number of useful people. I had never held a job, and I was scared. Yet, I knew we needed the money, and Mutti should have doctor's care. Well, I thought, "tonight I sleep in my new bed, and tomorrow, Vati and I will talk."

It was already 1 AM, but Vati said, "You know, I see all the little groceries still open, why don't you go down with me and I'll get some cold beer. It's such a hot night, and we could use something after all the landing excitement." Well, I wanted a soda and on the corner we saw a store with sodas and root beer. Vati said, "Look, there we get both your soda and my beer." He took one sip from the dark liquid and then went out of the place and spit out the sip utterly disgusted. "Is that what they call beer in America?" A guy who overheard our conversation enlightened us. Root beer was the extract from the roots of certain plants like sassafras, etc. Beer would be sold in cans in the little grocery across the street. Well, we thanked him, bought the cans and went home feeling like we had accomplished something wonderful for one night. [. . .]

We were finally ready for bed, put Mutti's, my, and Vati's shoes before the door to be cleaned, and retired. I think I was asleep before I hit the pillow. At 6 AM, there was a sharp knock on the door. I leaped out of bed fearing the worst scenario (after my German experience when the SS dragged Vati away at 4 AM).[8] Vati had put on his robe and opened the door cautiously. There stood our nice black elevator man and asked us to take the shoes in: "I have been watching them all night long. But, I am off duty now. Nobody is going to clean them in America, but they may very well steal them." We gratefully followed his advice and went back to sleep. Mutti hadn't even woken up.

At 9 AM, we all were wide awake. The noise of the street and the banging doors of the hotel guests give you no other option anyway. We figured breakfast at a hotel would be too expensive. We had seen a Horn and Hardart Automat[9] the night before and were going to try it. We promised Mutti a nice warm cereal. Vati and I went down and, with my superior English, asked the salesgirl for "Porridge." She looked at me as if I had descended from Mars and said, "What?" "Porridge, please." "Haven't got it." "Well, then give me bread and butter." She rattled off, much too fast for my ear to catch, "Whole wheat, white, pumpernickel, 3 grain, Italian, French, Kaiser roll" and on and on. I just said, "Thank-you" and walked away. Then she served another man before it was Vati's turn. He asked for three porridges. She heaved a sigh before answering, "Haven't got it." Vati said, "Yes you have. The man before me just got it." She said, "That was oatmeal." "Well fine, just give me three oatmeals and remember for millions of people it's still porridge." We also got three coffees out of the machine and returned to Mutti, highly satisfied with having completed our mission.

With the short errand, we realized that it would not be all that easy to adapt to the mores of another continent. Will we ever become Americans in every sense of the word, or do you have to be born here to absorb the vernacular with the mother milk? I can answer the question now at age 74, you have to be born here. My children and grandchildren look upon me still with a certain curiosity and correct my pronunciation and buy me occasionally German sausages to appease my foreign heritage. Only the second generation becomes totally American; the first generation works their fingers to the bone, lays very often the financial foundation, and is courted as a fountain of rather strange wisdom. I would have given anything to be thought of as typical American, because that's how I feel inside. However, we can't turn ourselves inside out. I am half American, half European, and it's not such a bad mixture. I am used to being half and half in everything.

The first day after oatmeal, I got a phone call from some Swiss friends from the Swiss Reinsurance Co. who were working here for two years and were living on the grounds of the Westchester Country Club. Mr. and Mrs. Habicht and Mr. and Mrs. Alther.[10] They invited me to come see them in Rye the following day. I liked the Alther daughters, Musy and Sybill, a little younger than I, very bright and pretty. I didn't know about the 10-year-old son, Tobey, of the Habichts. But the idea to see old Swiss friends was very nice. So, on the 14th, I took the train to Rye, where they picked me up by car. We had a nice lunch, went to the club's beach, and there they told me that Tobey's governess and teacher was returning to Switzerland. He needed all his lessons from math to history, etc. in French and German. Would I be interested to take the soon-to-be vacated job. Seeing the luxurious surroundings and knowing how much I liked the families, I quickly gave my assent before asking anything about pay or hours involved or anything at all for that matter. I was a real greenhorn, easily swayed by tempting appearances.

My job was to start in five days, on the 19th of August. I asked at the desk of our hotel, where I could buy a decent suit for my new job. I got an address on MADISON! What did I know? But, in spite of the high price, I did wear that suit for years and years to come. So, maybe it wasn't such a foolish thing after all. And the saleswoman let me pay it in installments.

On the 18th, a day before leaving for Rye, I visited Mrs. Scholle, Julian's mother. She was overjoyed and wouldn't let me go for hours. She talked about the difficult voyage. When Julian arrived with high fever and walking on crutches in Vigo, the ship's doctor refused to let him come aboard. Julian explained that he was a physician himself, he would sign a paper absolving the ship's company of any liability, and he would take care of all his own needs. After lengthy deliberations, the ship's doctor reluctantly gave in. Julian had to cut daily with scissors over a probe along the line of ever-widening infection. There were no antibiotics available, and he had no anesthetics and suffered excruciatingly. His mother helped and brought his food to the cabin. She worried every day, especially at the thought of leaving him behind, alone, in Cuba.

He made it to a rented room there and continued to treat himself. The landlady became very concerned and offered to take him to the Institute for Tropical Diseases. She helped Julian into a taxi, and they went there together—her Spanish was definitely superior. And there, lo and behold, sulfa[11] had just been introduced for experimental use. They tried it on Julian, and the first signs of healing appeared shortly on the wound edges. He was so happy and made fantastic progress from then on. It had been touch and go for so long and Margaret Scholle in New York City had no way to help him, which made her quite desperate as a loving mother. Mothers are supposed to be able to kiss booboos and that makes it all better. Well, not always!

She chatted away and told me about the other son Sigurd,[12] who lived in the same apartment hotel on 55th Street. He had gone to Washington DC to find out if there were ever people who refused the visa, and Julian could be given one of those to enter. He pleaded because of his need of care and also the age and precarious health of the mother. There were enough humanitarian reasons to let him leave Cuba as soon as possible. However, while they refused Sigurd his request, the official at the Immigration Department, with whom he spoke, sent a telegram to the Cuban Consulate: "Offered Dr. Scholle a visa to enter States earlier, stop, he refused." We only found out through a friend there what was going on within our diplomatic corps. I was livid when I heard it and so was the Scholle family.

I told Mrs. Scholle about my job starting tomorrow, and she was happy for me. And then I did a little sightseeing, ending with praying at the rear altar of the St. Patrick's Cathedral.

On the 19th of August, I went to Rye. At 7:30 AM, I had to get up to prepare breakfast for Tobey and me, then we read and played a while, and then I was asked to wash and dress him!! Oh my God, I never washed and dressed any boy, let alone a boy of 10. Well, if that was my job, I'll do it, and we'll make it fun time. We got along very well, and I was like a member of the family. [. . .]

On the 14th of October, Vati and Mutti visited me. I missed them. Vati had hoped to possibly find a job within the reinsurance field, but his age worked against him. Young, handsome, intelligent, recent college graduates were preferred over an old man with experience. It was a young country, looking out for its young people. Vati and Mutti had really aged a lot. And nobody talked about salary to me—I had nothing to give them. While I received room and board, my parents paid the same for our rooms whether I was there or not. I told Vati that if I didn't get anything by October 15th, I would look for other employment. The day came and went and nothing happened.

In the meantime, Sigurd Scholle, Julian's older brother, had asked my parents if I were available to stay with his mother and quoted compensation over the phone. I thought I would accept that offer. Tobey was bound to go back to Switzerland one of these days, and so I told Mr. and Mrs. Habicht that my parents needed me nearer and I would be leaving October 31 or November 1, 1941. They were astonished and sad but accepted my request quite cordially. On the day I left, they gave me a present with a little envelope on top containing what they called "pocket money" and a very lovely expression of their gratefulness. It was my first experience with the real world. You have to stand up for yourself and negotiate intelligently. Will I ever learn? I needed more than pocket money now. On the other hand, I was glad that they considered me a special friend rather than an employee. I was still a bit stuck up in my heart.

On November 2, I started at Margaret Scholle's. Our relationship changed somewhat. She was now the boss, and she knew it. Although she had maid service, I had to go over half of what they had already done. If after dusting, I had moved a vase an inch, she would go over and move the vase and nod to herself approvingly. I had looked at the job as companion, and she wanted one minute a maid, the next a slave, the next a companion. This was the time of food rationing, and she would send the butcher back three times because the piece of meat he showed her wouldn't suit her. If all the herbs were not available, she'd have a fit. What had I gotten myself into? I was patient and kind, but there are limits!

In the meantime, Julian wrote the sweetest letters to me, and after each letter, I acquiesced for a while and thanked God she wasn't my mother. Sigurd must have sensed my mounting dissatisfaction, because he took me out on the 23rd, flattering me all over the place!!! On the 30th, he took both his mother and me to the La Guardia Airport Restaurant and gave me tickets for Rudolf Serkin[13] the following day. He gave me more time off. [. . .] I felt better and took the little idiosyncrasies in stride. And Mrs. Scholle calmed down too.

On December 7, 1941, the Japanese attacked Pearl Harbor.[14] The whole nation was shocked, and an aura of mourning descended over the land. Who knows what will happen now? Every family sat glued to the radio night after night. America was quickly preparing for war now. I spent Christmas Eve with Margaret Scholle, then went to midnight mass and Holy Communion and returned to Vati and Mutti for our first Christmas in the New World. It was as worrisome as most of the others in the last few years. The "peace on Earth" escaped us for so long. [. . .]

Margaret Scholle and I got along much better now. Whatever it was that put her in a better frame of mind, I enjoyed it. We often sat in the early winter darkness with just a lamp by the desk lit, and she would tell me stories of the family. She herself was born Margaret Solmsen in Schneidemühl, Germany. She played the piano very well and loved classical music. [. . .]

I now came only every second day. I had the chance to look at other possibilities. What about my certification to be a French teacher? I called up a private school and made an appointment. I got the surprise of my life. If you want to teach here, you not only need French exams from a US school but also a teacher's certification to be allowed to teach anything at all. Here, I thought all along I had worked toward something useful, and it was for nothing. I wasn't strong enough to go to night school and do the homework, too, and couldn't afford daytime. Well so much for that.

Vati had in the meantime studied for the exam to become an insurance broker, passed the exam and formed, with two friends, the Allied Brokerage agency in downtown New York (70 Pine Street). It was not a job he liked, nor was he good at it. He wrote hundreds of letters to major corporations, hoping to get his foot into more lucrative and interesting work. But nothing came of these efforts, but polite refusals. And he was forced to do what he hated most, peddle from household to household, starting with friends and acquaintances, with tiny commissions. It was exhausting and for him, humiliating. By the time the furniture, office machinery, and office rent were paid, pitifully little, if anything, remained. It depressed him, and I was still dilly-dallying more or less.

I decided to talk to more people to put out their feelers. One offer came: sell the most delectable Austrian-style chocolates in a swanky shop on Fifth Avenue. They wanted somebody with language skills for their international clientele. Eighteen dollars a week. Well, the pay wasn't all that enticing, although in 1942, it bought a whole lot more than it does today. But, when I passed by the shop, just around the corner from Margaret Scholle's, I fell in love with the place. It was called Altmann & Kuhne.[15] Mr. Altmann had brought over from Vienna all the recipes and was also the architect for the place; a delightful Rococo confection, where you expected to see Mozart pick out his own Mozart Kugeln.[16] Poor Mr. Altmann had put too much money into establishing his own chocolate factory and furnishing this exquisite place on Fifth Avenue. He lost it all to a couple from South Africa and was now reduced to "window dresser."

I entered, spoke with the owners, Mr. and Mrs. Duvall,[17] and got the job. Required dress: black silk. Who could afford silk? Now, I had to tell Sigurd about my decision. He was very disappointed, but I was adamant. It was time to look out for myself. I promised to pass by often after work to see Margaret and cheer her up. She really didn't need me so much of the time.

The clientele was fascinating: Monty Woolley,[18] Ingrid Bergman,[19] Marlene Dietrich[20] with her friend Jean Gabin,[21] and on and on. Since I myself was a chocolate freak, I gave them mouthwatering descriptions of the various delicacies and sold very well. I had a lot of opportunities to speak French and German again and made extra money by doing overtime around the holidays. Mr. Duvall asked if my parents could come in for about a month around Christmas and New Year's to wrap packages in the basement. Mutti thought it was fun to make some money for the Holidays. A week after New Year's, they each got a box of chocolate and a handshake. We still hadn't learned!!!

After a few months of good work, Mr. Duvall approached me and asked if I wanted to become manager of the store. He saw that I was reliable, enthusiastic, and capable. "Well, Mr. Duvall, how much does that position pay?" "Twenty-two dollars." For four more dollars, I would have ten times the work on my shoulders. No way. When I came home and told Vati, he did not think I had made a good decision. I should have stuck it out as manager for a while, and if and when leaving, I would have had a better title on my resume: Manager of a Fifth Avenue Establishment.

While I was mulling over my faux pas, the phone rang. The son of one of Vati's colleagues, my old buddy from Nice, Freddy,[22] was asking me if he could come over. He had something to discuss with me. I said yes, of course. He came in a few minutes, looking a bit shaken. He had been drafted. He had just begun to learn how to cut diamonds. After the German invasion of Holland and Belgium, a big part of the diamond trade had relocated in New York City, and they needed a lot of young people to learn the trade. In the first stages, there were more bosses than workers available. Freddy had been an apprentice, but now he would have to leave for the Army. His boss did not want another boy-apprentice; he might be drafted, too. He was looking for a girl, would I be interested? "Well, how much does an apprentice get?" "Forty-two dollars a week." I thought I hadn't heard right. I would be learning a trade and get paid $42? I looked at Vati and Mutti. They weren't exactly thrilled about the diamond trade, but left the decision-making process to me.

I said yes without knowing anything about either what the work entailed or the caliber of the people involved with the trade. There were a few eye-openers in my future, but eh, a jump from making eighteen dollars to earning forty-two to start, with the prospect of making oodles more when the apprenticeship was complete. The place was unionized. I first needed a membership card. That took a while; lots of red tape. Seeing the actual shop was scary. Was the money worth the miserable working conditions? Yes, at this moment in our lives it was. [. . .]

In my eagerness to become Americanized and meet young people, I joined three American young women's organizations, the YWCA (Young Women's Christian Association),[23] the National Catholic Young Women's Club, and the National Security Women's Club. In the first one, I took golf lessons, which was fun, although I never played it later on. The second one was a service organization which at that moment in time came up with the idea to give mini courses in English to foreign men who wanted to see New York. The women's organization had a lovely building on the side of St. Patrick's Cathedral, and we organized a nice dance, together with lessons on how to ask your way around, how to order in restaurants, etc. It was fun. I took all the French-speaking sailors and officers. We really prepared them well and treated them kindly. I still got thank-you letters after the war from some of them, and one sent me a box of chocolates with a lid in the form of a sailor's hat including the pompom.

With my mother, I joined a third organization, the National Security Women's Club. It was a paramilitary organization, with uniforms and drills. I soon made it to staff sergeant and acting lieutenant, while Mutti was still corporal. It was fun to command her around and see her obey!! I was a little disappointed in their organization as a whole. Nobody had any experience, and the drills seemed a bit senseless, since they were not accompanied by any precise defense program for the City of New York. So, eventually I resigned. Playing war wasn't my idea of a useful occupation. Mutti stayed, sewed uniforms, and was one day congratulated by the Duke of Windsor, who was at that time governor of the Bahamas. She was thrilled.

I still complained to some of my friends that I felt isolated in many ways. I had finished my apprenticeship at Gissenger's diamond cutting place and for what reason? I don't remember—I think Gissenger's went out of town—I looked for work more uptown, nearer to home. I found a wonderful place, smaller, cleaner, nicer people and a good boss. I was pleased with my progress at work but not with my personal life. Freddy, who had originally introduced me to the diamond trade and was now in the Army, came home often enough on leave and would check on me. He also took me out to the nicest nightclubs. I had never seen any, and to dine, for instance, at El Morocco, was impressive. New Year's with a Canadian orchestra at some swanky hotel! I looked forward to those beautiful evenings, although we were just good old buddies looking for companionship while waiting . . . of course, those are often the nicest relationships. Absolutely no strings attached. Such good old friends are rare, I know, and I did appreciate our exceptionally beautiful evenings, which were like magic to me then.

One day in 1942, my old Munich friends, the Frei's,[24] introduced me to their friend Werner S.,[25] visiting them on leave from the Army. We found out that he had lived opposite of my house in Munich, but we had never met before. He was looking for things to do in New York while on leave, and we had a country picnic, saw some movies, and went for walks along the Hudson River. After a few outings, he became quite serious about our relationship, and I really didn't want that. I went out because I had nothing better to do. He was Jewish and had lost both his parents in a concentration camp. Naturally, he owed his allegiance to a faith for which they died. And I was serious about my faith, being a practicing Catholic. I saw only conflict ahead and hoped to keep the relationship on just a friendly path, without deeper attachments. Well, in spite of my trying to keep the relationship light, it led to on-and-off marriage talks, a broken marriage date, and to our final breakup in May 1943 to the relief of us both!! I really hadn't needed all that emotional commotion leading to absolutely nowhere anyway.

I had poured out my heart about all that in letters to Julian. He never believed I would marry Werner, and in the end, he was right. I moped through the summer of 1943, just concentrating on my work and not wanting to see anyone in particular. I felt constantly tired and the heat of New York in July and August doesn't exactly invigorate you. September 20, 1943, Sigurd Scholle called me, out of the blue. Julian was arriving on the 22nd, but Margaret was not well at all and would I come along to Penn Station (he was arriving by train from Florida) and sort of prepare Julian for the shock of seeing his mother in very poor condition. She had esophageal bleeding ulcers and the treating physician was pessimistic.

Well, I had not even heard that Julian was expected so soon. I was very sad about Margaret's illness just at this time, but in seventh heaven about Julian's arrival. From doldrums to seventh heaven, my, my! I got a new dress, very chic, but my knees buckled until the train pulled into the station. Julian had lost a lot of weight, and I saw a strong resemblance to Leslie Howard,[26] whom I had just seen in Gone with the Wind. When we saw each other up close, it was as if fireworks' sparks were going off in all directions. We both knew, that very instant, that this was it, although we acted very demure in front of Sigurd. How come I had never felt like that before about him? Perhaps I had, by now, seen more of life, had grown more mature and receptive. Perhaps we both had to be very lonely for a while. Perhaps we were both at the point where ready for a serious relationship. Whatever it was, we were attracted to each other and we knew it, without words, at this, our first embrace.

NOTES

1. The *SS Navemar* was a cargo steamship built in England in 1921. The Spanish freighter, built to carry 28 passengers at most, left Seville, Spain, with 1,120 passengers in 1941. Most of them were Jewish refugees fleeing German-occupied countries. Some had paid as much as $1,750 for their ticket; 345 passengers disembarked in Havana, Cuba; the remaining passengers arrived in New York, USA, 48 days after leaving Spain. According to US Public Health officials, 6 passengers died on the trip; upon arrival, 41 were placed under the care of the officials since they suffered from fever.

2. Bermuda is a British island territory in the North Atlantic Ocean.

3. With the German word "Vati" (dad) Ilse Scholle refers to her father Dr. jur. Simon Wertheimer (1882–1961), banker and later CEO of the Bavarian Reinsurance Co., who married Katharina Krenn on August 9, 1916. Together with his wife and daughter, he emigrated from Munich via Seville to the United States in 1941. Once in the United States, he became an insurance broker and formed with two friends the Allied Brokerage agency in downtown New York.

4. With the German word "Mutti" (mom) Ilse Scholle refers to her mother Katharina Wertheimer, neé Krenn (1892–1972), who was born and raised Catholic in Passau. Together with her husband Simon Wertheimer and daughter, she emigrated from Munich via Seville to the United States in 1941.

5. Claude-Ann Kirschen (1920–2012) was a young Belgian woman and fellow passenger whom Ilse met while waiting for the departure of the *S.S. Navemar* in Seville. They not only survived the voyage together, but remained life-long friends. Under her married name of Claude-Anne Lopez, she became a renowned writer and senior research scholar at Yale University, who specialized in studies of Benjamin Franklin.

6. Dr. Julian Scholle (1897–1975), World War I veteran, medical doctor, and eventual husband of Ilse, was born in Danzig as the second child of Emil Scholle (1858–1928), a well-to-do importer of coffee, tea, and spices, and his wife Margarete (Margaret) Scholle, neé Solmsen (1870–1943). Julian had been a physician in Berlin, but had lived in France for five years prior to emigrating to the United States. Ilse was 21 when she met him, 43 of age, at the beginning of her journey toward the United States in 1941. In May 1941, both—Ilse with her parents, Julian with his mother— were on board of the *S.S. Wyoming*, a cargo-mixed boat sailing from Marseilles/ France toward the Caribbean island of Martinique. Due to unexpected circumstances,

the passengers of the *S.S. Wyoming* were taken off the boat in Casablanca, Morocco, on June 7, 1941, and interned on a half-abandoned horse farm in Sidi-el-Ayachi. Since Ilse and Julian had been listed on the passenger list as "daughter" and "son," and the authorities did not look at the ages, they spent the next weeks together in the "children's camp."—On June 24, Julian and his mother left for Tangier from where they continued to Vigo, Spain, to board a liner for Cuba (for Julian) and New York City (for his mother). During the first part of their journey, Julian got an infected bite of a tsetse fly on his ankle, had a high fever and was thus afraid the liner at Vigo might not take him—news he had shared with Ilse in a letter. On July 5, 1941, Ilse and her parents left the camp to head via Casablanca, Morocco, to Seville, Spain, from where they had booked a new passage to New York via Lisbon, Bermuda, and Cuba on the *SS Navemar*, scheduled to leave on August 6, 1941, actually departing on August 7, 1941. Ilse and Julian reunited in the United States and got married on November 27, 1943.

7. Dr. Alfred Wertheimer, born in Munich in 1882, had been running a technical office in Munich since the early 1920s. With his wife Ella, née Friedmann (1894–1992), he emigrated to the United States via England in February 1939.

8. During *Kristallnacht*, at four in the morning, two SS men had rung the doorbell like crazy. When the door was opened, they brutally dragged Simon Wertheimer out, down the stairs and into a military van, while his mother and daughter stood helplessly by. For several weeks, his family had no idea where he had been taken, but eventually it turned out that he was in the Dachau concentration camp. Between Christmas and New Year he came home, thin as a skeleton. He hardly spoke a word (even in the future he would never talk about his experiences in Dachau) and was amazed at how much his wife had prepared on her own so that the departure for the family's safety could be planned for January 17, 1939.

9. Horn & Hardart was a food company in the United States known for operating the first food vending machines in Philadelphia and New York City.

10. No personal data known.

11. Sulfa drugs, also called sulfonamides, refer to members of a group of synthetic antibiotics containing the sulfanilamide molecular structure.

12. Sigurd Scholle (1893–1971), brother of Julian Scholle.

13. Rudolf Serkin (1903–1991), world-famous pianist who was especially appreciated for his interpretation of the works of Beethoven, Schubert, and Brahms.

14. The United States formally entered the European Theater of World War II on December 11, 1941, just a few days after the surprise attack on the US naval base at Pearl Harbor on Oahu Island, Hawaii, by Japan, an ally of Nazi Germany, on December 7, 1941.

15. Altmann & Kühne is a confiserie and chocolaterie founded in 1928 in Vienna, Austria. After the Anschluss in 1938, the owners Emil (Emile) Altmann and Ernst Kühne, who were Jewish, fled to New York City. In December 1939, they opened a chocolate shop at 700 Fifth Avenue, which was sold to an American investor in 1941 and continued under the Austrian brand until 1958.

16. Famous chocolate from Salzburg.

17. No personal data known.

18. Monty Woolley (1888–1963), famous American actor.

19. Ingrid Bergman (1915–1982), famous Swedish actress.

20. Marlene Dietrich (1901–1992), famous German actress, who emigrated to the United States in 1930.

21. Jean Gabin (1904–1976), famous French actor.

22. Freddy Kramer, son of a former Austrian colleague of Simon Wertheimer. No other personal data known.

23. The YWCA, today the largest ecumenical women's organization in the world, was founded in Britain in 1855 under the impact of the Industrial Revolution and in imitation of the Young Men's Christian Association (YMCA); the World YWCA was founded in 1894. The YWCA took a pioneering role in working to empower women and raise awareness of women's issues.

24. Could not be identified.

25. Presumably Werner Richard Stahl (1918–1976), who emigrated to the United States in June 1936.

26. Leslie Howard Steiner (1893–1943) was a British actor and filmmaker probably best remembered for his role as Ashley Wilkes in *Gone with the Wind* (1939).

Chapter 11

Tossed by the Storms of History

Experiences of a Survivor

Charlotte Haas Schueller

Charlotte Haas was born on June 30, 1912, in Munich. Her father was the distinguished surgeon Dr. Alfred Haas; her mother Elsa Haas was the daughter of the well-known Munich brewery owner Joseph Schülein. Charlotte, who lived with her parents and her younger brother Gerhard on Richard-Wagner-Strasse, not far from her parents' clinic, attended the Municipal Girls' Lyceum on Luisenstrasse from May 1922 to March 1931. Shortly after Adolf Hitler's appointment to Reich Chancellor, Charlotte Haas emigrated to England to study at the renowned London School of Economics. Later, she decided to study languages and ancient history. Her brother Gerhard, born in 1917, also went to England to study in Cambridge. After her parents, Alfred and Elsa Haas, had emigrated to the United States via England in the spring of 1940, Charlotte also decided to relocate to New York. She arrived in the country in 1941 and became a citizen of the United States on January 30, 1953. Later that year, there was an election, and Charlotte was thrilled to be able to exercise her right as a citizen to vote—for the second time in her life. The first time had been in 1933, when Germans had voted overwhelmingly for the National Socialists. Charlotte, who had married the native Viennese and widower Otto Schueller (1901–1976) in New York in 1959, did not let the bond to her old homeland break after 1945. Until her old age, she visited Munich regularly every year to meet her numerous friends. On June 5, 2010, she died in a hospital in New Jersey, shortly before her 98th birthday.

Her memoirs, written in English, were completed in 2002 and comprise 112 typewritten pages. In the passage included here, Charlotte Haas Schueller reflects on the challenges associated with her decision to emigrate, the time she spent in British exile (where she experienced the outbreak and hardships of World War II), and the difficulty she encountered while applying for an American visa, which, ultimately, arrived and opened the way to a new life in the United States.

Figure 11.1   Charlotte Haas Schueller as Young Woman, Undated. *Source:* Stadtarchiv München.

[. . .] In 1933 we had our last summer that was normally and fairly peace-fully spent in Bernried.[1] The outside world was already hostile. I decided that summer to leave Germany and in fall[2] I went to England to stay with Doris H.[3] as her guest and companion. I matriculated at the London School of Economics and spent one term improving my English essay writing. I had no trouble with the language, in fact, not at any time in my further studies at London University or, in Gerhard's case at Cambridge, did either of us have to pass a language exam.[4] We were interviewed and were accepted thanks to our parents' foresight giving us English as a second language.[5] We were way ahead of most other refugees, something that I've always appreciated.

Leaving what I had believed to be home and going to England was not an easy decision. It was a brutal break. I had grown up the granddaughter of Josef Schülein,[6] a prominent citizen of Munich with a square and a street named after him as well as the daughter of an extremely well known and popular physician.[7] And, after all, somebody in my own right. In London I was nobody. Still, it was better than being what the Nazis labeled us to be, which was a cockroach to be exterminated.

To leave Bernried and the mountains was hard, as it was to live on sea level where I have always been miserable. I have been doomed to live on sea level for the rest of my life. I became dependent on Doris H. who turned out to be a very possessive and domineering woman. My position with Doris was very ambiguous. She gave me refuge and gave me a roof over my head in a comfortable place. I was her companion but she also tried to own me, which is not a healthy thing. [. . .]

I had previously been in England as a visitor but in 1933 I arrived as a would-be student and I got a student's permit but had to promise never, ever to be a liability to the British labor market.

After one semester at the London School of Economics, I switched to University College on Gower Street. I matriculated there for a major in French and minors in Latin and Ancient History. I thought I was going to teach. In addition to functioning as a companion to Doris, I was a student at University College until I took my Bachelor's three years later. [. . .]

Making friends was difficult. Being an alien in England was like being a hunchback. "Poor thing, she can't help not being British." It was considered a birth defect. This was the time of Chamberlain's appeasement policy, fervently embraced by the majority of Brits.[8] I was not allowed to mention what was happening at home. Any mention was branded as "spreading atrocity stories." England's rude awakening came later.

Fortunately, I had some connections dating back to the days when British surgeons stopped in Munich to watch Father at work. Peter Wright,[9] for instance, had quite a crush on my parents and used to visit us in Munich and Bernried frequently. He was a surgeon himself, married to Helena Wright,[10] one of the pioneers in the birth control movement. [. . .] Their house was home away from home. It was warm, full of humanity, and pleasantly quirky. [. . .]

Doris and I first lived at Grosvenor House, a very ritzy hotel on Park Lane. Eventually, she rented an apartment in the Boltons, a garden square in South Kensington, off the Old Brompton Road.[11] She hired a decorator at Harrod's[12] and bought all the furnishings at that world famous emporium. We had fun choosing colors and making mistakes. Neither of us had any experience. We chose blue paint for one of the bedrooms that ended up looking like an aquarium and had to be redone. Then she hired a cook and a maid and the household was launched.

The first few years that I was in London, Doris and I used to go back to Munich every year in the summer. This was feasible up through 1937. We would stay with the parents in Bernried. It was a very strange sort of double life for me. Things in Germany became very difficult and our horizon became more and more restricted. The village of Bernried itself remained comparatively peaceful and people continued to be nice to us. The mayor was a social democrat and kept unpleasant and active antisemitic symptoms away from us. But one became more and more isolated.

In the spring of 1938, at Easter time, my grandfather [Joseph Schülein] sent me a message in England. He had advanced Hodgkin's disease, which was incurable at that time. He let me know that he wanted to see me. I thought that he had become senile and that he was bringing me back to Germany to say goodbye. It was risky but I felt that I had no choice. My passport had run out and new passports issued to Jews were now stamped with a large "J" which made you easy prey to every horror.[13] I went to the consulate general in London and saw an elderly civil servant who said he couldn't issue me a new passport without a J. I told him I had to go back and see my grandfather. He asked me if I knew what might happen to me once there. I said yes, but I have no option. So he did something unheard of and extended my old passport by three months. So, I gathered up my passport and went back into Germany.

It was too dangerous for me to stay too long in one place. I spent two or three nights in Munich and two or three nights in Bernried, then I went to Kaltenberg[14] and then started all over again. What I found, to my consternation, was that Grandfather wasn't at all senile and not at all sentimental. When I arrived at Kaltenberg, he had Onkel Fritz[15] go to the office, open the safe and bring back a box that contained the family jewels. It wasn't much because he had really fed his wife mediocre baubles as I mentioned before. But there were some good pieces and Grandfather told me to take it abroad. He said, "If I don't give it to you now, I know you'll never get it."

I then had the scariest trip in all my life because I had to take the bloody jewelry out of the country and there was a death penalty for smuggling valuables out of Germany at that time. I put it in my luggage and was sick all the way to the Dutch border because I was so scared. The pass controller and the luggage controller came in and they never opened my bags. They looked at my peculiar passport, gave me a strange look, and gave it back to me. Nothing happened. I went over the frontier, went to the toilet and took some time to be able to leave it again. And that is the story of the jewelry. That was the last time I went to Germany and the last time I ever saw my Grandfather. [. . .]

On many weekends, we went down to Blofield[16] to Doris' home. [. . .] Here, I should explain that at that time in England, and maybe even still today, language was really your passport and your label in society. While you might be a highly educated person, your accent always gave away your origin. There was no eradicating it and the barriers between the classes had not broken down. We were lucky because we had always had governesses with the right accent! So, there wasn't any problem in that department. But society was extremely bigoted. [. . .]

But English society also had some admirable features. The "upper class" and intellectuals displayed serious concern, knowledge, and true involvement in political problems and their treatment. They were informed and took action. In German society, the upper class, the middle class, and intellectuals did not participate actively in the political life of the nation. "Politics" was almost a dirty word [. . .]. These people (including my own) did not wake up until politics touched their personal lives and comfort. The British tradition of charity and philanthropy practiced as a duty by those lucky enough to belong to the upper crust impressed me enormously. Social work, voluntary and often demanding, was routinely considered the responsibility of the "leisure classes." Please note that I am discussing English society, not British. The social structure in Scotland is very different and I don't know enough about Ireland. [. . .]

In September of 1938, Grandfather Josef died. The parents prepared, late as it was, to leave Germany. In November, there was a big round up of Jews[17] who were taken to the various concentration camps [. . .]. On that day, my Father was at the tailor getting measured for suits to take abroad, for after they left they were going to be penniless. Jews were allowed at that time to take only 10 marks out of the country. A former patient came to the tailor's and warned Father that they were looking for him. Father found refuge in a very romantic way, the sort of thing you read in a book but never really believe. A very old lady, a former patient, who was actually the sister of one of the dignitaries of the Catholic church in Augsburg, had seen him many months before and had given him a key to her apartment. She told him never to leave the house without that key in his pocket. She wouldn't and couldn't tell him more than that.

When he got the warning at the tailor, he took out the key and went to the old lady who lived alone with a housekeeper and a dog. Those two women hid him. The storm troopers came and just like in fiction the ladies hid him in a cupboard. He wasn't found but during this time a list appeared in the *London Daily Mail* of prominent men who had been taken to Dachau or killed. My Father's name was on this list and we didn't find out until quite a few days later that indeed he was still alive. Father came out of hiding when Peter Wright, the surgeon from London, arrived in Munich and started negotiating for a permit for Father to leave the country. He succeeded by promising the *Gauleiter* (the regional boss)[18] a racehorse. The trade was one Jew for a horse. I am glad to say the *Gauleiter* never got his horse. Peter Wright and his wife had worked for many years as missionaries in the interior of China. They had become proficient in an obscure dialect not on the list of the Gestapo's censorship. Negotiations in that language enabled the Wrights to best the horse crazy *Gauleiter*.

Father came to London late in November and Mother stayed behind to supervise the packing of the things they were allowed to take. Not very long afterwards, they arrested Mother and took her to prison. They tried to intimidate her into confessing that the family's jewelry had been taken abroad which would have condemned her at once. But she was very firm and denied any such thing. Then, very mysteriously and probably through the machinations of another ex-patient, she was released. It took several weeks to deal with the painful and humiliating formalities required to claim a fraction of our possessions. Michel, the chauffeur, took her to the train station and she left for London. We had all spent an appalling month waiting for her to arrive safely. Father was frantic with fear for her. She finally arrived in London on Christmas Eve of 1938. Once again, the family was together all in the same country.

The parents stayed in Doris' apartment for a few days and then she shipped them off to the little house she owned in Bexhill-on-Sea[19] and made them stay there with the old housekeeper-caretaker. She gave them very little money to manage on their own. They were humiliated and helpless and unable to take up their London connections and thereby their hopes for a halfway normal life. But once we were nobodies and had nothing to offer, Doris was a changed person. Eventually, Onkel Hermann,[20] who had left Germany earlier for New York and had been able to take most of his fortune with him, sent money to England, which enabled the parents to rent a tiny apartment in London and finally take up their connections. [. . .]

I was dependent on Doris and, up to a point, so were the parents. I was walking a diplomatic tightrope, which was not comfortable. The parents waited a year for Father to get a permit to practice and then one day Father decided he'd had it. Within two weeks, they dissolved their household and went to America. They had a visa due to the fact that Onkel Hermann and great uncle Julius[21] already lived there and were able to sponsor them. England was already at war but it was the "phony" war.[22] Things hadn't really erupted in the West. The parents left just before the Germans invaded the Netherlands.[23] So, they were able to cross in a normal passenger ship to America. That left Gerhard [who had come to England in 1936 to study at Trinity College, Cambridge] and me, who had applied for British citizenship, or rather to become subjects of his Majesty.

The solid relationship between Father and Mother prevented one disastrous change common in refugee marriages. Britain would not allow anyone to take any work other than domestic service. The men were stuck. But the women got permits to become servants and thus became the breadwinners. The normal balance of a German Jewish family was disturbed as the women became the dominant element in the household. This destroyed many marriages and made trouble in a great number of families. Our family was spared that because my mother never stopped looking up to my Father as the dominant member of the household. She never doubted him.

Early in 1939 we received a copy of a German government gazette. It contained a list of prominent individuals who had been expatriated by name. All four of us shared that privilege. To be deprived of your birthright, to be state-less, is an experience that defies description. Father was hit the hardest. [. . .]

WAR, AGAIN

In some ways, I had led a privileged life in England. [. . .] Many intelligent and educated people showed me great kindness and did not share the general and official prejudice against aliens. My brother, who was part of the intellectual establishment in Cambridge, has never lost his affection for England in spite of internment and its indignities. He lived among the elite and never experienced the everyday bigotry prevalent among the rank and file. [. . .]

At the outbreak of war in 1939, Doris joined the Censorship Office and became a censor of international mail. A few months later, the censor's office was moved from London to Liverpool. So, Doris' household was moved to Liverpool, and I of course had to move with her. [. . .] Gerhard was in Cambridge until the Germans invaded the Netherlands and the British went crazy. The only battle they could win at that time was against the helpless German refugees so they arrested all the men on the east coast and interned them as "enemy aliens." Mind you, we had all already faced a tribunal when war broke out and been declared harmless but that was all forgotten.[24] Gerhard was picked up in Cambridge and taken to various sub-human camps. Eventually, he emerged in a camp outside of Liverpool. I was able to do the impossible—I finagled a permit to visit him in that disgusting place. They had no decent food, suffered unsanitary conditions, and were treated in the most undignified manner.

In Liverpool, I had been permitted to work because there were very few teachers. I found employment as a stand-in teacher in the public school system in French and Latin. I also ran a course in German at the University of Liverpool. That was the first money I had ever made in my stunted life. I was able to buy fruit for Gerhard and, most importantly, a sleeping bag, which made his life a little more bearable. We had a short, loving, and productive meeting and decided to apply for visas to go to America. If his Majesty couldn't do better than lock us up there was no point in staying. That visit cemented our already close bond even further. We would not see each other again for four long years.

Very shortly after this, the English government decided to ship its internees overseas. [. . .] I had no idea where Gerhard had been shipped to [. . .]. The parents in America kept calling and asking for his whereabouts. I was frantic. [. . .] Two weeks later, it emerged that Gerhard had been taken to Canada and that he was safe. He remained behind barbed wire for a long time, and it was very difficult for him to come to America. He ended up spending two years in Cuba before he finally obtained a visa to enter America.[25]

Now, I was the only member of the family still left in Europe, except for the ones who had been swallowed up by the various concentration camps. My time in Liverpool was overshadowed by the parents' departure for the United States, Gerhard's deportation, and a feeling of helplessness. But I was able to teach. Teaching has ever been one of my passions. Early in 1940, we returned to the Boltons. Doris left the censorship office and joined WVS, the Women's Voluntary Services, a uniformed civil defense organization [. . .]. I was not able to join as a full member, being ever an enemy alien, but did join the workforce of the organization. I was graciously permitted to wear an overall of the right colors, but not a uniform.

In the spring of 1940, the Luftwaffe staged a devastating attack on the city of London.[26] It was a moonlit night in May. I joined a WVS crew manning a mobile canteen to feed the rescue diggers. We worked all night. On the underground, going home in the morning, a young man said to me, "Don't go down in the mine again, mother." I was pitch black from the fires and the dust. Back at the Boltons, I suddenly had the conviction that the house was doomed. I refused to spend another night in the place and stood my ground. We moved to Grosvenor House but were able to get a room only on a high floor. So, every night, we went to the shelter in the basement. I was young and small—two chairs and an eiderdown made a good bed for me. [. . .] There were raids most nights, weather permitting. One night, the Boltons were hit. The ceiling over what was my bed in the basement collapsed. I would no doubt have been killed. Sometimes it pays to be stubborn.

Life under siege and bombardment is very educational. It leaves you two options: either you break or you adjust. By nature, I am a physical coward. But the general atmosphere of stoicism and defiance and the responsibility for the welfare of comrades under siege proved to be a complete antidote to fear. An old friend and colleague of my Father gave me enough morphine to take if the Germans staged a successful invasion. Having secured this bit of insurance, I honestly stopped worrying. During attacks, I calculated the odds against my being hit and if not on firewatch or other duty, simply went to sleep. Bombardment of civilians is counterproductive. It stiffens the backbone of the population and enhances their solidarity with the fighting forces. War generally strikes me as the most idiotic human pastime. [. . .]

Food became scarce and severely rationed: one egg a week, minute amounts of fat and meat. I had been a tea drinker all my life but tea was rationed so I switched to coffee and used my tea rations as currency in all sorts of transactions. My parents sent me occasional food packages from New York and Gerhard, poor as he was, sent me some tidbits from Cuba. A can of Spam was an event. Some packages got lost. I finally mentioned the missing packages to our mail carrier, a woman. She simply said, "I have four children." So?!

I remember watching a dogfight between a German bomber and some of our planes and my feeling of triumph and elation when the intruder was shot down. It dawned on me only much later that he might have been a former friend or neighbor. I cheered his death and he was ready to kill me. War! It dehumanizes everyone. [. . .]

When the battle of Britain began to tilt in the British direction and the air raids subsided, my job changed. I worked for a long time in a clothing depot, also manned and organized by ladies of the WVS. [. . .] It was a regular factory located in a mansion on Eaton Square. We worked full time and the ladies who ran it were remarkably knowledgeable. They were very kind to me but I always remained a second-class person, even in their eyes. [. . .]

Mobilization was complete late in 1941. Able-bodied females had the choice of joining the forces or working in a factory engaged in the defense industries. Aliens, previously banned from working, were now subject to conscription. I did not join up because I wanted to be free to use my American visa once it was granted. Since I was a full-time civil defense worker, albeit an unpaid volunteer, I was exempt. Our two maids however were called up. [. . .]

My American visa finally came through in the fall of 1941. To validate the precious key to a new life you had to be interviewed and medically examined at the American consulate. Long lines of aspirants queued up in all weather outside the consulate. The asylum seekers were admitted one by one during office hours, which were never long enough. [. . .]

Finally in possession of the visa, I began the search for passage to America. A friend referred me to a Quaker who worked at Cook's, the travel agency. Through the formidable networking power of the Quakers, this man got me passage on a ship to Trinidad.[27] From there, I was to fly to New York. Everything appeared to be under control. I started to make my farewells. Then came Pearl Harbor[28] and all visas were cancelled. I thought my world had come to an end. But listen to this: the ship that was to carry me to Trinidad was torpedoed and sunk by the Germans. There were no survivors. I learned never to force an issue against fate.

Once I had adjusted to the loss of my American visa, I settled down to work in the WVS, sporadic bombardments and occasional visits to Blofield. [. . .] Blofield changed. The front of the mansion was commandeered as a rest home for wounded officers. The family kept their bedrooms and otherwise was confined to what used to be the servant's quarters. Most big houses were filled with "evacuees" from London or other beleaguered cities. [. . .]

Never will I forget the feeling of elation when the first American planes flew in formation over London town. Soon, G.I.s on leave showed up on the streets of London. We were not alone any more. The atmosphere changed in countless subtle ways. The G.I.s created a lot of goodwill by sharing their smokes, sweets, and other more basic supplies with their civilian contacts. Some of them were rowdies but most showed typical American generosity, good nature, and an endearing form of naivety.

Early in 1944, my new American visa came in the mail. Once more, I set out to find passage. And once more, a member of the Society of Friends, a Quaker, found a spot for me. This time, my berth was on a ship that had been sunk in Valetta[29] harbor, raised, and was being sent to the United States for repairs. She had been built for the Australian sheep trade, had a big hold, and a few staterooms for ranchers accompanying their merchandise, sheep, wool, etc. She was unable to carry any ballast. Since we crossed during the period of equinoctial storms, this made for a rough passage.

Once more, I made my farewells. Doris feigned a heart attack in a last attempt to change my mind. [. . .] The back door was my place of exit from my longtime home in London. I was accompanied by an old friend, Peter Wright's housekeeper. She went with me to Newport in Wales from where the ship sailed. The vessel was only marginally seaworthy. One day out, we lost our convoy. A brief revival of the U-boat attacks at this time added to the feeling of uncertainty. We zigzagged all the way south to near the Azores and all the way up to Newfoundland. We had to wear life jackets most of the time. There was no stewardess on board, only men. I shared a cabin with a pregnant war bride, who was sick most of the time. Whenever feasible, I stayed on deck. I was not seasick and actually had a good time. I flirted with the ship's officers and since I was the only likely female on board, I had fun! [. . .]

We approached New York City on a warm day in April. I did not go to bed that night. To see the lights was magic. After four years of blackout this was brilliant. They told me it was a brownout——little did they know. We landed in Hoboken, which was crammed with ships of every description.[30] [. . .] Sailing up the river edged in lights was one of the most moving experiences of my entire life. I took it as an omen for my future in the New World.

PART II—THE NEW WORLD

Arrival

When we docked, the ship got a telephone connection. Prior to security clearance, I could not use it so one of the officers called my family. When I finally set foot on American soil, Mother and Gerhard were waiting for me. Father had also been part of the reception committee but had had to return to his patients before Immigration finally cleared me. Seeing my family again after four years of anxious uncertainty was exciting, moving, and thrilling beyond words.

We drove from Hoboken to Manhattan through the Lincoln Tunnel, which at that time had just two lanes. Gerhard said it was the longest, most modern such tunnel in the world and that the Hudson River tunnels were unique. I pointed out that the Mersey Tunnel in Liverpool predated them and probably outsized them. We had a heated argument and I knew I was home. The family had recently moved into a six-room apartment on the 10th floor of the Rheinlander building on Lexington Avenue between 88th and 89th Streets. Father's office was in the same building. I moved into the maid's room, my abode for many years. The apartment had a grand view of the East River and was located in Yorkville, the city's German quarter.[31] I had not spoken German in years and had lost my German accent. Otherwise, it would have been a bit risky to work in shelters and canteens during air raids. Now, I landed in a German-speaking neighborhood. The tradesmen, shopkeepers, restaurants, and many of Father's patients spoke German rather than English. And we spoke German with our parents of course. I reacquired my accent in no time at all.

A few days after my arrival, the parents' receptionist was out sick. I was filling in for her when a large Bavarian type came to the door and asked, "Is this the Haas who married the Schuelein?" I said yes, and he asked for an appointment, in German of course. And this in wartime! I could not believe it. Living in Yorkville after London took some adjustment.

The parents had performed a minor miracle. Father was sixty years old when he arrived in the United States. He arrived in May and in September he passed the medical licensing exams in the states of New York, Maryland, and Massachusetts. Mother had such faith in his immediate success that she wasted no time renting an office and then scouring the second-hand stores to furnish it. So once he had qualified, his office was waiting for him, including the "help," which was Mother! They were an amazing team. They received some financial help from Onkel Hermann and a loan from HIAS (Hebrew Immigrant Aid Society), which they were able to repay within a few months. Onkel Hermann, who was the head of Rheingold brewery, spread the word of Father's arrival among the German innkeepers and tradesmen. In those days, Yorkville functioned in some ways like a village. Many Germans knew Father's reputation from the Old Country. In other words, the core of his initial practice was in the German-speaking community. How is that for irony? [. . .]

NOTES

1. The summer home of the Haas family was located in Bernried, a small community on Lake Starnberg.

2. Charlotte Haas Schueller's memoirs give the impression that she had emigrated to England as early as the fall of 1933; however, the legally required deregistration required when moving away from Munich did not take place until September 28, 1934.

3. Doris H., a British friend of the Haas family. The name was made anonymous by the editors.

4. Gerhard Julius Haas (1917–2013), brother of Charlotte Haas Schueller.

5. Alfred Haas (1878–1978) was a German surgeon and founder of a hospital in Munich. In 1909, he married Elsa Schülein (1886–1982), daughter of the brewery owner Joseph Schülein (1854–1938). The couple had a daughter and a son and emigrated in 1940 from Munich via England to the United States where Alfred Haas maintained a private practice in New York City and served as a consulting surgeon at Misericordia and Wyckoff Hospitals, among others.

6. Joseph Schülein (1854–1938), brewery owner; owner of the Union Brewery and of Löwenbräu; Munich benefactor, married Ida Schülein, née Baer (1861–1929), in 1881.

7. In 1910/11, Alfred Haas had a surgical-orthopedic private clinic (Klinik) with residential wing built at Richard-Wagner-Straße 19, which he ran from 1912 to 1938. The clinic initially had room for 45 patients.

8. Appeasement was the name given to the British policy in the 1930s that allowed Hitler to expand German territory unchecked. It is associated primarily with Neville Chamberlain (1869–1940), a British Conservative Party politician who served as prime minister of the United Kingdom from May 1937 to May 1940, and is today widely discredited as a policy of weakness.

9. Henry Wardel Snarey, known as Peter Wright (1892–1976), general surgeon, served in World War I and as Rockefeller Professor of Surgery in China before being appointed to a number of positions in England.

10. Dr. Helena Rosa Wright, née Lowenfeld (1888–1982), married to Henry Wardel Snarey, was an English gynecologist and influential figure in birth control and family planning both in the United Kingdom and internationally.

11. The Boltons is a street and lentil-shaped garden square in the Royal Borough of Kensington and Chelsea, London, England.

12. Harrods is the most famous department store in London; it is one of the largest, most famous, and exclusive department stores in Europe.

13. The so-called *Judenstempel* was a stamp in the form of a red "J" affixed to German passports by German authorities starting in 1938, identifying the passport holder as a Jew. The basis for this was the Ordinance on the Passports of Jews of October 5, 1938.

14. Joseph Schülein had given up his position on the Löwenbräu board of directors in 1933 and retired to his Kaltenberg estate, where he died on September 9, 1938. The family estate, Schloss Kaltenberg, was "aryanized" during the "Third Reich" and not restituted until 1949.

15. Fritz Schülein (1885–1963), son of brewery owner Joseph Schülein, emigrated to the United States in 1939.

16. Blofield is a village in the Broadland district of Norfolk, England.

17. In Munich alone, about 1,000 Jewish men were arrested in the course of the *Kristallnacht* and interned in the Dachau concentration camp.

18. Gauleiter (head) of the traditional administrative division of Nazi Germany Munich-Upper Bavaria was Adolf Wagner (1890–1944).

19. Bexhill-on-Sea is a town and seaside resort in the county of East Sussex in the south of England.

20. Dr. Hermann Schülein (1884–1970), son of brewery owner Joseph Schülein, emigrated to the United States via Switzerland in December 1935.

21. This probably refers to Dr. Julius Schülein (1881–1959), son of brewery owner Joseph Schülein, who emigrated to the United States in December 1938.

22. The "phony war" was an eight-month period at the beginning of World War II in which there was only a limited land military operation on the Western Front.

23. On May 10, 1940, the German army invaded the Netherlands.

24. An interesting contemporary perspective on these developments can be found in Maximilian Koessler, "Enemy Alien Internment: With Special Reference to Great Britain and France," *Political Science Quarterly* 57, no. 1 (1942): 98–127.

25. Gerhard J. Haas was interned as an "enemy alien" at Pentecost 1940 and subsequently deported to Canada. It was not until May 1941 that his father obtained his release, which enabled him to leave for Cuba. In 1943, Gerhard entered the United States where he worked as a microbiologist and in the field of food technology for both industry and research.

26. After the German Luftwaffe (air force) had been attacking mainly airports in the south of England since July 1940, Hitler gave the order on September 5 to fly day and night raids against the major cities. By May 1941, London was the target of almost daily German air raids.

27. Trinidad is an island in the Caribbean Sea and the largest island of the Lesser Antilles, as well as part of the territory of the island nation of Trinidad and Tobago.

28. The United States formally entered the European Theater of World War II on December 11, 1941, just a few days after the surprise attack on the US naval base at Pearl Harbor on Oahu Island, Hawaii, by Japan, an ally of Nazi Germany, on December 7, 1941.

29. Valletta is the capital of the Mediterranean island nation of Malta.

30. The city of Hoboken is located on the Hudson River directly across from Manhattan; it was the most important dock in New York Harbor for liner shipping with Europe in the late 19th century.

31. Yorkville was the German quarter in the Upper East Side of Manhattan. It was possible to live there and never learn English. The Haas Family lived there amidst all the non-Jewish Germans.

Chapter 12

Memories

Hanns Peter Merzbacher

Hanns Peter Merzbacher was born on December 4, 1910, in the apartment of his parents Otto Friedrich Merzbacher and Emmy Elisabeth Helene Merzbacher, née Herz, at Elisabethstrasse 38 in Munich-Schwabing. His father was a master furrier and trade official with the ready-made clothing and smoking goods store "E. u. O. Merzbacher" at Theatinerstrasse 42, later at Promenadeplatz 6.

Hanns Peter Merzbacher's school years began in the middle of World War I. After finishing elementary school, he attended the Old Realgymnasium on Siegfriedstrasse in Schwabing. This was followed by a few weeks at a private commercial school and in his father's office, as well as some time in Switzerland and England, before he moved to his maternal uncle's house in Berlin and worked as an apprentice in his uncle's prestigious export business. In 1931, he returned to Munich for five years, to his parents' business and his parents' house.

As early as 1935, his younger brother Wilhelm Eduard (1913–1994) emigrated to South Africa. Hanns Peter Merzbacher turned his back on Germany at the end of 1936. On December 5, 1936, he traveled as a "Commercial Traveler" on the "Highland Chieftain" from London, England, to Rio de Janeiro, Brazil, where he disembarked on December 21, 1936. He initially lived in Rolandia, but left Brazil on September 24, 1948, to move to New York, USA, where his parents had lived since early 1946. Here, Hanns Peter Merzbacher married Miriam Blumenthal (b. 1927), a Theresienstadt survivor who had emigrated together with her mother to the United States in 1947. They had two children. In January 1954, he received American citizenship and died on July 7, 2006, in Greenwich, Connecticut.

Hanns Peter Merzbacher wrote his memories in book form for his immediate family. The passage selected here, the end of the second and the beginning of the third part of his three-part report, "Germany—Brazil—USA," was written in German in 1996, after he visited the Munich City Archives. These selections focus on his time in Brazil, his departure from there, and his arrival in the United States ten years after leaving Germany. The account paints a unique picture of the dynamics and significance of transmigration and the role of migrant networks.

Figure 12.1   Provisional Police Registration of Hanns Peter Merzbacher in Londrina, February 23, 1937. *Source:* Stadtarchiv München.

[. . .]

ARRIVAL AND STAY IN RIO

On the day of my arrival, December 21, 1936, I woke up with unpleasant sciatica, a problem that had troubled me earlier in Germany. Nervousness?

Perhaps. After all, I was facing a decidedly critical moment. I didn't notice anything about the entrance to the world-famous Guanabara Bay. A certain restlessness had set in on the ship. People were packing up and getting ready to land. It was high summer and very hot. A barge was approaching. Officials, mostly of brown complexion, disembarked. Tables were set up in the social rooms. Loudspeakers gave orders. Queues formed, myself among them.

A few minutes later and I was without a passport. It had been taken from me and replaced by a green piece of paper with illegible data and a stamp. Down from the ship, my never-before-seen relatives[1] were waiting for me and greeted me kindly.

As far as my passport was concerned, they were calm and confident. There were only a few formalities to take care of, but everything would take care of itself. A few days to get used to it would certainly not hurt me.

I was accommodated in a kind of pension, in a large old house in the historic Flamengo district,[2] the setting for famous romantic novels of the turn of the century. I did not get to feel anything of the romance. There was a great water shortage in Rio. Pipes and toilets ran only a few hours a day. It must have been uncomfortable, tense days for me. My relatives' assurances did little to calm my nerves. [. . .] They didn't go so far as to suggest a "trip" to the interior of the country, but they didn't exactly resist when I mentioned the idea either. I had become more and more impatient. Finally, I decided to take my fate into my own hands and to vamoose. It was a very far-reaching decision with long-lasting, drastic consequences. [. . .]

After a 7-hour ride, we reached the outskirts of Sao Paulo—factories, workers' settlements, warehouses, railroad tracks that separate, cross, come together again. The train entered the "Roosevelt" station. [. . .] I was alone in a big city, where I knew no one, had no connections, and where there was no place for me to stay anyway, without papers. But someone had recommended to me a hotel in Rio, Hotel Aurora in Rua Aurora. It was small, clean, and inexpensive, and apparently popular with German travelers. [. . .]

THROUGH NIGHT, THROUGH FOREST
TO THE LAND OF RED EARTH

I didn't want to fool myself or others. It was an escape, a necessity, not at all romantic adventurousness, that made me leave the city of Sao Paulo. Papers, which I did not have, played a role there. Without them, one could not find work. In the interior of the country, I was told, no one would ask for them; they drove cars without identification numbers. One would be safe there, they said. [. . .]

IN ROLANDIA

With one suitcase in hand[3]—I had checked more luggage—I was now standing next to the train.[4] The disembarked passengers began to disperse. I looked around. No one was there who looked like he wanted to pick me up. I had only the name of my hoped-for host-employer, but no address—not so unusual in an area without a post office. A not very knowledgeable looking figure finally suggested a direction that he thought would at least lead me close to my destination. But it was far, about 1½ hours on foot. It was hot, early in the afternoon. With a suitcase to carry, the direction not even quite sure, I began to make my way. It was not an encouraging or promising start. I crossed the railroad line, passed a small sawmill. Hoping to be somewhat relieved of my uncertainty, I went in and asked again. I didn't seem to have sounded very idiomatic, because a man answered me in a strangely colored, but at least well understandable German. Yes, I was on the right track. The road was flat, and so, somewhat encouraged, I went on. A horse-drawn cart, a kind of large ladder wagon, came toward me. The driver, no doubt not a native Brazilian, probably had the same impression of me and stopped. At the same moment, it became clear to both of us that this encounter represented the contact that both parts had been looking for. Yes, he was the one I was looking for, and he was on his way to pick me up. [. . .] He suggested to go on immediately and pick up my belongings from the station. The way gave sufficient opportunity to get acquainted. The eagerly sought contact was now established. A new, completely unfamiliar life began for me.

ON THE WAY TO THE NEW PLACE TO STAY

[. . .] When we arrived at the farm, we were met by a worker who unharnessed the horse and took care of it. We went back uphill to the house [. . .] and to a little house made of boards, that I had been assigned. There is not much to describe, because there was not much inside. The gaps between the rough walls may or may not have been covered with the usual slats. The room had no ceiling. Above me was a steep roof covered with wooden shingles. It did not lie directly on the walls but left a space free for the passage of air of any temperature and also allowed free entry to the rich fauna of winged nature. My description of the walls is also valid for the floor. It is not clear to me today how it was possible for me to live for more than a year without any furniture, except for a simple cot. Did the room have a shelf? Was everything I owned stored in suitcases and boxes? Every memory is erased. What is certain is that there was only a minimum of necessities for my daily needs. However that may have been, I had my privacy.

After this short description, I will skip the night and move on to the next day. K.[5] had to go again to the village, but this time without a car. So, we used the most popular means of transportation—we rode. This was my first ride here in Brazil and my first acquaintance with Rolandia, a tiny center that German-speakers usually referred to as "town square." Every place in the CIANORTE territory was planned and divided into zones. All streets ran dead straight. They were still unpaved, but they already had names, the houses even numbers. A small business center had already formed around the station, centered around the ARMAZEM DE SECOS E MOLHADOS, ubiquitous in rural Brazil—a mix between a hardware store and a general store. There was everything you needed there, and you met everyone you wanted to meet or not meet. It was a kind of news exchange bourse. There was also an ice cream parlor (with its own generator), a textile store run by Syrians, a barber shop, and a pharmacy. [. . .]

The ride to the "town square," which lasted about one hour, gave me the opportunity to have a clarifying and explanatory conversation with K., who had been insufficiently informed about my situation so far. He understood that I had not landed here to pursue an agricultural career, but to escape the claws of the immigration authorities and finally to obtain my settlement permit. For my part, it was clear to me that I had to work and could not count on any earnings. [. . .]

I spent more than two years on this farm. They were the most difficult years as far as my physical adaptation to this life was concerned. There was hardly any work in which I did not participate, by no means always with enthusiasm, still less always with consummate skill. I raked the driveways that had to be maintained, I fed the pigs, and I spent a lot of time harvesting corn, which required carrying the cobs to the roadside in large piles. I learned, to my own amazement, rather quickly to pick up heavy sacks and load them on a wagon. Some progress brought me a good dose of satisfaction, such as learning to mow after repeated failed attempts. [. . .] The most unpleasant work was to keep the planted areas free from weeds. It was a Sisyphean task, on humid days in a veritable cloud of mosquitoes, against which one tried to defend oneself by covering one's head. If some of what I report sounds a bit melodramatic, I will hasten to correct a false perspective. There were many things that at least alleviated the misery of the very earliest period, and later even more than compensated for it. [. . .]

For the sake of completeness, it should be mentioned here that the experiences I recount were not all acquired at K.'s plantation. I also worked and lived elsewhere, providing opportunities to learn a lot. My daily work program was not always the same. Gradually, I had more to do with animals and had many opportunities to ride around the area. Some of the acquaintances I made would later prove to be quite useful.

For a very short time, I worked in the central bureau of CIANORTE in Londrina, where I had to replace an English-speaking employee on a temporary basis. The executives there were people of some influence, and I told them about my delicate situation. They advised me quite strongly to turn the money I had brought into a piece of land. I would then be considered a "lavrador" (= something like a land agent) and would be practically exempt from serious difficulties with the immigration authorities. And so, I became the owner of about 20 hectares of land. It was available for sale at any time, and there was no risk for me. The piece was much too small to ever be worked profitably. I was promised that they would try to do something for me, which I however took note of with skepticism. I was to be proven wrong for a change. [. . .]

The post office was a case of its own. There was no post office in Rolandia. Mail was carried only as far as Londrina, from where it was sent, unsorted in a sack, to Rolandia. There, the contents were simply piled up on a large table. Everyone could rummage around in the pile at will to see if there was any mail for them. The chaos was great and caused a lot of trouble, sometimes despair, especially in those hellish times in Europe. Loss of letters, which also affected me, was inevitable. [. . .]

DEUS EX MACHINA

At the beginning of my third year in the CIANORTE region,[6] I received a completely unexpected message from Curitiba,[7] the capital of the state where I lived. The sender was the local representative of a law firm. The content was a request that I go to Curitiba as soon as possible and report to the police department. A permanent residence permit awaited me there, provided I could show the title to my "country" and a receipt for the amount paid. I had both. It seemed clear that the company in Londrina had indeed taken steps to assist me. Ingrained skeptic that I was, I had never seriously believed that people would go out of their way for me. In this case, money would not have done much, but the company had something more important, namely relationships and influence.

Anyway, I didn't need to be told twice and set off. It was a long and circuitous journey. [. . .]

Once there, I met the CIANORTE representative who accompanied me to the police station. I was received politely, presented my papers, whereupon— a true miracle—my old confiscated passport was returned to me, with an impressively stamped note that I was entitled, according to § so and so, to permanent residence in the country. Happy and grateful, I was able to leave the police building. [. . .] Then back to Rolandia. [. . .]

BACK TO LIFE IN THE CITY

While in Rolandia, I searched in vain for a cure for my climatic wounds[8]—there was no real doctor there—while I loitered unemployed with friends where I had worked. [Healing was only possible in Sao Paulo. Half nolens, half volens, a great change entered my life.][9] Saying goodbye to friends, to the place, but really to a whole way of life was extremely difficult for me. It was the third difficult farewell in my life. What I did not know was that it would not be the last. [. . .]

After arriving in the city, I hardly had time to "catch my breath." People I had met in Rolandia were waiting for me with the pleasant news that they had already rented a simple, furnished room for me. So, I was relieved of this problem, which was a great relief for me, even more so when, by unusual luck, within a few days I found a modest position, but one sufficient to live in.

Unfortunately, things did not go so smoothly. Shortly after my arrival in Sao Paulo, but before taking up my position, a telegram arrived from New York. The sender was my mother's brother-in-law,[10] who had emigrated some time before. The telegram was urgent and asked me to immediately transfer all the money at my disposal to the United States to pay for my parents' passage to Cuba.[11] I have no recollection of any details of the transaction, in which a Jewish aid organization obviously played a decisive role.

The telegram woke me up like a thunderclap from my unsuspecting, thorny sleep. Having just arrived from the jungle, I was extremely unaware of the seriousness of my parents' situation. Naturally, I did not hesitate for a moment to comply with my uncle's request. I knew well that my "land" was immediately available for sale at any time. But it was necessary to attend the transaction personally, and so I was forced to return to Londrina in a great hurry. And so it happened, without the slightest loss of time. I took the proceeds to Sao Paulo and had the amount, which I do not remember, transferred to the United States through a bank. [. . .]

THE FATE OF MY PARENTS

So, my parents' trip to Cuba was paid for. They took the very last opportunity to leave their homeland and escaped Germany in October 1941, traveling via France to Barcelona. On October 31, their ship "Isla de Tenerife" left Barcelona. Details of this trip do not belong in this report. I will only let it be said that they had to live through a truly hellish time, especially [since] inhumane conditions prevailed on the ship.

They spent 4½ years in Havana where, without work permits, they were tolerated and depended on the support of family and Jewish organizations. Apart from that, they had it good. Some emigrants were able to earn pocket money by moonlighting. My mother also managed to do this to a small extent. She did sewing work but was quite handicapped by poor eyesight. For my father, a fur and skin specialist, the situation was hopeless. In a warm country like Cuba, the demand for furs was not exactly overwhelming.

In June 1946, they finally managed to obtain a regular immigrant visa to America. Although he was already 70, he still expected something from America, which he knew well from his youth and a later visit. He spoke fluent English and had even maintained relationships with old friends. Thanks to them, he managed to find a subordinate position in the fur department of a prestigious fashion house, in an industry in which he was leading and respected. It was an arduous life, but for a short time it went well. One day, however, he went home on foot in a heavy snowstorm, with recklessness that cost him a coronary thrombosis. [. . .]

FIRST WORK IN THE CITY

After this unavoidable detour into the life of my parents, I can now continue with my report:

The position I was able to take up after my return from Londrina was a cross between gatekeeper and payroll clerk in a spinning and weaving mill belonging to an Italian family. It was a one-story factory building in an area of unpaved streets, most of which were lined with very modest little workers' cottages. Many people in our workforce lived there and enjoyed the convenience of walking home. I moved to the vicinity of the factory, which also brought advantages for me.

The technical manager of the factory was a young German emigrant who had already learned the trade in Germany. The factory may have employed about 100 workers. My supervisor and I were the only Europeans among the staff. I later learned that I was a welcome replacement for my predecessor, who seemed to have been a big "greyhound." There was a lot of mischief to be made in this position and having a trusted person in this position was a great relief to the plant manager. My work was not exactly demanding but required great accuracy to avoid friction with people. I had a lot to do with the workers, which was nothing new to me after my Rolandia experience. When I joined the factory, in April or May 1940, the war in Europe was already in full swing, but Brazil had remained neutral until then. My supervisor and

I were considered Germans. The average Brazilian had no real idea of our status as emigrants.

BRAZIL AT WAR

This was soon to change. When the Brazilian government realized that all was not well with the "Axe,"[12] it was considered advisable to side with the Allies, even to send Brazilian troops to the theater of war in Italy. For us emigrants, the consequence was that we were suddenly declared enemy aliens. We were all lumped together. Didn't we all speak German? Fortunately, nothing changed for us in our company. The day after Brazil's declaration of war on Germany, the entire factory staff was called together, and the management tried as best they could to explain our somewhat delicate status. It was vigorously emphasized that we enjoyed the unchanged confidence of the management and were to be treated accordingly, which was done.

Outside the factory, however, the changed situation had very noticeable consequences—also for emigrants since in Brazil no distinction was ever made. I had long since lost my German citizenship as a result of the Nuremberg Laws (but not my German passport, which did not even have the famous "J" stamped in it), but no notice was taken of that here. The use of the German language in public was forbidden (which, however, caused some emigrants to sit on their pants and finally start learning Portuguese). We were no longer allowed to leave the city without a special permit. Trains and buses were then controlled. Any small or large excursion required a "salvo conduto,"[13] which, however, was easily obtained without much harassment. Apart from the ambivalence of our situation, emigrants (even non-emigrants) could not complain about bad treatment.

How and where did I live during the three years of my work at Fiaçao e Tecelagem Sant'Ana? In the beginning, I had a small room that required me to get up very early in order to be at work on time. At dawn, I had to board a streetcar (open on both sides), which, cold as it often was, was quite uncomfortable. I finally managed to find a similar room not far from the factory, from where I could walk. It was again an emigrant household, a Viennese who struggled through life by tailoring.

However, my life—at least my workday life—did not take place in emigrant circles at all. Apart from the Brazilian milieu in which I worked, I had my daily lunch in the house of a very simple Brazilian family, an inheritance that my "greyhound" predecessor had given me. I had always been attracted to simple Brazilians of all colors, and it was no wonder that my daily contact with this family continued for a long time, even leading to an occasional picnic on the seashore. I now spoke very idiomatic, perhaps even too idiomatic at times, Portuguese.

In many ways, I was satisfied and comfortable in the textile factory, but although I had received a raise, I earned very little, just enough to get by. Apart from that, I had no opportunity to make use of what I had to offer. Luck and a friendship threw a change into my lap. I had the opportunity to change my position. What was in store for me was more money but also much more grueling work at a company that was a mixture of factory and import, run by a mixed team of Germans, emigrants, and Brazilians. [. . .] When the supposed possibility of further improvement presented itself, I changed positions again with the result that I failed and, even worse, became unemployed for the first time in my life for three weeks. I do not remember being seized by panic. Why should I? I was a bachelor, without any responsibility except for myself, and the general job situation was favorable. After two more failures, I finally landed my last job, which, I didn't know when I started, would be my last in Brazil. There, in an Anglo-Brazilian working environment, I had it very good. The salary was poor, but the atmosphere was better, and the field of work—railroad material—was of some interest to me. [. . .]

LEISURE-TIME ACTIVITIES

I want to touch the social side of my Sao Paulo weeks and months only superficially, but I cannot skip it completely.

Already from Rolandia, I had brought with me certain contacts, mainly people of my age or older. Contacts with younger people that I created myself. My visit to a school maintained by the BRITISH COUNCIL played a certain role in this. The British Council is similar to the Goethe Institute and Alliance Française and has the same goals. Although I had been fairly fluent in English for a number of years, I wanted to keep up my skills and improve them, if possible, in order to advance professionally. There were also social considerations. I started taking courses very soon after taking my first job, continued for a long time, and one day was in possession of the CAMBRIDGE CERTIFICATE.

My "traditional" social relationships were stimulating. The people with whom I socialized were, without exception, educated and diversely interested. All of them had been thrown off course by emigration. There were musical evenings, drama readings with distributed roles, a puppet theater, and even a real theater group to which I belonged. In general, I would like to mention here that Central European emigrants at that time gave a very noticeable boost to the cultural and industrial life in Sao Paulo.

But my leisure life was not limited to "culture." Around the city there were many excursion possibilities, of which I made use in suitable company. A two-day excursion made it possible to visit a mountain landscape similar to the Alps [. . .].

ENDING IN BRAZIL

[. . .] I began to feel restless and uneasy, regardless of my satisfaction in my work. [. . .] At about the same time, I received a letter from my mother in New York, informing me of my father's worsening condition and, without pressuring me, asking me to come to America. It was only a formality for parents to obtain immigration permission for a child.

A year earlier, the receipt of such a letter would have put me in a serious quandary. Even now I felt a certain dilemma, but not a really heavy burden. My old adventurousness and the disappointment with what I had just experienced[14] had begun to loosen my roots somewhat.

[. . .] So, after a short transitional period, I decided to emigrate for a second time. The decision was absolutely incomprehensible, especially to my superiors and colleagues. Hadn't I made quite a satisfactory impression? But in the end, I was not exactly irreplaceable; they put a good face on the incomprehensible game and showed themselves from the best and most generous side until the last moment.

In a kind of trance between deep sadness and expectation, well aware of the gravity of my decision, I decided to make a short farewell trip to the state of Minas Gerais,[15] an area of great cultural, historical, and art-historical interest. [. . .]

A few colleagues from my resigned position took me in their car to Santos[16] and to the ship, a gesture of great stature, a kind of golden ending to an important chapter of my life.

On September 24, 1948, the ship left the port of Santos. It was an ordinary U.S. cargo ship that was allowed to carry 12 passengers. I have little memory of the trip. The other passengers were young Americans. The cabin was basic but comfortable and clean. There was only one general lounge where meals were taken. The food was excellent.

The next day we docked in Rio, but only for a few hours. Then the ship (I can't even remember its name) sailed to Victoria,[17] a city whose location is almost equal to Rio's. Otherwise, Victoria's importance lies only in the fact that it is an important ore export port. Then we continued directly to New Orleans in always wonderful weather. We were traveling for a total of 21 days.

ARRIVAL AND ENTRY INTO AMERICA

When I awoke in my cabin on the morning of October 15, 1948, something struck me as unusual, namely an unaccustomed silence. The ship's engines could not be heard. No movement whatsoever could be perceived. I got dressed and went out on deck, where nothing could be seen but dense fog. One thing was certain: we had anchored, so we seemed to have arrived in America. Slowly the curtain of fog lifted, and the first scene gradually became visible at dawn. Some life came to the stage in the form of a couple of mosquitoes. In the water, a few dolphin-like creatures began to circle the ship expectantly. To the extent that daylight was able to penetrate the fog, piles and pile-like wooden shacks protruding from the water became visible. Large pelican-like birds sat motionless on the pilings. For them, the sight of the ship seems not to have been unusual. We had reached the delta of the huge Mississippi River and with it the American sovereign zone. The picture was not what one would have imagined as an immigrant—no skyscrapers, far and wide not even a modest stone house.

The crew told us that we had to wait here for the arrival of the American pilot who would accompany us upstream to New Orleans. My assumption that New Orleans was a seaport proved to be a sign of ignorance. It was to take almost a full day to reach the city. Since I had a regular immigration visa, the formalities went off without a hitch, with the exception that after the customs check, I found that a bottle of "cachaça" I had brought from Brazil was "stuck" there. The hotel reservation I had made from Sao Paulo didn't work out, and I had to spend the night in a not very attractive, at best second-class hotel. I have no memory of the city itself. I had planned the trip via New Orleans because I wanted to see something of the country before arriving in New York, which happened only to a very limited extent.

My young American fellow passengers seemed to be looking forward to the landing with impatient anticipation, at least as much as I was. I had the impression that they were literally craving for special American delicacies. They introduced me to one of them shortly after arrival. It was a huge, thickly stuffed roll dripping with mayonnaise, called a "sandwich,"[18] intended as a snack, but sufficient for a meal. [. . .]

From this evening on, my memory lets me down again. I went by train—my first train trip in the USA—to Atlanta, and from there in a long and exhausting trip by bus to New York. Little of that bus trip has stuck in my memory. There were no expressways at that time. The rest stops at which the bus occasionally stopped were not inviting. As uncomfortable as this trip may have been, it was interesting and gave me an unaltered picture of a small part of the country and its people. During the night trip, there was no question of sleeping. Not only was it cold, but the endless procession of headlights of oncoming trucks was disturbing. Really unforgettable for me is the entrance to the suburbs of New York, located on the New Jersey side. The dawn had already broken. The bus was driving on a four-lane road, brightly lit by arc lamps reflecting on the wet asphalt. I had never seen such a wide stream of traffic. Finally, the silhouette of the city emerged, but we ducked into one of the tunnels under the Hudson River. On the other side, there was a confusing series of winding viaducts, and finally the entrance to a not very impressive bus station. [. . .] As the bus passed through the tunnel under the Hudson, I may well have guessed, without now being able to recall, that getting off that bus meant entering a radically changed phase of my life. [. . .]

REUNION AND FIRST DAYS IN NEW YORK

A revolving door pushed me out of the terminal and I was now face to face with my father, whom I had not seen for twelve years. One cannot reconstruct one's own feelings. My father must have been aroused, at least inwardly. He hailed a taxi, and we drove through the confusing, brightly lit maze of streets to my parents' flat, where my mother was waiting for me. Her inward reaction could hardly have been different from my father's, but she was not inclined to melodrama. As for emotions, I will leave it at this.

It is different with the visual impressions. Looking back, it is clear to me that it was not really possible for anyone involved to gauge the extent of the unavoidable gulf that a merciless time had created between us. Enormous was the material abyss on the edge of which I now stood. Very poor was the small flat in which they lived. No less miserable was the house, and no less miserable the neighborhood in which it was situated. The contrast with my previous dwelling [. . .] could not have been more striking. My parents, when they came from sunny Havana, must have had similar feelings. On the other hand, they left no doubt about their satisfaction at being free and, at least theoretically, independent. It gave my father great pleasure to show me the city he had known so well in his youth. It was a New York that no longer exists: Long-demolished elevated trains. Newspapers at 5 cents a copy. Fast food vending machines. Last but not least: rarely a feeling of insecurity. I visited my uncle and aunt,[19] who were much better off than my parents. They were younger and had emigrated two years earlier. I also visited distant relatives,[20] who treated me with indifference, which did not diminish my self-confidence. Despite their very limited means, my parents had a positive attitude. After all, they had been through terrible hardships. In material terms, I was able to adapt.

In other respects, it was not so easy. There was a certain dichotomy. My parents could not shed their habit of looking at me as a son = child, whereas

I was used to an independent bachelor life. The resulting tension was eventually resolved by my marriage.[21] To elaborate further on this problem would take me off-topic. I will confine myself to my intention to report on how this emigrant from Schwabing continued to "make his way."

In New York, I had the same experience as in Sao Paulo: I hardly had time to look around. Within a few days, I had a position, albeit an unsuitable one. Here's what happened: My employers in Sao Paulo represented, among others, a large American company in the field of water purification. My boss gave me a letter of recommendation to this company. And it only took a short visit, and I was employed. I was not fulfilling an urgent need, and I would like to think that the people here felt somewhat obliged to show goodwill toward their Brazilian representatives. So, for a few weeks, I worked as a translator of technical specifications, of which I didn't understand a word. I also didn't like the milieu of engineers sitting at big drafting tables. My departure must have been accompanied by a mutual sigh of relief. At least, I had the opportunity to take a look at an American working environment, and I came into possession of a social security number that will accompany me for the rest of my life.

What had prompted me to give up this first small position so quickly? As was my duty, I read through the—at that time quite meager—job offers in *The New York Times* every day. And I was not a little surprised to discover one day the advertisement of a Brazilian company, a large forwarding company. I was under the impression that it was worth submitting a letter of application, and indeed, after a few days, I received a request for an interview. It would be arrogant to say that they were waiting for me. Nevertheless, there was a certain interest on their part, and a tremendous interest on my part. The open position didn't exactly fit me "like an old shoe." In some respects, I seemed to meet the requirements. I spoke and wrote English and Portuguese. In other respects, there was a lack. Although I had not yet forgotten the German standard shorthand, it took some improvisation to adapt it to English or Portuguese. I succeeded to a certain extent. When a gap in the recorded dictation was reached, my memory had to come in and help me. What finally tipped the scales in my favor and led to my employment was, above all, the warm recommendation my previous employers sent in writing to New York. I had been an obscure unknown and, understandably, people wanted to know who they were dealing with. The work was quite interesting but exhausting, sometimes until late in the evening (but with overtime pay). And I had the opportunity to continue speaking Portuguese. As a bonus, so to speak, I made the acquaintance of a person there for whom I did stenographic and translation work in the evenings in a hotel and was well paid. This allowed me, in collaboration with my wife (I had married in the meantime and she was also working), to put some money aside for purchases.

I kept that job for about two years. Then, unfortunately, the bureau in New York had to be closed. Two more positions followed in New York, one of which had to do with Brazil. Fortunately, I was never out of work. At least I had some experience now, and—equally important—a reference to refer to. [. . .]

Of course, "one" (we) was on the way to becoming somewhat Americanized but still clung to the emigrant sphere, especially when it came to consulting doctors or shopping in a bakery. Of course, solidarity with fellow emigrants also played a role. [. . .]

NOTES

1. Could not be identified.

2. Flamengo, the Portuguese word for Flemish, was one of the first residential (beachside) neighborhoods of Rio de Janeiro.

3. A total of about 400 German families lived in this jungle plantation, named after Bremer Roland.

4. The events take place starting in 1937.

5. Anonymized by the author.

6. *Deus ex machina* (Latin), literally "the god from the (theater) machine" (in ancient theater, the gods floated onto the stage on a crane-like flying machine). In this context, this expression refers to an unexpected helper appearing at the right moment in an emergency situation or the surprising, unexpected solution to a difficulty.

7. Curitiba, as of 2020, is the eighth most populous city in Brazil and the largest in Brazil's South Region.

8. After engaging in forest felling work in untouched virgin forest areas to establish a coffee plantation in 1939/40, Hanns Peter Merzbacher suffered from festering spots, especially on his legs, that would not heal.

9. Addition from a previous chapter of the memoir, not included in this selection.

10. This probably refers to Dr. jur. Alfred Selz (1879–1956), who was married to Emmy Merzbacher's sister, Alice Margarethe, née Herz (1896–1941). He emigrated to England in August 1939; she was deported on November 20, 1941, from Munich to Kovno (Kaunas), where she was murdered. Their daughter, Martha Leonore Dachs (1919–2015), had emigrated to New York in October 1937. Daughter Antonie Valerie Friedlein (1920–2007) emigrated to England.

11. Otto Friedrich Merzbacher (1874–1950) and his wife, Emmy Elisabeth Helene, née Herz (1887–1961), emigrated to Cuba in 1941 and from there to the United States in 1946.

12. This refers to the Axis powers, a coalition led by Germany, Italy, and Japan, that opposed the Allied powers (France, Great Britain, the United States, and the Soviet Union) in World War II.

13. *Salvo conduto* (Portugese) means safe conduct.

14. Hanns Peter Merzbacher had been living for some time with an emigrant couple, his dentist and his wife, an arrangement made impossible after the husband's suicide.

15. Minas Gerais (Portugese: General Mines), so called because of the various mines in the area, is a large inland state of southeastern Brazil.

16. Santos, only 70 km from São Paulo, is the most important and largest port in South America.

17. Vitória, spelled Victória until the 1940s, is the capital of the state of Espírito Santo, Brazil.

18. The local name for this traditional sandwich from Louisiana is "po' boy."

19. Could not be determined.

20. Could not be determined.

21. Hanns Peter Merzbacher married Miriam Blumenthal (b. 1927) on February 16, 1949.

Chapter 13

A Family History
For My Children and Grandchildren
Lotte Bamberger

Lotte Sophie Bamberger, née Kohn, later Krafft, was born to Gustav (Gustl) Kohn, a World War I veteran and Freemason, and his wife Marie (Mize) Kohn, née Zwiedinek, in Saaz, Bohemia, on December 28, 1904. At the time of her birth and the birth of her brother Hans two years later, this provincial town of less than 20,000 inhabitants was part of the Austro-Hungarian Empire. Even though all their close relatives and friends were Jewish (with the exception of a very small part of the family on their mother's side), both children were confirmed in the mother's Protestant (Lutheran) faith in 1920, the same year that their father, who had been baptized in 1914, decided to change the family name to Krafft. After completing eight years at the Gymnasium, a school that prepares pupils for university entrance, Lotte Bamberger studied business administration, economics, and languages in Vienna, Grenoble, and Munich.

In 1926, Lotte Bamberger married Siegfried (Fred) Bamberger. The couple had two children, Frank in 1927 and Liesbeth (Li) in 1931. Siegfried Bamberger was one of five brothers who further developed the parent company founded by their father Jakob Bamberger (1849–1918) in Worms in 1876. He managed two men's clothing stores in Munich and Cologne until their immigration to the United States in 1939. The Munich branch of Bamberger & Hertz (B&H), which opened in 1914, was the company's youngest business house; others were in Frankfurt am Main, Saarbrücken, Stuttgart, Cologne, and Leipzig. After the April boycott of Jewish stores in 1933, all these stores experienced a decline in sales. The store in Saarbrücken closed in 1934; the one in Frankfurt was sold in 1935; and the stores in Cologne, Stuttgart and Leipzig were forcibly sold or dissolved in 1938. After creating a legal basis for "Aryanizations" in mid-1938, Johann (Hans) Hirmer, who had joined the Munich store of Bamberger & Hertz as a salesman in October 1915 and rose

*to become head of purchasing for all six Bamberger & Hertz stores by 1933,
and Emil Haller, together with the main investor Theodor Döring, took over
the Munich store of the Jewish owner Siegfried Bamberger on August 25,
1938, thus founding "Hirmer & Co. KG."*

*With support from relatives in Salt Lake City, Lotte and Siegfried
Bamberger emigrated with their two children on the* Britannic *via Liverpool,
England, to Los Angeles, USA. On May 11, 1940, they arrived in Hoboken,
New York, where Frank and Li went to school for the six weeks that they
stayed there. Advised by the family not to stay in New York, where there were
already too many refugees, Lotte Bamberger and her family drove in a 1938
Ford, which they had purchased secondhand for $450, to Southern California
in the hopes that there would be more opportunities for her, her husband,
and their children. After three weeks, on July 24, 1940, they arrived in Los
Angeles, the city that was to become Lotte Bamberger's home for the rest of
her life.*

*Lotte Bamberger died peacefully at home on August 14, 2006. Her
English-language memoirs, which she wrote for her children and grandchil-
dren in 1990, are divided into five parts. The excerpts included here are from
Part 4, which begins with a description of the family's immigration to Los
Angeles, and continues with their life in the United States and the fates of
relatives and friends.*

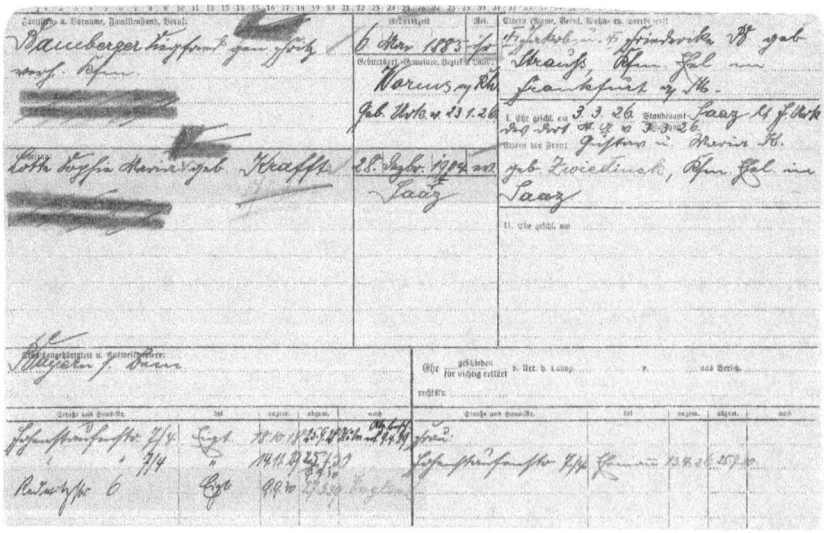

**Figure 13.1   City of Munich Registration Card for the Bamberger Family, Created in the
1920–1930s**. *Source:* Stadtarchiv München.

[. . .] 1940 had certainly been an eventful year—leaving England, six weeks in New York, driving through the states, four weeks in the tiny Ojai apartment, finally moving into Havenhurst apartment on August 21, Frank and Li starting school in America, Grandpa [Siegfried Bamberger][1] trying to find a job, any job and I trying to run a household, of course without any help.

What probably made our situation easier was the fact that so many people we knew or met were in the same boat [. . .]. The lawyers had a very hard time—at best, they could become consultants, but most had to switch to jobs far removed from law. [. . .] The physicians at least were admitted, after going through internship at no or minimal pay, and after a language exam. Some co-immigrants started chicken farms, some went into business like we did, on a very small scale. Very few of our contemporaries found jobs, any jobs.

In many ways, life was easier—not only cheaper—than today. Many times, I took the streetcar when Grandpa needed the car. There was no smog—the sky was bluer than blue. It was hot but not humid, and when we first drove to Riverside,[2] there was nothing but orange groves. We went often to the beach that first summer, and we went to the concerts at the Bowl[3] and paid one dollar, high up on the benches. [. . .]

Our children had no keys for the house—the door was left open when they came home from school. We knew the milkman well, and especially the mailman, with the fitting name Maile. [. . .]

Our Finances and Opening the Stores, 1941 and Later

In August 1940, we received a letter from Clarence [Bamberger],[4] suggesting that we meet at the Mission Inn in Riverside—he would be on the way back home from Coronado. I remember the drive to Riverside—the sweet smell of the orange groves, which have long since disappeared. Dressed in our Sunday best, we presented ourselves with our extremely well-behaved children to the scrutiny of our sponsor Clarence. I believe he resented our having passed through Salt Lake City (we spent one night there in a small motel) without contacting him. We thought it would have been an imposition to have asked him to receive the five of us,[5] looking a little disheveled after driving a couple of thousand miles.

A few weeks after this rendezvous, we received a letter from Clarence, asking us to sign a promissory note to a corporation, for the money we had received in England and on our arrival in the United States [. . .] we could not sign the note, not knowing if we would ever be able to pay back the money we had lived on.

I repeat what I have said before: Clarence's first letter to England, with the ominous "advanced," meant that, instead of Joe's freely given promise, we would have to accept an American loan.[6]

We finally composed a letter, explaining why we could not sign this note to a corporation, not knowing into whose hands it might fall, for money that we needed to live on. The answer was devastating: in this case we shall have to stop supporting you.

I persuaded Grandpa to go to Salt Lake City ad talk personally to Clarence—it was probably the hardest trip Grandpa ever had to make. But we had no choice—there was no chance of Grandpa's getting a job, nobody was willing to help us. He went to Salt Lake, and was greeted by Clarence: "What are you doing here, Fred?" To ask for money from somebody so inconsiderate must have been most depressing. Clarence finally said he would continue to support us with $150 instead of the previous $200 monthly, if Grandpa went to Julian Bamberger[7] and asked him for the difference of $50. Did he do this to humiliate Grandpa, to show him his power, or to punish him for not signing the note? Who knows. Grandpa went to Julian, who raised his hand toward the picture of his father Simon[8] and said: "HE would have wanted me to do this for you." After ten months—his loan had come to $500—Julian started to send reminders about our debt to his corporation, till we paid it back at the very first chance.

In the meantime, Walter Feldberg[9] and Grandpa had decided that there was no chance for a job for men their age, and that they would have to go into business for themselves. As both had been involved with men's clothing, they investigated these possibilities but found that it would involve too much capital. It seemed that women's sportswear, however, could be managed on a smaller scale.

Walter Feldberg had left Germany one year before we did, and at that time it was still possible to transfer some money. They also had gotten out all their furniture, including some antiques, etc. Walter never missed an opportunity to mention how he had sat in Grandpa's beautiful office in the 1930s, trying to persuade him to sell his business, as he had already done. Walter had some capital to invest, and Grandpa finally managed to get a loan of $2,000 from the Salt Lake cousins, and another $2,000 from some friends. The loans were paid back as soon as there was some profit from the new business.

In May 1941, they found a small store in North Hollywood which they called "Fields," translating the Feld from Feldberg. They opened the new store on June 7, 1941. It did quite well once war broke out, as many young girls had jobs in the defense industry and could buy inexpensive but pretty clothes. Grandpa and Walter later added three more stores in other suburbs, till they sold all of them in 1955. Grandpa would have liked to continue, but Walter did not want to. And doing it alone, at age 70, would have been too much for Grandpa. It had always involved a lot of driving, from North Hollywood to Pasadena, to South Vermont, to Manchester Avenue—but we had very good managers. [. . .]

After we had paid back everything to Julian, and repaid the loan with interest to Clarence, and after Grandpa had many attacks of paroxysm tachycardia, I wrote a letter to Clarence, explaining why we had not paid back the money that had been given to us for our living expenses before we had a chance to make a living. (All this was before we got money out of Germany.)[10] Amazingly enough, Clarence answered that he understood—although he addressed me as Mrs. Bamberger. Many, many years later we very briefly considered paying back that money for which they had taken responsibility, but we decided for many reasons against it. [. . .]

V. OUR LIVES AS AMERICANS

Los Angeles, 1941–1951

[. . .] The United States declared war on Japan December 8, and Germany declared war on the United States December 11. When war broke out, that was the end of our efforts to get anybody out of Europe—at least out of Germany, Austria, and Czechoslovakia. We did not even know at that moment what the day meant for the Jews of Europe. We could correspond for a while via Switzerland, till everything stopped.

We became enemy aliens, permitted to travel only within a radius of five miles, and had to observe curfew at 7 o'clock at night. While Grandpa (probably also the Feldbergs and I) got permission to go to his store in North Hollywood—which was beyond the five miles—Li and I would stand anxiously in front of the door at Havenhurst, worrying if Grandpa would make it back by 7. [. . .] There were rumors flying around that we would not be allowed to stay near the coast. We discussed with friends where we would go. We considered Denver, and some other places. We had to turn in our radios. It was pretty depressing to accept these restrictions after having escaped from Germany. Eventually, a congressional committee, called the Tolan Committee, arrived in Los Angeles, and I believe Truman was on it. They held hearings, and people like Thomas Mann,[11] Bruno Frank[12] and many more pleaded for all of us.[13] In the end, we were allowed to stay. I do not know when the curfew was lifted.

Li went to Bancroft Junior High School in Hollywood after Laurel Elementary School. I remember talking to her classroom teacher, who was full of praise. When I told her that Li was not always that helpful, that diligent at home, she said: But you would not <u>want</u> her to be perfect.

Frank started Fairfax High School in 1942—he joined the ROTC, and the debating club of which I attended many sessions. Frank made many friends [. . .]. In Li's classes, when the teacher asked whose mother had time for a certain job, Li always volunteered: My mother has time. [. . .] With all these activities and driving Li to the dentist and to the Girl Scouts, and going to the North Hollywood store to help, it never occurred to any of us that I could try to find a paying job. [. . .]

On January 17, 1943, we moved to La Jolla Avenue, which for the first time gave Li and Frank a room of his (and her) own. On June 6, Frank was confirmed at Wilshire Temple. On February 3, 1944, Frank graduated from Fairfax High, half a year before he was actually supposed to graduate. This gave him, under war conditions, the chance to put in three semesters at UCLA before he was drafted into the Army on April 13, 1945. [. . .]

In the spring of 1944, our landlord on La Jolla Avenue told us that he was selling the house—were we interested? We laughed at the idea, and thought that it was a mere threat to raise our rent. One day, he came to tell us that the house had been sold to a lady who wanted to move in right away. (She was allergic to the orange trees surrounding her present home.) We finally got an extension of three months, and I went every single day for weeks to find an apartment. But there were few apartments available and nobody wanted to rent to a family with teenagers, although I told all landlords that MY teenagers were different from all the others. We thought it was the biggest catastrophe possible, and while we thought we could definitely not afford it, we decided to look for a house to buy. I looked at many, many houses, from east to west and from south to north. When we found the house we still life in now, where the price and the down payment seemed more reasonable than the others, we did not know that it was the best move we ever made. The price was $12,000, but we had to take $7,500 out of our three-year-old business for the down payment of $5,000, and for the $2,000 it cost to fix up the house. We moved to Warnall Avenue on May 31, 1944.

For the first time, Frank had a room with his own bath, and a door that opened into the garden. We had very little furniture, and ate in our dining room around a bridge table, with just barely room for four. But when my parents[14] arrived from England, we had to buy a table that seated six. As the Feldbergs had left at a time when you could take all (more or less) your belongings, they had more than they needed to decorate their house. So, they gave us some beautiful Delft tiles for our empty dining room walls which started us on our blue-white china. [. . .]

On September 7, 1945, we had our hearing and examination for citizenship. We had studied very hard and knew, albeit very temporarily, everything about the US Constitution, presidents, etc. Our witnesses, Walter and Ellen Feldberg, accompanied us downtown. Grandpa always told a story about this event, and to this day, I don't know whether it was true or a joke. His interrogation followed mine, and the examiner said to him, "I have only one very difficult question for you: where did you get such a charming wife?" Anyway, we both passed, and were sworn in as citizens on March 8, 1946. It was a very solemn and important moment for us. Frank had been sworn in in San Louis Obispo while stationed in Camp Roberts, and Li got her papers a little later. On the evening of March 8, we celebrated at our house with a little party [. . .].

Our little Fields stores (ladies ready to wear) enabled us after a while to live quite decently, but when we had to take the down payment of $5,000 for the house out of the weakly blossoming store, it seemed enormous, and we felt very daring.

Looking back at the decade of 1940 to 1950, when we had very little money, I don't feel we suffered, or felt very deprived or to be pitied. It must have taken some courage to travel across the States as we did, to buy a house, to start a business—but I don't think we ever felt that we were courageous or brave or anything of that sort.

Negotiations with Mr. Hirmer, etc., 1950, 1951, and After

In 1950, Grandpa decided to go to Munich to settle his affairs with Mr. Hirmer[15] and some other questions of property. He had worked on his claims for a long time. [. . .]

I would have liked to wait a bit with our departure for Munich, because Ami and Apu had their important birthdays—70 and 80 respectively—in the middle of August. But Grandpa all of a sudden found the trip most urgent, and so we left by plane—no jets at that time—on July 27. We changed planes in Boston, and then flew directly to Shannon, Ireland, without the usual stop at Gander, as we had a favorable wind and hardly any passengers. I think there were no more than 20 or 22 people in the huge cabin. We asked ourselves if possibly war had broken out and only we did not know about it. (Korea was on the horizon.)

From Shannon, we flew to Frankfurt, where we had to go through passport control, and here was the inspector, looking at Grandpa's beautiful American passport, saying: Ah, auch ein guter alter Deutscher. (Another of the good old Germans.) It made me furious, and I would have liked to shout: Forget about the good old Germans, we are Americans. (Later, when I went to a little seamstress in Munich, she said: Isn't it wonderful to be home again?—as if nothing had happened between 1933 and 1945.) From Frankfurt, we flew to Munich, where we stayed at the Vier Jahreszeiten. [. . .]

In Munich, the discussions and negotiations with Hirmer dragged on end-lessly, Mr. Hirmer repeating again and again that without him there would be no store and noting to return, and Grandpa maintaining that without him Mr. Hirmer would not have a store to negotiate about. [. . .] Hirmer even threatened to open a store under his name, if Grandpa wanted his store back—on the other side of the street. He also offered a partnership, but under his conditions—no interference, no monthly reports, just a check every so often. Of course, financially, that would have been very favorable, but Grandpa would not even consider becoming a silent partner in HIS store, his creation, his baby, without his say. In the end, we left with the main question unresolved, with some money in our pockets, transferred at a miserable rate.

The laws[16] the Americans had established in our favor were excellent, but we had to deal with people who only wanted to tell us what THEY had gone through. [. . .] Let me say *en passant* that nobody asked us how we had fared, how we felt about our losses, how we managed to start in America—for THEM we had been safely in America while they were bombed out by the English and Americans. [. . .]

We also went to Ascona for a few days to interrupt these endless discussions. I was always worried that they might do harm to Grandpa, who was suffering from paroxysm tachycardia. [. . .] Mr. Hirmer was a realist and financial success was his *raison d'etre*. For Grandpa, the reputation, the quality of the merchandise, the high caliber of the advertising, were all important. But I am sure that some of what Grandpa had preached for 25 years, was not lost on Mr. Hirmer completely.

We stayed in Munich for three months—very exhausting and tiring days. We visited everybody [. . .]. We had dinner at the Hirmers, where Mrs. Hirmer served us without sitting down with us.

On the way home from Munich, we went to Sevenoaks,[17] where we stayed with Hans and Tim.[18] That was the low point of Hans' existence—the children were all home. We sailed home on the Ile de France, first class, to make up for the voyage on the Brittanic—and I must say I felt better on the Brittanic.[19] I had one black short dress which I wore every evening, and did not feel very comfortable among the few but very elegant passengers. We were seated with a couple from Portland, Maine, who I am sure are convinced to this day that they and we were served caviar and foie gras only because we spoke French to the waiters. (I believe we were seated with this couple because we and they did not belong to the "Ile de France-crowd.")

We stopped in New York, Baltimore, and Philadelphia to visit friends and relatives before returning home after a four-month absence. [. . .] On October 30, Mr. Hirmer arrived, after a voyage on a big American steamer where nobody talked to him—evidently, there were no Germans (or very few) on the boat, and as he had nothing to read, he studied the English notices on his desk and finally made out what "custom" meant (which he pronounced like a German word).

The atmosphere in Los Angeles was much better than in Munich. Maybe he felt more relaxed, not having to worry about his store, and Grandpa certainly was less frustrated, sitting in his living room on Warnall Avenue instead of facing Mr. Hirmer across HIS old beautiful desk where everything reminded him of the past. I had the feeling that Mrs. Hirmer, a very simple and straightforward woman, had said: Hans, you go alone [. . .] to Mr. Bamberger and talk to him and settle your affairs. And that he did.

The idea of a partnership had to be abandoned as the prospective partners could not reconcile their views, but he offered a payment of a lump sum and monthly payments which he later augmented when he saw how well the business was doing. In the end, the monthly payments were converted into one cash payment.[20] Mr. Hirmer came back to visit us for two weeks in 1960. We took him [. . .] to a very nice stay in San Diego. [. . .]

Mr. Hirmer visited us again in 1974, this time with Mrs. W., his indispensable helper, and our old bookkeeper from 1937 till we left. [. . .]—they loved it and Los Angeles altogether.

Whenever we came to Munich, in the 1960s and 1970s, we were greeted royally at the airport [. . .], followed later by a very elegant dinner in a restaurant. The ceremony was unchanged when I later came alone, and the dinner was extended to the Hirmer nephews and their wives, but we were never joined by Mrs. Hirmer, who was probably too shy and reticent. There was always a car at our disposal, he always had some cash ready for us, the hotel was paid [. . .].

In 1980 (to finish the Hirmer story), Mr. Hirmer was suffering from leukemia and was in and out of hospitals. When I called him one Sunday in April (he just happened to be home from the hospital) and asked if I could come and visit him in June, he said: Yes, by all means come—I have a surprise for you. Two days later, he died. I decided to go to Munich anyway and to pay my respects to Mrs. Hirmer. The first evening was the usual big dinner. Next day, Max-Peter, the nephew, better known as Dr. Hirmer,[21] came to the hotel to tell me that I had inherited from his uncle eine Eigentumswohnung—a sort of small condominium. Then I was taken to Mrs. Hirmer and learned that Mr. Hirmer had always intended to leave the apartment to me in his will, but he had always postponed writing it down properly. But Mrs. Hirmer and the nephew had decided to honor his intentions, so here I was, proprietor of an apartment that I was shown the next day. It is situated in a very crummy neighborhood, and when I was told I had the choice of living there, renting it out or selling it, I decided very soon to sell it. Next day, I was taken to a notary public (a much more important position than in the United States) to declare my intentions. Eventually, Mrs. Hirmer bought it from me and after a few months I got the money. [. . .]

I should tell you that Grandpa was never completely satisfied with the Hirmer arrangements, not even after Hirmer had decided to make a gift of

$30,000 each to my children and grandchildren. Grandpa never quite got over the loss of HIS store that he had created, and that, from very difficult beginnings during the First World War, had become, under his guidance, one of the most important men's clothing stores in Germany. Their advertisements had been written up in trade magazines, and today, in 1991, the posters, created by Ehlers, are exhibited in museums and sold at enormous prices. [. . .]

Receiving money from Hirmer, and restitution from the state of Bavaria for the loss of occupational income (Berufsverlust) certainly made life easier for us.[22] We could do a little more for my parents, although they still lived very modestly. (They also got some supplement from the state of California, after they had become US citizens in May 1950.) [. . .]

NOTES

1. The title Grandpa is reserved for Siegfried Bamberger (1885–1976), Lotte Bamberger's husband and the grandfather known personally by the grandchildren for whom the memoirs were written.

2. Riverside is a city in California located about 50 miles (80 km) east of downtown Los Angeles.

3. The Hollywood Bowl is an amphitheater in the Hollywood Hills neighborhood of Los Angeles, California, and has been the premier venue for live music in Southern California since its opening in 1922.

4. Clarence Bamberger (1886–1984) of Salt Lake City was the son of Jacob Bamberger (1852–1928), who was born in Germany and came to New York in 1865, and his wife Bertha, née Greenwald (1858–1939), who had provided the affidavit required for immigration to the United States for Siegfried Bamberger and his family. After her death, daughter Dorothy Allen, née Bamberger (1894–1985), eventually gave them the affidavit. Jacob's father, Emanuel Bamberger (1805–1897), had seven children (two with his first wife, five with his second wife) who all emigrated to the United States in the 1800s, as did he; he became the founder of the Salt Lake dynasty. Lotte Bamberger's husband Siegfried Bamberger was a descendant of Emanuel Bamberger's brother, Loeb Bamberger (1809–1899), his grandfather, who remained in Germany in the 1800s.

5. Siegfried and Lotte Bamberger had asked their friend Thea [Dispeker], who also wanted to explore the possibilities in California, to drive across the country with them. Thea Dispeker, née Schlesinger (1902–2000)—concert agent, pianist, accompanist, piano teacher, and musicologist—immigrated to New York City in 1938, where in 1947 she eventually founded her own artists' agency, Thea Dispeker, Inc. Artists Management.

6. During their stay in England in 1939–1940, Jacob Bamberger's third son, Joseph (Joe) Bamberger (1878–1961), who had taken on the obligation to support them while they were in England until their quota numbers for the United States came up, invited the Bambergers to their estate outside London. When Siegfried and Lotte

Bamberger informed them that the Home Office guarantee was not pro forma, Joe, originally a stockbroker, told them that his brothers in Salt Lake City were so much richer than he was and would send them any money they needed. Since they said at the time they needed $200 a month, Joe's brother Clarence Bamberger from Salt Lake City agreed to provide that sum, but told them when he sent the first check that the money would be "advanced" to them, signed by a corporation, which meant they had to pay it back.

7. Julian Bamberger (1899–1967), second child of Simon Bamberger (1845–1926) and Ida, née Maas (1863–1936).

8. Simon Bamberger (1845–1926), father of Julian Bamberger and brother of Clarence's father, Jacob Bamberger, arrived in the United States in 1859. According to family records, he became a member of the Board of Education, a State Senator, and finally in 1916 the Governor of Utah.

9. Walter Friedrich Feldberg (1895–1968), born in Stettin, Germany, arrived in California via England in June 1939. He was married to Ellen (Eleonore) A. Feldberg, née Landauer (1912–1968).

10. After the end of the war, Lotte and Siegfried Bamberger filed claims on the basis of the Law for the Reparation of National Socialist Injustice. For more information, see Bayerisches Hauptstaatsarchiv, LEA (Landesentschädigungsamt) 42197, Restitution File Lotte Bamberger.

11. Thomas Mann (1875–1955)—German writer, winner of the Nobel Prize for Literature, and vocal critic of the Nazi regime—did not return from a trip abroad in 1933, was expatriated in 1936, and went from Switzerland to US exile in 1938, from where he returned to Switzerland in 1952.

12. Bruno Frank (1887–1945), a German author persecuted by the Nazis, fled Germany and lived in Austria and England for four years before emigrating to the United States in 1937.

13. The House Select Committee Investigating National Defense Migration, commonly known as the "Tolan Committee" held hearings in February and March 1942 in four cities about the possible removal of Japanese Americans from the West Coast. History, Art & Archives, US House of Representatives, "House Select Committee Investigates Japanese Evacuation and Relocation," accessed June 19, 2021, https://history.house.gov/Blog/2018/May/5-8-tolan-committee/.

14. Gustav (Gustl) Kohn (1870–1955) and his wife Marie (Mize) Kohn, née Zwiedinek (1880–1966), later Krafft, emigrated to England in 1938, from where they moved to Los Angeles in 1944; they are referred to as Ami and Apu, as this is how Lotte Bamberger's son Frank called them.

15. Johann (Hans) Hirmer (1897–1980), purchasing manager for all six B&H shops by 1933, took over the Munich shop from owner Siegfried Bamberger in 1938 against the backdrop of anti-Jewish measures in the Nazi state, thus founding the "Hirmer & Co. KG." In 1946, Bamberger initiated legal steps for the restitution of his company, which had been "aryanized" in 1938, a move that caused a lot of antagonism, as Hirmer resented the legal approach. On November 21, 1949, a settlement was reached in the restitution proceedings before the Wiedergutmachungsbehörde I, Oberbayern (Restitution Authority I, Upper Bavaria) and the joint reestablishment of the Hirmer &

Co. company with Hans Hirmer as personally liable partner and Siegfried Bamberger as majority shareholder implemented. See Hans-Diether Dörfler, "Von Bamberger & Hertz zu HIRMER: Ein respektables Stück Wirtschaftsgeschichte," accessed June 21, 2021, https://www.hirmer-gruppe.de/download/presse/pressemappe/hirmer_gruppe _geschichte.pdf.

16. What is meant here is probably the state laws passed in the American occupation zone as early as 1946, which provided for provisional payments and benefits for the restoration of health, for vocational training, for the establishment of an economic livelihood, or for the prevention of hardship, as well as pensions for persecuted persons and their surviving dependents for the purpose of reparation.

17. Sevenoaks is a town in Kent situated south-east of London, England.

18. Lotte Bamberger's brother Hans Kohn, later Krafft (1906–1997), and his family, mentioned here is his wife Mary Eileen (Tim), née Woodward (1913–1989), lived in England.

19. In 1940, the family had crossed the Atlantic on the Britannic.

20. After difficult negotiations and a personal visit by Hirmer to the United States, an agreement is reached on November 2, 1951. According to the agreement, Siegfried Bamberger left the company retroactively on December 31, 1950, in return for a severance payment of 688,000 DM. Dörfler, "Von Bamberger & Hertz zu HIRMER."

21. In 1980, Dr. Max-Peter Hirmer and his brother Walter Hirmer took over the sole management of the Hirmer parent company from their great uncle Hans Hirmer. Since 2011, the cousins Ulrich Hirmer and Dr. Christian Hirmer have represented the interests of the family as the dual leadership of the Hirmer Group. Hirmer Gruppe, "Geschichte," accessed June 19, 2021, https://www.hirmer-gruppe.de/ueber-uns/ geschichte.

22. For more information, see Bayerisches Hauptstaatsarchiv, LEA (Landesentschädigungsamt) 42197, Restitution File Lotte Bamberger.

Chapter 14

The Lost Home

Charlotte Stein-Pick

Charlotte Stein-Pick was born in Munich on October 22, 1899, as the daughter of the Munich dentist and Sanitätsrat[1] Friedrich (Fritz) Baron and his first wife Constantine Clementine, née Scherbel. She spent her childhood and youth in her hometown, where she experienced World War I and the devastation of postwar Germany. Here, she also met her husband Herbert Stein, a dentist who ran his practice with his father-in-law in the house at Sendlinger-Tor-Platz 6a. During this time, Charlotte Stein-Pick was actively involved in the Jewish Women's League, including serving as chairwoman of its household school in Wolfratshausen (1932–1938). She watched the rise of the Nazi Party and Adolf Hitler's coming to power in 1933 with great concern.

Charlotte Stein-Pick personally experienced persecution by the National Socialists and the terror of the November pogroms in 1938. During Kristallnacht, her husband's dental practice was closed, and he was taken to the Dachau concentration camp. She eventually was able to obtain his release from the Nazis, and with further great difficulties, the couple managed to leave Germany in August 1939. Shortly thereafter, they boarded a ship in France, which carried them to the United States. They made a new start in Seattle, Washington. After studying dentistry a second time, her husband opened a new practice. It was not until after his untimely death in 1950 that Charlotte Stein-Pick visited Germany, in the following year. A few years later, in 1954, she became married again, to Ludwig Hermann Arthur Pick. She last lived in Oakland, California, where she died in 1991.

With the help of her diary entries, Charlotte Stein-Pick wrote her memoirs in 1964. It was her intention to show that even those who were able to save themselves and build a new life suffered greatly because, even in the case of positive integration in a host country, the old homeland could not be

*fully replaced. Its violent loss left a deep and lasting wound. The previously
unpublished memoirs were first edited and made available in Germany in the
early 1990s. The selections included here are excerpts from the later part of
this memoir, translated into English by the editors of this volume.*

Figure 14.1   Charlotte Stein-Pick, Passport Photo c. 1938/1939 (Kennkarten-Doppel).
Source: Stadtarchiv München.

It moved, it sailed, it left the harbor. It was no illusion. We hadn't even
noticed the departure, so smoothly did the gigantic ship glide along.[2] Soon
we noticed a war escort boat constantly following us at a short distance.
But everything was somehow frightening. We had to line up for roll call
on deck, equipped with gas masks and life jackets. The sinking of the sister
ship weighed on everyone and, in addition, when the *Aquitania* reached
the open sea, she began to race and kept this pace until the end of the
voyage, constantly zigzagging.[3] After two days, the protective escort boat
left us. A cannon was mounted at the front of our ship, and in the evening
all the hatches were covered. But in case of an emergency, these precau-
tions would not have helped much. Both of us were very cold because our
wardrobe was only configured for a short stay in Europe and, as we learned
later, the *Aquitania* took a northern course, passing close to Iceland and
Greenland.

On board, the mood was excellent. Most of the passengers were Americans and happy to be leaving wartime Europe. [. . .] The rooms of the *Aquitania* were furnished with old-fashioned pomp, but at the same time were quite beautiful and elegant. Expensive carpets and paintings, a large library, constantly changing entertainments, concerts, lavish balls, and, last but not least, the rich food must have made such a crossing a pleasure in normal times. We, however, felt only heartbreak among all these happy, carefree, and dressed-up people. The voyage coincided with our high holidays—New Year. We had hoped to be able to celebrate these in the United States. Deep down in the ship, two cabins had been hastily prepared for a Jewish service, which we attended. The prayer was led by an old man, and the worshippers were mostly European Jews. There we all sat, filled with grief, and our prayers were for the loved ones who had been left behind in hell. Some members of the crew were also present, including the first cook. One could not think of a greater difference than we few sorrowful Jews, compared to all the other joyful, noisy, happy travelers. We were treated very badly by the staff, who probably knew from previous experiences that the Hitler refugees had hardly any money and therefore their tips were minimal; and on the other hand, to the English, we were German . . . enemies. After the incredibly fast time of 4½ days, the *Aquitania* was constantly running at full engine power, we approached New York.[4] We both stood arm-in-arm at the nose of the ship. The Statue of Liberty suddenly appeared on the horizon, powerful and compelling, and we were overcome by previously unshed tears.

Countries and seas had to be crossed to find it—the freedom that had once ruled our faithful homeland and broke our chains. Now, it was gagged and trampled underfoot, and we had to seek in a foreign land that most precious thing, freedom.

PORTLAND 1940

It was extremely difficult to get a job in those years, especially for unskilled workers, to which group I belonged. After a few temporary jobs, I was finally accepted as an apprentice in a tailor's shop. How often had I wished in Munich that I would soon find work, any work but sewing—because I knew how little I could do in it. And now it came nevertheless, and I accepted, obeying the need immediately. Apart from me, there were 15 women working, all of them trained tailors. Doctors' gowns, nurses' dresses, and all kinds of serving dresses with aprons were produced on a large scale. The machines ran electrically; it had to be worked very fast.

Here I was, still weakened by a serious illness, completely inexperienced, still inhibited by the foreign language. Of course, I was met with open mistrust at first. Today, I do not recall why this mistrust soon turned into friendliness and later even into warm cordiality.

One thing I still recall today is the palpitations and fear with which I went to work every morning. At first, I did everything wrong. How often did the older forewoman quickly overlook these errors. She was a very kind woman, who soon noticed that I was trying hard. The owner—our boss—on the other hand, had no understanding at all. I feared him, and when he watched me, I made even more mistakes than usual.

Very soon I was able to speak to my colleagues during our lunch hour about my old home and our fate. I have never had more interested listeners before or ever since. We also had long conversations about politics and work, and I kept reproaching them for not uniting enough. Their whole goal was to live well, without thinking of their fellow Americans or of the future. Very soon, however, I got the proof of a strong sense of solidarity.

I was gripped by the flu and had a fever for a few days. When I came back, the boss told me he didn't need me anymore. While I was working, I cried quietly to myself. The dismissal meant starvation for us in no uncertain terms. Mother[5] and I lived on the small wages I received. My husband had to do hard labor in a hospital at night to support himself and raise funds for his studies. During the day, he was fully employed at the university for dentists.

So, I was deeply depressed about the loss of my job. My female co-workers asked me the cause of my grief but kept silent when they learned the reason. Our company belonged to a union. I was not affiliated, however, because my boss knew how to prevent it until now, since he was paying me below scale. When lunchtime came, all the workers went out. Otherwise, we sat together, and one or the other always slipped me a few cookies or fruits. I could not afford it. Today, I was alone with my grief. When everyone came back, the boss called me into his office and let me know that the employees had forced him through the union to keep me. I would be taken on immediately, and my salary would be brought into line with the pay scale. For me, it was like a beautiful dream.

A few days later, after closing time, all my female co-workers took me to a union meeting, where I officially became a member, now protected from all arbitrary actions of the employer. After I was inducted, each one kissed me. "Sister," they said, "now you belong to us completely." As a surprise, they had ordered a table in a restaurant and invited me to dinner. It was an event in my life that I will never forget. Here I sat, a Munich child, so far spoiled by fate, the so-called "Frau Doktor," who always had a cook, howling and laughing with happiness and pride that she now belonged to a union and wanted to be nothing but a worker.

RETURN 1951

My husband and I had already decided in mid-1950 to take a trip to the old homeland in the spring of 1951. Dear relatives and friends asked us to come, and although grief and pain almost prevented us from doing so, we wanted to dare. But in December 1950, I suddenly lost my beloved life-companion to a heart attack. So, I was alone, and all the more, this urged me to carry out the plan. In April 1951, I sailed on an English ship, the *Mauretania*, to France.[6] I sat at a table with a very old American woman. She had once lived in Germany for many years and was happy to brush up on her German with me, so we had a very stimulating chat. At the next table sat a larger group of Englishmen. To my astonishment, the next day I got English answers from my neighbor, and I found out that a complaint from the English people demanded that we not speak German. I was outraged by this, and I let them know in turn that they were confusing a language with a system that has not existed for six years. I have the right to speak in any language that suits me, especially as a persecutee of Hitler.

From then on, I didn't talk much at all. In any case, the closer we got to Europe, the more I preferred silence and contemplation.

In Paris, I stayed for a few days with relatives who had saved themselves by going underground. Oh, what they all told me: how much agony and hardship they had gone through! I wandered haphazardly and aimlessly through the city, and though the traces of the heavy years of occupation were still visible everywhere—the uniformity of the architecture, the spacious squares and boulevards, the bridges and monuments—it really overwhelmed me. I had completely forgotten how beautiful Europe was. America is too young a country; its distinguishing features are in other areas.

When I boarded the Orient Express[7] one evening, which was to take me directly to Munich, I noticed a gentleman entering a compartment who had just said goodbye to a lady in the next carriage. Without thinking much about it, I approached him and asked: "Excuse me, but are you not Hans Albers[8]?" To my astonishment, he extended his arms and called out, "My dear madam, how long has it been since we met?" I mumbled something and went back to my seat, barely able to suppress a smile. He certainly didn't know me, whereas I had seen him very often on film, but we had never met in life. When I stepped to the window, I heard to my amusement how the lady—his wife—called out to a group bidding her farewell on the platform: "She is a Viennese, who did a film together with Hans and recognized him immediately." Yes, that's how you become famous easily and quickly.

By the next morning, we were already in Germany when I awoke. An incomprehensible defiance seized me. Now, I didn't want to speak German anymore, after having given a good lesson to others. In the dining car, I ordered coffee from the fluent English-speaking waiter, which was undrinkable, so I asked for tea. To my silent amusement, I then heard him say to his colleague, "Again, such a crazy American, who does not know what she wants."

From Stuttgart, the train raced through Württemberg, and from Ulm onwards, I found myself in my familiar homeland. I stood at the window and saw the austere beauty of spring. It was only the beginning of May, the trees showing their first, fresh green. The land seemed unchanged. [. . .] Alone, I returned—alone, alone, alone hummed the beat of the wheels in my ear. At noon, the train pulled into Munich's station, and from here on, looking at the completely destroyed station hall, I knew how Germany's cities had suffered.[9]

When I got off the train, I was embraced by three people—my husband's cousin,[10] who escaped being killed as a result of her marriage to a Christian doctor, as well as my own cousin,[11] who would not let go of me while crying, and her kind husband. When I looked into their eyes, I knew one thing: I was no longer alone.

That very afternoon, I went to see Resl,[12] who had bought a small grocery store. We couldn't say much to each other at first as we were too moved. But soon, she urged me to visit the various neighbors with her. My coming seemed to be awaited with joy and curiosity in the surrounding small stores. Resl took me by the hand and led me to the butcher's, to the smoke store, to the old goods dealer, and each time she went into the stores first and announced, beaming, "There she is, the Lotte." Then, I had to let myself be examined very carefully, was offered something everywhere, and on we went to the next neighbor. How proud she was of me, the good soul; and one thing I knew for sure—none of these people had ever been Hitler supporters!

RETURN 1951—PART 2

My first trip the next morning was to my father's house.[13] The night before our emigration, my husband had just thrown his house keys in a suitcase. When I looked at him questioningly, he told me that his belief in the fall of the Third Reich was unshakable. We would come back and use those keys to open our house again. So, I stood in front of my father's house, hesitating and trembling. I already knew that the new owners had had the small, very nicely carved figure of a saint above the entrance gate torn down. How dilapidated the building looked! I was now trying to open the heavy front gate with my keys when a hand came down on my arm. "Stop, what are you doing here, breaking in?" an indignant male voice asked me. I looked into his face and replied with the defiance that still controlled me, "No, I'm not a burglar, but I want to enter my house." His anger turned to surprise when I told him my name; he suspected I was in deepest America. This man was the director of a bank that had bought the house in 1939. He now asked me very politely to come into his office. I cannot describe my feelings when I now climbed the old curved Biedermeier staircase with him and entered our former apartment. It was almost too much for a human heart. I then sat opposite him in the small room that was my room from childhood until my marriage. If a fortune teller had prophesized this situation to me 12 years ago, how impossible it all would have seemed. I searched with my eyes for the old branched ash tree behind the house and the vines that once climbed over the window. But all that had disappeared, vanished . . .

Then, as if in a dream, I walked through the other rooms, quietly stroking the beautiful marble windowsills and the bronze doorknobs, all of which displayed the monogram of the first owner. The old Biedermeier house had only two owners, my father bought it from the heirs of the builder.

It looked sad, but it stood, despite several big fires from bombs and detonations, the only surviving house in this part of the large square. Some neighbors, I was told, had whispered to each other, "The Jewish house outlasts all others. God is probably protecting it."

But to me it was dead, dead like most of its former inhabitants, and no attachment remained for me to this house I had loved. Two of the old parties were good and cordial to me, but I still decided to sell, especially since great burdens and difficulties were imposed on me by the tax and other authorities. In any case, how could I afford the high cost of restoration? I was single and lived 10,000 km away. It was the same with the Starnberg house. It was in very bad condition, yet in order to get it back at all, I had to make a huge monetary sacrifice for alleged improvements, such as a "champagne cellar" that the Nazi residents had added on.[14]

On top of all this, I had been defrauded of many thousands by the so-called trustee, who had been appointed to manage our estate. Although I could prove it, there was no way to get at him. So, I gave it away for very little money, which I regret today, since—due to the renewed rise of Germany—I actually lost a large fortune. What security that would mean for me today. But I am not an exception. Many German Jews have acted the same way, especially widows and orphans facing all the disappointing impressions and hurdles of restitution. Some of them live in constrained situations while, of course, the new owners have become rich. This is how we came to lose our possessions for a second time.

STAY 1951

The most beautiful part of my visit was spent at Tegernsee.[15] At first, everything seemed very small and cramped, quite different from what I remembered. I had already become accustomed to the dimensions and vastness of America, especially the American West. Seattle's surroundings, the city I lived in, are wonderful; large lakes and high mountains encompass it. But almost all the terrain is without trail or footbridge, completely desolate and undeveloped, no village, no inn, nothing. I always say that the landscape, even in other American states, seems to me like a painted lunch—you can't eat it. But I quickly got used to the old familiar picture again. The shores of Lake Tegernsee[16] and Lake Schliersee[17] soon appeared to me as they once had, but no longer so close together, and the dwellings no longer like dollhouses. My relatives often visited me, and we spent pleasant hours together. There were hikes to alpine pastures where we rested and ate a sandwich, always having to shoo the cheeky chicken folk away from the table. On such days, I almost felt at home again. I could almost imagine that time had stood still, that the wounds could heal. But when we walked back to my little guesthouse and passed the ridiculously metropolitan hotels, in whose front yards sat preened, loud, completely carefree German people, who were served by waiters in "tailcoats," then I knew it was only a dream. There was no turning back. Germany had still not awakened from its bloodstained past. [. . .]

In August, I went back to the city. I still wanted to visit some places that I thought of with melancholy. So, I went to Wolfratshausen[18] with my relatives. The building that once housed the school had been returned to the Jewish community. It had served Nazi purposes since 1938. Now Jewish DPs [Displaced Persons] were temporarily housed there. It was horribly run down, this once beautiful, well-kept house. Frightened people looked at me, and I did not dare to go far. We then drove to the nearby Foehrenwald camp, a primitive settlement for Jewish refugees.[19] Only when I identified myself as a member of an American relief organization did they let me in. It was shocking, gruesome, to see these obdurate people vegetating here, crammed together, still in unshakable fear. At first, I was met with open distrust, even hatred. They thought I was a spy or something like that. They were all Eastern Jews, and I could not speak Yiddish. I walked through the camp with the deepest sympathy. More and more inmates, who had escaped the hell, followed me. I turned to an old man, pathetic and dirty, who had been watching me suspiciously for a long time. "Brother," I said, "believe me, I am also a Jewess, why God spared me, I do not know." He shook his head, so I made one last attempt and said our prayer of faith, "Shma Yisroel . . . Hear Israel, the Eternal . . ."[20]

He stared at me, then burst into sobs. "She is a Yiddin; she is a Yiddin," everyone now shouted and surrounded me. Everyone wanted to shake my hand. I was ashamed of how well I was doing. I felt only one desire. I would have loved to kiss these wretched, ragged people. [. . .]

PARTING THOUGHTS 1951

Four months had passed, and my time in the old Heimat was coming to an end. The next morning—it was the last days of August—I had to leave for Paris to catch my ship in Le Havre.[21] I lay awake all night and let all the many impressions pass me by again. What had happened? Had I found the old Heimat again, now that it was open to me and freed from madness and tyranny? No, was the answer, and again No. The landscape remained the same, lovely and at the same time powerful, unspeakably beautiful the meadows and the mountains, the little villages and churches. But the poison that had been sown for so many years had eaten into the souls of the people and destroyed them. To be sure, some brave and upright men had been found, who resisted the general insanity and now guided the destinies of Germany. They will always be a heartening thought for us outcasts. Nevertheless, the generation around Hitler will probably first have to disappear from the eternal coming and going until a new and innocent German world can arise again. I found dear old friends, who had never been caught by the poisoning; but too many others still were, and my ear heard all too quickly the wrong tone. "Hitler would have won the war if not for the Americans" or "it is an infamous lie that six million Jews were killed—who counted them?" In the beginning, I tried to set the record straight; later, I kept silent. People did not want to know the truth at all. They did not want to feel guilt. They only regretted one thing, that they had lost the war. But the worst were the hypocrites, whom I often knew had been devoted to the Nazi regime and had gone along with it. They now affirmed again and again that they had never, never ever believed in the thousand-year Reich and had always belonged to its opposition. How often they told me: "You had it best. You were able to go to America and didn't have to go through all that terrible bombing and starvation. How good you had it." I looked at them and thought of our heartache and the fear for our loved ones, who had been eliminated, and our longing and the hard unfamiliar work in the foreign country. I just shook my head and kept silent. Everything was in vain here.

And my sadness grew when I walked through the city and often could not find my way in old familiar streets that still lay buried. Who was I looking for here? Jewish relatives and friends had almost all been murdered or had emigrated, and some of my Christian friends had also been swept away. The terrible hustle and bustle, the wild chase for money and power, the people ruthless and without mercy for each other, all these were ways of life, so foreign, so unknown in my old Munich. Yes, I had to accept the bitter truth . . . the old homeland was lost.

The next morning, before I left, I went to my Resl again. I didn't want her to come to the station. So, we stood wordlessly in the little room behind the store. How frail she had become! "You no longer have a mother," she said softly, "so, I will bless you. I only know the blessing of my faith, but your mother would not mind." I lowered my head, and she crossed, and her blessing words made me happy. I kissed her old wrinkled hands and quickly ran out. Even this last true sense of home, which had radiated from her to me since I was a child, would soon fade away. I knew that.

So, I stood again at the carriage window on the train that would take me away, but this time I was alone. I did not cry, but I was sad without end . . .

NOTES

1. *Sanitätsrat*, German, medical councilor, a courtesy title awarded by the king of Bavaria.

2. Charlotte Stein-Pick fled Nazi Germany together with her first husband, Herbert Stein (1895–1950); de-registration from Munich to United States occurred on August 29, 1939. In 1954, she was married a second time to Ludwig Hermann Arthur Pick (1906–1997).

3. From 1939 to 1948, the *Aquitania* was used as a troopship; later, it was returned to Cunard Line service from May 1948 to November 1949. *Ancestry.com*. Passenger Ships and Images [database online]. Provo, UT, USA: Ancestry.com Operations Inc, 2007.

4. Herbert Stein and his wife of 18 years arrived in New York on September 16, 1939.

5. This probably refers to Getta Baron, widowed Heymann, née Stein (1879–1950), second wife of Friedrich (Fritz) Baron (1873–1937) since their marriage in 1919 (a year after the death of his first wife, Constantine Clementine, née Scherbel, 1865–1918) and stepmother of Charlotte Stein-Pick. She emigrated from Munich to the United States in 1940 and settled on the West Coast.

6. Charlotte Stein-Pick left for Europe from New York on April 28, 1951.

7. Founded in 1883, the Orient Express was a passenger train that took passengers on long-haul journeys across Europe. It operated until 2009.

8. Hans Philipp August Albers (1891–1960) was a German actor and singer and the biggest male movie star in Germany between 1930 and 1960.

9. Munich was badly hit by 73 air raids (1940–1945). A total of 6,632 people were killed; 45 percent of the buildings were destroyed, comprising about 60 percent in the city center, 74 percent in the train station area. "Atlas zum Wiederaufbau: München," Haus der Bayerischen Geschichte: Bavariathek, accessed June 17, 2021, https://www.bavariathek.bayern/wiederaufbau/orte/detail/muenchen/2.

10. The cousin (name not identified) of Charlotte Stein-Pick's husband lived in Nuremberg. She was saved from persecution by the prudence of her spouse, a doctor. Supposedly, a high Nazi official, his patient, made her personnel file disappear, which enabled the cousin to go underground.

11. Charlotte Stein-Pick's cousin, who lived in Munich with her husband, a lawyer, was like a sister to her. During the Nazi regime, she had to do forced labor for years; her non-Jewish husband stood by her and was sent to a labor camp. She died in 1962. (More personal information could not be identified.)

12. Resl was the family's Catholic cook and housekeeper, who had already served Charlotte Stein-Pick's grandmother. (More personal information could not be identified.)

13. Friedrich (Fritz) Baron had been the owner of the house at Munich's Sendlinger-Tor-Platz 6.

14. Charlotte Stein-Pick and her husband had owned a house with yard in Söcking near Starnberg, a German town in Bavaria at the northern end of Lake Starnberg, about 30 km southwest of Munich. This appears to be the house property (with inventory). For the restitution proceedings concerning the Starnberg house at Prinzeneiche 16 and the settlement reached before the Restitution Court (Wiedergutmachungskammer des Landgerichts München I, Ref.: I WKV 102/49) in 1951, see Bayerisches Hauptstaatsarchiv, LEA (Landesentschädigungsamt) 3441, Restitution File Herbert Stein.

15. Tegernsee is a town in the Upper Bavarian district of Miesbach, directly on Lake Tegernsee.

16. The Tegernsee is a lake in the Bavarian Alps in southern Germany, located 50 km southeast of Munich, and is the center of a popular recreational area.

17. Schliersee is a natural lake in the Bavarian Alps, about 50 km southeast of Munich.

18. The town of Wolfratshausen belongs to the Upper Bavarian Region and is located about 30 km south of Munich.

19. Föhrenwald was one of the largest Displaced Persons camps in post-World War II Europe. It was established in 1945, was made an exclusively Jewish DP-Camp in October of that year, and was the last to close, in 1957.

20. The Jewish *Shma* or *Shema* (Hebrew: hear) prayer is an affirmation of Judaism and a confession of faith in one God, recited daily in the liturgy and, customarily, before sleep at night.

21. Charlotte Stein-Pick returned to New York on the steamship *Mauretania* on September 4, 1951.

Chapter 15

The Tragedy of Emigration

Koppel Family Letters

On the first day of 1923, Carl (Karl), also called Carlo Koppel (1885–1958), who was a merchant born in Altona, married Carola (Karola), also called Carla Wagner (1903–1941), in Munich. Within the next few years, they had six children. Three of them were born in Hamburg, where the newlyweds had lived since 1923, and three were born after the family moved back to Munich in November 1931.

To escape the anti-Jewish policies of the Nazi regime and the increasingly violent exclusion and persecution of Jewish Germans, the Koppel family tried to leave the country and intended to emigrate to the United States. Carl Koppel was the first family member to succeed in July 1940; he arrived in San Francisco via Yokohama, Japan, on August 28, 1940. The plan was to bring the rest of the family to the United States as quickly as possible. However, only the sons Alfred (1926–2013) and Walter (b. 1928), who since 1938 had lived with their aunt Lola Goldschmidt, née Koppel (1887–1944) in Berlin, managed to escape via Spain to the United States. It was mainly the events of the war on the European continent and the bureaucratic obstacles set by the German authorities that derailed the plan. Ultimately, Carola Koppel and her four children, Judis (b. 1939), Ruth (b. 1937), Hans (b. 1936), and Günther (b. 1924), all of whom had stayed behind in Munich, were deported to Kovno (Kaunas), Lithuania, on November 20, 1941, together with almost 1000 Jewish children, women, and men, and were victims of a mass shooting at Fort IX outside the city on November 25, 1941.

The letters that Carola Koppel wrote from Munich to her husband Carl in the increasingly hopeless situation were in Al(fred) Koppel's possession for many decades. Behind partly ambiguous formulations, which were due to the strict censorship by the National Socialists, his mother hid important information about everyday life for Jews in the "Third Reich," described the constantly changing situations of the widely scattered (extended) family members, and reported her feelings as well as her desperate efforts to find a way for herself and her four minor children to escape their life-threatening existence in Germany. Only in old age did Al(fred) Koppel find the strength to read these letters and deal with the painful events of the past. In 2010, he published excerpts from the letters in English translation under the title My Heroic Mother: Voices from the Holocaust *with Trafford Publishing.*[1] *A small selection of these letters is shared here.*

Figure 15.1   Carla Koppel, 1920s. *Source*: Private Collection.

Carla to Carlo, September 9, 1941

My dearly beloved Carlo!

Thank you very much for your dear letter postmarked 08/26. I was very pleased with it, especially as it arrived rather quickly. Unfortunately, the contents were not very pleasant. I would not have thought that I would have to taste all the suffering to the end. I no longer believe in my emigration, and you can then figure out when we will meet again, if that is ever the case. Do the authorities in Washington have no sense and no mercy? After all, it is an inhuman cruelty to condemn me and my four children to stay here. How can a family with so many children be separated for years? I spent more than an hour with Dr. Schäler[2] today and reproached him and the Reichsvereinigung.[3] But what good does that do me? I can't leave with that. The Spanish and Portuguese consulates insist that they must first receive official notification from the American consulate in their country that we could get the American visa on arrival.[4] They won't give us an interim visa without an assurance of the final visa, as I've already telegraphed to you; Washington must have some sympathy for us. The consequences for us are unthinkable. Dr. Schäler said that you should try to obtain a Cuban visa for us with the help of a bank, namely a tourist visa. However, he is of the opinion that you would have to go to Havana first. You can now get the Cuban visa again in Germany at the Cuba Embassy in Berlin. You would then have to send a certified photocopy to the USA for presentation in Washington. W[ashington] would then have to hand over the visa to them before we arrived in Havana. Dr. Schä[ler] thinks this is the only possibility at the moment. But nothing can be done from here. So, you can only do it from over there.

Don't forget that Günther only has 5 months left to emigrate.[5] The difficulty with me is my age, and I don't know whether I will get the booking from the H.V.[6] because of that. [. . .] But I think that if you can get all the difficulties out of the way over there, it will be possible to overcome this difficulty here too. If there's no other way, you'll have to see if you can get Günther or Günther and Hansi out, even if I don't know what will become of me and the little ones. But that must not hold you back. For those who are with you, it is a life. [. . .]

I have altered all our clothes a little to make room for a modern decoration, in the same color as my good jumper, which dresses me well. I'm thinking of writing to the American consulate in Barcelona to ask for my papers from the American Embassy in Berlin. Maybe they will do that.

One clings to the thinnest thread of hope. I hope to receive a telegram from you soon [saying] that you have solved everything successfully. It's a pity that Löwenstein[7] is still ill; that also takes one back a lot. [. . .]

The Spanish Consul here is so overcrowded that you can't even see him anymore. But I will try again and again. My mood yesterday and today is worse than ever. It's no wonder, considering all the things that come at you every day. The only thing you mustn't do is think. [. . .] I don't know whether I have already congratulated you on the coming holidays.

I can't keep going. [I] almost can't open my eyes anymore.

The children send you their love, too. I will write more on Sunday.

Give the children my warmest regards. The little ones and Günther also send you their love and a kiss.

From me, my dearly beloved Carlo, take many greetings and endless kisses from your longing little wife,
Carla

PS. I have just written a very urgent letter to Löwenstein and also an urgent letter to the American consulate in Barcelona. I have included your address, in case they have any queries, and have written that they can request telegrams and postage from you as I cannot send anything by letter. [. . .] When will I get pictures from you?

Carla to Carlo, September 17, 1941

My dearly beloved Carlo!

I had very much expected to receive mail from you today, but unfortunately in vain, so we are hoping for tomorrow. [. . .] In my last letter, I wrote to you that I had once again written in great detail and urgently to Löwenstein, to which the answer is still pending. I asked him to contact the Hilfsverein ["Aid Organization"] in Spain, so that they could procure the entry permit for us to Spain. I also immediately touched on the question of passage and asked whether it would be available immediately if needed, also possibly if you were able to somehow get the visa for Cuba first (which can be obtained in Berlin from the legation). The Jüd. Blatt [Jewish newspaper] said that you can get the visa for Cuba by means of a bank loan. If you can take care of everything over there and we can get the visas, then there is still the almost insurmountable difficulty for me of being able to leave. Whether this difficulty can be overcome is more than doubtful, so don't get too excited.

I have also written a detailed letter to the American consulate in Barcelona. Hopefully, they will reply. I made my case very clear and wrote that we could no longer get the visas due to the closure of the consulates, but that the certificate and booking had already been submitted. I asked them to request our entire file from the Embassy in Berlin and to hand over my visas. They should inform the Spanish consulate in Munich that the American visa is ready for me in Barcelona so that I can get the transit visa. Hopefully, it will help, and they will do it. I have also given your address because of possible queries and in case of expenses, which I cannot transfer.

How is Alfred?[8] I would be very happy to receive lines written by him. I hope you received my congratulations for the holidays in time. We have already received your beautiful gift and will wear it with dignity. [. . .] I wish we were already eight weeks further along, then I would be a bit calmer.

When [I] get mail from you, I'll write to you again in more detail. Now [I'm] too fidgety. [. . .] I sent Günther to the hairdresser again today so that it will last for a while. I had my perms done yesterday. They'll last 5–6 months, and then we'll see. Write to me often and a lot, that's the only thing I have now. Best wishes to all my loved ones, especially the children.

To you, dear Carlo, I send my warmest greetings and an infinite number of sweet kisses,

your little wife Carla,

dying of longing.

Carla to Carlo, September 24, 1941

My dearly beloved Carlo!

Today I have a lot of mail from you to answer, and I was very happy about it. Your New Year's mail arrived very promptly on the 18th. I hope our mutual wishes will come true and that we will soon find an opportunity to get together again. You have received my telegram in the meantime, and you can believe me that it was an SOS call. If you don't find a way to get us out of here, I don't know what will happen. It is now at most a question of four weeks until we have to move [. . .].

You can imagine what that means for us, especially since we will all be separated. My flat has already been visited several times [. . .]. I asked Josef[9] to go to Prof. Berliner[10] or Dr. Braun[11] for me, who are now authoritative, but Josef of course didn't manage to go there. He only spoke to Dr. Freitag[12] and told him that Günther and I (and I assume the children as well) must [obtain] a visa from the American Consul in Spain. Only then can the Hilfsverein [H.V.] do something for me. As soon as I have this paper, I have to let the doctor examine me, and then I can get out. It is especially urgent for Günther because there is no possibility for him to get out after his next birthday.

I thank you very much for your telegram. You are right, I had hoped for a somewhat more favorable content.

Hopefully, Washington will give an answer soon. Somebody has to have mercy and show some understanding. Wouldn't it be alright if you went there yourself with my telegrams and letters? I could also make a petition from here, but I don't know how to do it. I have not yet received an answer from the American consulate in Barcelona. Dr. Schäler said today that you could get the visa from a Central American country, I think Trinidad, and then get the transit visa for 20 days from Spain within two days. When I told him I would also take such a route, he told me that was out of the question. The H.V. does not do that, where the responsibility is also there for four children. I could then be stuck in Spain and possibly deported. I could not persuade him to do so. If I had something from Washington in my hands, I could risk it more, because then I could assume that I would get the final visa within this period. I would also have to have official proof for the Spanish consulate that our living expenses during our stay in Spain are taken care of. Please send me a certified copy of this. I will explain our whole matter to the Spanish Consul again in writing, as he won't let me talk to him at all.

It's really maddening. Dr. Schäler says that the safest way for us is via Cuba with a tourist visa. Of course, it is also the most expensive. That is, the money is paid back, except for a very small amount. The point is that you might have to borrow it, and that costs interest. You should also get in touch with a bank. He thinks that perhaps something could be done with the committees over there in our case. Maybe Rolf and Gerda[13] can get something done with their rich relatives. After all, everything is only borrowed and not given, it is only deposited in a bank. Please, put everything into play so that you can help us.

My bad luck was and is, of course, that Löwenstein is still ill. Günther is working outside this week. Windows have to be put in and everything should be ready by Friday. [. . .]

If we do not find ways ourselves to emigrate, depending on the H.V. will be absolutely useless [. . .]

I received your letter of the 8th/9th on the second holiday and thank you very much. [. . .] I am really looking forward to Alfred's letter. Now, [I] have to hurry so that [we] can get to Spain.

Ms. Goldschmidt[14] from the community died, liver cancer. Otherwise, it's been seven here this week, so you can probably guess why.[15] I'll write again soon.

Many greetings and kisses from the children, also for Hanna[16] and Lea.[17]

To you, my beloved Carlo, the most intimate and many, many kisses from your infinitely longing
little wife Carla

Carla to Carlo, October 2, 1941

My dear, dearest Carlo!

Due to the holidays, today's letter is delayed. Today, I first want to tell you that Günther and I have fasted well, despite everything. Günther could not go to Schul[18] until 6 o'clock in the evening, as he did not get home from work until half-past six, like most of the others. [. . .] Günther now works at the workshop,[19] outside. He has to get up at 5 o'clock in the morning, because he has to get out of the house before 6 o'clock, because he has almost 1 hour on the tram and then another 20 minutes to walk. He starts at 7 o'clock, until he is at home in the evening. [It is] usually 6:30 o'clock, and he is terribly tired and hungry then, and he goes to bed right after dinner. So, you mustn't be angry with him if he doesn't write. [. . .] I took the precaution of not going to Schul at all because there are always visitors[20] there, and I don't want to make their acquaintance in the first place.

On Sunday, I wrote to the Spanish consulate again with a detailed letter and received a reply yesterday morning. The Consul wrote that he would see me today at 12 o'clock and that I should bring all the papers in my possession! So, I went there today with great hope, but was sorely disappointed. In spite of this, the Consul did not allow himself to be spoken to. I could only speak to Count Bassenheim,[21] who was extremely amiable. I promised the blue of heaven and in spite of everything could not achieve what I wanted. The only thing I was able to achieve was that Count Bassenheim, after he had spoken to the Consul again, told me to send him a letter immediately, officially asking under what conditions and in what form they could grant me the visa. They will then immediately send me an official letter saying something like that they are prepared to issue the visa for the purpose of temporary entry into Spain as soon as they (the Spanish consulate) are notified by the American consulate in Barcelona that we will receive the final visa there as soon as we arrive. I will then send you this document immediately by registered mail so that you can use it to approach Washington, in Count Bassenheim's opinion best in person.

He said that if he is so accommodating as to issue the Spanish visa on the basis of a written assurance from the American consulate, [moreover] without first having a final visa, then you would also have to manage to get the State Department to issue this assurance when you have a document in your hands from the Munich Spanish consulate that they will issue the visa as soon as they have the confirmation from the American consulate. [. . .] Washington would then also have to cable Barcelona, and I think it would be appropriate if Washington would also send a notarized cable to the Spanish consulate here. I probably don't need to ask you specifically to send me a telegram afterwards. The Spanish consulate also requires me to present the certificate of registration before I can be issued a visa, and I will have to deal with this because unfortunately Löwenstein is still very ill. [. . .] Count Bassenheim also asked whether I had any relatives or acquaintances in Madrid who could contact the Ministry of the Interior there. It would not be out of the question that an exception could be made.

Dr. Schäler recently mentioned that the Joint[22] now has a permanent representative in Madrid, who looks after the Joint's interests there and looks after the people who pass through Spain. Perhaps you can speak to the Joint so that they can get the gentleman to speak to the Ministry of the Interior. Perhaps he can obtain our earlier entry there. I haven't been able to find his address yet, and I can't tell him everything like that—you can write much better. Try everything, and remember that Günther's birthday is coming up.

The Van Wiens[23] have been evicted as of 15 XI. The people actually wanted our flat, but since I have even smaller children than van Wiens, this time they took that into consideration. But I have to reckon with the fact that our flat will be the next reflection, and then only a place like Edi's[24] will come into question; there is nothing else. By the way, the latest news is that Dr. Schäler has a visa for Cuba and will certainly be leaving soon. Then, [I] won't have anyone left to look after me a little. It's funny that it always works better with those who sit in front. We don't know yet who will be the successor. Maybe no one at all, because the H.V. is falling asleep.

If you ask Baby now, what's your name, she says nicely: "Judit Koppel, that's my name." She understands every word you say to her. The children are in the yard a lot now, and Baby is at the window. People are decent for the most part but you feel embarrassed when people stare at you like that and you only leave if you have to.

It worries me a lot that I still haven't received a direct message from Alfred. I'm worried about that; he should write. You're not hiding anything from me, are you? As soon as I have the letter from the consulate, [I] will write again. I am already waiting for mail from you again.

Best wishes to the children and Hanna. Further happy holidays to you, my dearly beloved Carlo. The warmest greetings and many, many kisses in infinite longing,

Your loving little wife Carla

Carla to Carlo, October 8, 1941

My dearest, dearest Carlo,

This time my patience is being severely tested again, for it is already the third week that I have had no mail.

In the meantime, I have received the promised letter from the Spanish consulate. Unfortunately, due to the holidays, I can only send it today by registered mail. To be on the safe side, I had three photocopies made and had them certified by the police. I showed the letter to Schäler this morning, and he was very enthusiastic about it. He absolutely expects success from it. [. . .]

You must have the letter with the corresponding cover letter submitted to Washington, or perhaps, if you think you can, take it there yourself. With G-d's[25] help, you will then also be successful. Everything else that is required will then somehow be procured here. The greatest difficulty will be whether I get out. Once we have reached that point, it will probably be possible to achieve that as well. In any case, Schäler gave me a lot of hope today in response to this letter. [. . .]

Dr. Schäler told me, however, that he thought it would be wrong to take Günther to Cuba alone, as he did not believe that he would get the American visa there if he left me and the children behind as blood relatives. [. . .] However, it would be best and easiest if the thing with Washington would work out now. So, do your best and do it quickly because of Günther. [. . .] I got an invitation from Aunt Meloche[26] today for Friday. I just don't know what I'll do with the children then. Well, I have to go there first and see what I can achieve. [. . .] I am very worried that I have still not received any direct news from Alfred. Please send me some mail from him.

Thank G-d, the children are well. So, the letter should get sent off in a moment. Mrs. Gold[27] is here today, so I can leave right away. I also want to go shopping with Hansi [. . .].

More on Sunday, G-d willing. Until then, I hope to have mail from you. Best wishes for the children and Hanna. [. . .] My dearly beloved Carlo, accept my warmest greetings and many, many kisses from your little wife Carla, who loves you very much and longs for you endlessly.

Enclosure

1 Letter from the Spanish consulate.

Carla to Carlo, October 10, 1941

My beloved dearest Carlo!

Today, I can confirm your dear letter No. 48 of 9/16 and was very pleased with it. Today, I was with Mrs. M. E. Loches,[28] and I still have time until next Friday. I was not able to achieve anything more.

Today, I spoke to Koronczyk,[29] and he agreed to employ me at the community. I'm pretty sure I'll get the authority's approval. I've already talked about it. Now, I had to send in a written application with a photocopy of my certificate from the commercial school, which he was very enthusiastic about. I'm supposed to come back on Monday, and I'll get a definite answer then. Hopefully, it will work out since the reduction in civil servants is generally quite big there. But I hope that after Hechinger[30] has to decide about it, it will probably go well. Only after I receive this notice can I worry about what to do with the children.

I will certainly put Baby in the Antonienheim,[31] which would be very hard for me, and the others from morning to night. I can probably tell you about that in my next letter. It will be a lot for me—employment, household, and taking care of the children. If that doesn't work out, I'll find something else to do. [. . .]

I received the enclosed letter from the American Embassy yesterday (I kept the photocopy). Perhaps you can do something with it. I have sent the certified photocopy of the letter from the Spanish consulate to Löwenstein with the request that it be forwarded to the committee there so that they can take steps in Washington to support you. Perhaps it will be of some use. I can't write to Hochfelds[32] until Sunday. I don't know what to do first. [. . .]

I hope you can send me a good telegram soon. I will deal with the rest of your letter in my next letter. Now, it's almost Saturday. So warm greetings to all.

To you, my dearly beloved Carlo, the warmest greetings and many, many kisses from your very loving and longing for you more and more

little wife Carla

Enclosure:

1 Original letter

Carla to Carlo, October 24, 1941

I want to take advantage of this opportunity and start a letter during my mealtime, as it is quicker with the typewriter.[33] Today, I can confirm your dear letter of 9/26. I was very pleased with it. Unfortunately, I cannot send you the confirmation you had in mind for the children and me [concerning a transport]. The departure will be determined on a case-by-case basis, and Löwenstein will certainly see to it that he gets it through—for the sake of the children—to put me on a transport to Spain. The difficulty with the age only exists for permission to join a transport to Spain. In any case, Löwenstein is very hopeful at the moment, after I sent the certified photocopy of the letter from the Spanish Consul. I hope you have received it in the meantime and sent it to Washington as an addendum to your request. I am thinking about sending the same photocopy and the AC [American Consul] certificate to the American consulate in Barcelona. I will draft a letter and then write it here on the machine. Regarding Cuba, I am sending you the following copy of a message from Löw[enstein].

"To obtain a tourist visa for Cuba, the following are required:

a) $2000—deposit
b) $500—further deposit
c) $150—deposit for onward travel
d) $275—visa procurement fee

The deposit for a) of $2,000 can be replaced by a bank guarantee, which costs $150. In total, $1,075 will then have to be paid, of which $425 (namely $275—procurement fees and $150—for the bank guarantee) will be lost, while $650 will be returned. To obtain the visa on the basis of these last requirements, one must contact a reliable intermediary company. Such can be named without liability 1) Ignatz Rosenack, 233 Broadway Woolworth Building New York; 2) Herbert Seeliger, c/o American Lloyd Inc. 55 West 42nd Street New York."

Perhaps you could get in touch with these people if you have not heard anything from Washington so far. [. . .] Thank G-d the children are doing well. I visited them last Sunday, and they were happy. This Sunday, Günther will go because he has the bike, and I have to rest my legs, because it would be a three-hour walk there and back.[34] So, now I have to wrap up for now and will continue writing at home.

So now, [I'm] already at home and have to finish right away because it's about to be Saturday. Tomorrow, I'm off, but on Sunday I'm on duty from ½ 9–½ 1. Next week, [I] will get my identity card, which [I] am very happy about. One cannot know how one might still need it. You do understand me.

Carla to Carlo, November 6, 1941

My dear, dearest Carlo!

Today, I can confirm two letters from you at once, one from October 3 and one from October 10. The one from the 10th arrived two days earlier, so to speak. Of course, I was very disappointed by the message concerning Washington. Unfortunately, I received a similar message today from the American consulate General in Barcelona. They are only responsible for people in their area and are not allowed to give me any confirmation that they will grant me the visa on arrival. It can only be done on explicit instructions from Washington. They see no way to help me at the moment and write that I will have to wait for a better situation in Europe. All in all, a lot of polite phrases and no help. This lack of understanding of our situation from all sides is simply incomprehensible. If the help comes too late, then it is really no longer necessary. I am really completely hopeless concerning our emigration at the moment, and I think there is no point in you working on it any further at all. You are just spending a lot of money unnecessarily. At the moment, emigration is impossible anyway because all five of us fall under the restricted age (0–60).[35] So, we have to wait for a change. It would take a miracle. By the way, it is also possible that an emigration will take place for us very soon. The route would then be the same as the one you took at the time. [. . .] I am working very hard. I leave the house at 7 o'clock in the morning and come home at 7:30 in the evening at the earliest. Then, [I] also have to do the most necessary household chores. Washing dishes, mending, washing, ironing, writing, and so on. So, you mustn't be angry with me if I don't write as diligently as you are used to. Of course, I don't get enough sleep, and it's just fortunate that the three little children are in the children's home. I couldn't do that as well. Günther goes to bed at 8 o'clock in the evening because he is always so tired from his exhausting work. For me, one of the worst things is the walk. I have to walk for two hours every day, and you can imagine what my legs look like. [. . .]

Now comes the main thing, congratulations on your birthday. This is the fourth time we've been apart.[36] I can't even think about it. In any case, we wish you all the best from the bottom of our hearts. May all our fondest wishes come true and may we, with G-d's help, soon be reunited. That is what I pray for, day and night.

Thank G-d, the three little ones are doing very well in the children's home. They have settled in very well, and [there are] a lot of children there due to the time constraints. Unfortunately, I can only visit them very little because the way for me to walk is a very long and exhausting one. But I know that they are in good hands, and I often talk to them on the phone. My work in the community is a lot of fun but very exhausting. Hechinger has given me quite an extensive job (statistics and housing department), and I have a lot to do. I have a lot of fun doing it, and I'm glad when I don't get to think during the day. It's quite good sometimes when you don't have time for that. [. . .] If the letter has a second sender, don't worry. In the morning, when I go to the office, the post office is not yet open, and in the evening, it is already closed, so if I can't slip away in between, I hand the letter to someone to take with them wherever they go to run errands. I hope you have more good news from Alfred. I'm curious when the first letter from him will arrive. Walter hasn't written for a long time either. Günther is doing well, praise G-d. He is also long and thin, no wonder. He could do with the care Alfred is getting now! At that age, the body needs all kinds of extra things. But now, I have to stop. I want to write to Lola,[37] Bernhard,[38] and Lene,[39] so that we can send each other a sign of life, otherwise we'll get scared.

And then, I have to go to bed, otherwise I won't be able to get up in the morning. So, give my warmest regards to the children, Hanna, Lea, Walter, Morrisons,[40] and so on. But you, my dearest Carlo, accept my warmest greetings and many, many heartfelt kisses from your infinitely loving little wife Carla.

I am still consumed by longing, and only the thought that I must be here for the children keeps me going.

Carla to Carlo and Hanna Koppel, November 10, 1941

My dearest Carlo and dear Hanna![41]

When I send my letters to Hanna's[42] address, you already know that it means something special. This is the last letter I can write to you here, as we are all leaving tomorrow. I can't give you a new address yet, but I will do so as soon as I can. Lola will keep herself informed and keep you up-to-date. You don't need to worry about me. I was desperate at first, but now I'm over it. You never get more than you can bear. I am also in great company, so that [I] will always have help and support.[43] [. . .] I have also just received a card from Bernhard—he and Ulli have left [. . .]. They left on Thursday. Perhaps we will meet.

We'll probably pass by Reißens[44] on the way. My great wish would be if I could at least get some mail from you before then. I have received all my papers, including my passports. If necessary, you can have photocopies made over there. Surely, there must be ways and means now. I have to be present at everything. I can't write to the Hochfelds anymore; you are in correspondence with them. By the way, Mrs. Oberdorfer is also going. She is very anxious because she has not yet heard from her daughter that the child has arrived.[45] Praise G-d, the children are doing well and will be a distraction and pastime for us.

Now [I] have to end, because [I] still have a lot of work to do. Always think of us. Greetings to all of you and do what you can. Give my regards to the Hochfelds, too. Many warm greetings to the children. I hope Alfred continues to be well.

Now, take my dear Carlo and Hanna the warmest greetings and many many kisses from your very loving and infinitely longing little wife Carla

Friedl and Lotte[46] came to see me today, and you will receive the mail as soon as it is possible and there is an opportunity. Please write to the Hochfelds. They should also tell Benno Sarsky[47] about Gertrud. Günther is still out, running errands for me. I am very glad that I have him with me now.

Letters from Carla Koppel took four to five weeks to arrive in New York. Because of the delay in mail delivery, Carlo Koppel had not heard about the deportations of his wife and four minor children at the end of 1941. He, along with others, was still working feverishly to free his family from the clutches of the Nazis. Below is the one surviving letter from Carl Koppel to his wife, dated December 8, 1941, with a postmark of December 10. Again, at this time he had no news of the horrific events that had taken place in Munich. This letter was returned to him four months later with the note "Delivery not possible. Return to sender."

Carlo to Carla, December 8, 1941

My dear little Carla:

Now the fifth week begins, and there is no mail from you, which upsets me very much since I do not know the reason. I very much hope that tomorrow something will come from you, and then I will immediately add a confirmation. I hope that you received my various letters, and I am eagerly awaiting your answers. [. . .] Your last letter is dated 10/24, and Uncle[48] had one dated 10/30, in which there was also something for me, which he should then pass on to me.

I am trying to get the money for Cuba together, and only hope that I will succeed, since it is the only way. Even today, nothing has come, and I really don't know what to think. My thoughts are with you day and night, and I have no interest in anything. The latest events have certainly not improved my mood. Alfred writes very often, and [he is], thank G-d, very well; the doctor is quite satisfied. Alfred has new wishes every moment, which I fulfill according to the purse. Enclosed are letters for Bernhard and Lola. [. . .] Uncle Siegfried[49] has another case of nerves but is already on the mend. How do you like your work and can you do it? What are my little ones doing? How are Günther's working hours?

We don't know now how it will be with Cuba. I have only a third together. Hopefully, it will not be too late. I would love to have a real picture from you, but it will hardly be possible. The only distraction for me is the cinema, but I don't go anywhere else. [. . .]

Now, I've been gone for almost a year and a half. It's terrible, this being alone. Walter has grown a lot and is still such a big cuddler. [. . .] Alfred has been in Denver for four months now: how time flies. How is your health? Is everything as before? I miss you so very much, and [until you are here] I can't really do anything of substance because I don't know whether we will stay here or whether we will go to the West because of Alfred. Right now, we always eat in the evening at 6 o'clock. I make my own food for the mornings and evenings, and we still eat at Max's[50] for lunch. Our apartment is generally admired, but the furnishings are missing; there is always room for improvement. There is no point in buying anything if one does not know positively that one will stay, not to mention the money. I can't write because of my restlessness and will only be able to write in detail again when I receive more mail from you. I am sending this letter today, and should anything arrive tomorrow or in the next few days, I will write again immediately.

So, my dear Carla, please continue to write very diligently, so that I always know what is going on with you. Many warm greetings and kisses to the children and to you.

Yours, in great longing and love. Only thinking of you and living for you,
Carlo

Your mail of 10/30/1941 has just arrived, and [I] am very glad to have a sign of life from you. Whether there is still a possibility via Cuba, I would have to doubt. The next few days will probably clarify this. You can imagine my mood in this regard. I will write to you again at the end of the week, provided it is still possible, which I very much hope. [. . .]

So, for today again greetings and kisses,

Your Carlo

NOTES

1. Alfred Koppel, *My Heroic Mother: Voices from the Holocaust* (Victoria, BE: Trafford Publishing, 2010); and Alfred Koppel, *"Dies ist mein letzter Brief. . .":Eine Münchner Familie vor der Deportation im November 1941*, ed. Ilse Macek and Friedbert Mühldorfer (Munich: Volk, 2014). The German publication served as the basis for the editors' translation of the letters written in German.

2. Dr. jur. Joseph Schäler (1885–1943), until 1935 chief magistrate, from February 1941, deputy chairman of the Jewish Community of Munich; from April 1941, deputy chairman of the Reich Association of Jews in Germany (*Reichsvereinigung*), under whose umbrella all Jewish communities and associations were forcibly united. He was deported to Auschwitz on March 13, 1943, and murdered there a few days later.

3. The Reich Association of Jews in Germany (*Reichsvereinigung der Juden in Deutschland*) came into being in February 1939 and was a continuation of its predecessor, the Reich Representation of Jews in Germany. As a result of the intensification of the antisemitic policies of the "Third Reich," its objectives became increasingly linked to Jewish survival and, in particular, emigration until its liquidation in July 1943. See Reichsvereinigung der Juden in Deutschland: Records (microfilm), 1939, *The Wiener Holocaust Library,* GB 1556 WL 604, accessed June 28, 2021, https://archiveshub.jisc.ac.uk/data/gb1556-wl604.

4. In June 1941, all US diplomatic missions in Germany and occupied Europe were closed. From then on, emigration to the United States was only possible for those people who could reach an American consulate in Spain, Portugal, or the unoccupied part of France.

5. Günther would then reach the age of 18 and would no longer be considered a child for the purposes of family reunification.

6. *Hilfsverein der Juden in Deutschland* was a Jewish aid organization, founded in Berlin in 1901 for the purpose of supporting Jews abroad, especially in Eastern Europe. Later, it was an important aid organization for Jewish emigration from Germany.

7. Victor Löwenstein (1885–1943) was an important contact for Carla Koppel as an employee of the Reich Association of Jews in Germany in Berlin. He was killed in an air raid on Berlin in March 1943.

8. During the four-week ship journey from Spain to the United States, Alfred Koppel had contracted tuberculosis and was therefore transferred to The National Jewish Hospital in Denver, Colorado, for treatment.

9. Joseph (Josef) Goldschmidt (1872–1943), husband of Carlo's sister Flora, called Lola Goldschmidt, née Koppel (1887–1944), lived in Berlin. In 1942, they

were deported to Theresienstadt, where Joseph was murdered. Lola was deported to Auschwitz in 1944 and became a victim of the Shoa.

10. Prof. Dr. Cora Berliner (1890–presumably 1942), employee of the Reich Association of Jews in Germany in Berlin.

11. Dr. Leo Braun (1877–1942) presumably worked in the *Reichsvereinigung der Juden in Deutschland* in Berlin; he was deported to Theresienstadt in 1942 and was murdered in Treblinka on September 26, 1942.

12. Dr. Freitag worked in the emigration office of the *Reichsvereinigung*; nothing more could be determined.

13. This refers to Carla Koppel's cousin Dr. jur. Rolf Hochfeld (1907–1988), later Ralph Holt, and his wife Gerda, née Reich (1914–2001). The couple emigrated via Great Britain to the United States, where they arrived on February 5, 1940.

14. Cilly Goldschmidt (1890–1941), employee in the administration of the Jewish Community.

15. This is an allusion to the often covered-up suicides.

16. Hanna (Hannah) Koppel (1888–1970), sister of Carl Koppel, emigrated to New York in the 1930s.

17. This is probably Lea Baer, née Rosenthal, who came from Hamburg. She was already living in New York in 1940 and was closely related to Carl and Hanna Koppel.

18. Going to the synagogue or prayer room.

19. Presumably the Jewish Vocational Training Workshops in the rooms of the former synagogue at Reichenbachstraße 7.

20. This refers to SS and Gestapo.

21. Probably Waldbott von Bassenheim (1883–1952), who in 1941 was an employee of the Spanish consulate in Munich.

22. American Jewish Joint Distribution Committee (JDC), a Jewish aid organization.

23. Dr. med. Otto van Wien (1886–1941) lived with his wife Frieda, née Majer (1894–1941), and his two children, Gertraud Babette (1925–1941) and Dittmar (1928–1941), at Thierschstraße 7, like the Koppels. They were deported from Munich to Kovno (Kaunas) on November 20, 1941, and murdered there.

24. Here, Carla Koppel refers to the fate of Edward (Edie) Koppel (b. 1894), the youngest brother of her husband Carl Koppel. He escaped from Germany to France in 1939, where he was caught and imprisoned before being deported to Auschwitz in 1942. Initially, she seems to have suspected that she and the children would be transported to a camp in France; however, she later indicated that the latest information seemed to suggest that they would be transported to "the other city." It can be assumed that she was talking here about deportations to the East.

25. The original German reads "G'tt," translated here as "G'd." Religious Jews do not write out the word God, so as not to dishonor the word. They either use a Hebrew designation (e.g. Adonaj = my Lord) or express reverence by omitting a letter.

26. "Aunt Meloche" refers to the "Aryanisation Office" at Widenmayerstraße 27, which summoned the persons intended for forced labor in writing. "Meloche" is the Yiddish word for work.

27. Selma Gold, née Falk (b. 1890), was deported to Piaski with her husband Julius (b. 1883) and her son Fritz (b. 1926) on April 4, 1942, and became a victim of the Shoa. Their son Martin (1920–1984) emigrated to New York in January 1939.

28. "at M. E. Loches," Meloche, cf. note 26.

29. Theodor Koronczyk (1898–1956) was the head of the Munich district office of the Reich Association of Jews in Germany and, from summer 1942, head of the Jewish Community and very controversial because of his role as a liaison to the Gestapo.

30. Dr. jur. Julius Hechinger (b. 1895), lawyer, head of the Jewish Community, and a liaison to the Gestapo. Deported on July 13, 1942, with a so-called punitive transport; victim of the Shoa.

31. In her letter to Carlo Koppel of October 20, 1941, which is not included here, Carla Koppel confirms that she placed the three youngest children in the Antonienheim. "Kinderheim der Israelitischen Jugendhilfe in der Antonienstraße 7," accessed June 28, 2021, https://gedenkbuch.muenchen.de/index.php?id=kinderheim.

32. Carla Koppel's uncle and aunt, Siegfried Hochfeld (1873–1952) and his wife Else (Elsa) Hochfeld, née Wassermann (1880–1952), emigrated to the United States in 1939. Else Hochfeld was the youngest sister of Selma Wagner (1876–1931), Carla Koppel's mother.

33. The fact that this letter bore neither salutation nor signature and repeated information already given before is interpreted by her son Al(fred) as a sign that his mother was particularly upset or confused at this time.

34. Carla Koppel had problems with swelling in her legs. Nevertheless, she walked one and a half hours each way from her house to the Antonienheim to be able to spend time with her small children. Since October 26, 1941, the use of public transport for Jews had been forbidden by decree of the Gestapo through Munich's Lord Mayor Fiehler.

35. On October 23, 1941, a ban was issued on Jews leaving Germany. (The ban on emigration did not affect the implementation of mass deportations of the Jewish population to concentration and extermination camps in the East.)

36. By this time, Carl Koppel had been in New York over a year and a half, where he had "celebrated" his birthdays in 1940 and 1941. The reason Carla Koppel talks about having been separated from each other for four birthdays is that in the year 1938 Carl Koppel spent his birthday in the Dachau concentration camp; in 1939, he was incarcerated in Stadelheim prison in Munich.

37. This refers to Carlo's sister, Lola Goldschmidt, née Koppel (1887–1944).

38. Bernhard Koppel (b. 1884) and his wife Juli, called Ulli, née Neuwahl (b. 1883), lived in Hamburg-Altona; they were deported on November 8, 1941, to the Minsk Ghetto and became victims of the Shoa.

39. Helene (Lene) Oettinger, née Koppel (b. 1883), lived in Frankfurt/Main; she was deported toward the East in 1942 (location unknown) and became a victim of the Shoa.

40. Max Morrison (1899–1996) and his wife Else (1899–1971) lived with their nine-year-old son Gerd in Brooklyn, New York; they were of German descent. From spring 1941, they had Carl Koppel as a subtenant. From November 1941, Walter and Carl Koppel had their own apartment but still went to the Morrison's home for lunch.

41. Apparently Carla Koppel was housebound in Munich and could not go to the post office to post a letter to her husband overseas. Instead, she sent this domestic letter to Lola Goldschmidt, her husband's sister, in Berlin, so that she could forward it to Carlo Koppel in New York.

42. Carla Koppel writes (probably due to commotion) "Hanna's" instead of Lola's address.

43. Following this statement, Carla lists the names of all the families who had lived with them in the "*Judenhaus*" at Thierschstraße 7 immediately before the deportation; they were all deported to Kovno (Kaunas) and murdered there on November 25, 1941.

44. Marta Magda Reiss, née Griesbach (1887–unknown), and Isaak Reiss (1881–1941) had been deported in the course of the "Polenaktion" in 1938 and were later deported further east. Mrs. Reiss was used in the letters of Carla Koppel and Lola Goldschmidt as a cipher for the deportations to Poland and the East, respectively.

45. Toni Anna Oberdorfer (1884–1941) was murdered in Kovno (Kaunas); her daughter Nelly Recha Mendle (1909–1994) had emigrated with her husband Emanuel Mendle (1903–1991) to the United States at the end of the 1930s, where she became a mother in 1941.

46. Amanda Franziska, called Friedl Koppel, née Modey (1894–1953), from Hamburg was the non-Jewish wife of Carl Koppel's brother Siegmund, called Siete Koppel (1881–1963); Lotte was Friedl's sister.

47. Benno Jonas Sarsky (1884–1972), concertmaster, emigrated to the United States in December 1938. Benno Sarsky was the brother of Henriette Gertrud Schäffer, née Sarsky (1885–1941), a friend of Carla Koppel.

48. This probably refers to Nathan Leipheimer (1860–1952), Carl Koppel's uncle, the brother of his mother Jette (Jetta) Koppel, née Leipheimer (1859–1931). He had emigrated to the United States in 1891.

49. This refers to Carla Koppel's uncle, Siegfried Hochfeld (1873–1952).

50. Max Morrison (1899–1996), former landlord of Carl Koppel in New York.

Chapter 16

"Wanderer between Two Worlds"

Hans Lamm

Hans Lamm was born in Munich on June 8, 1913, as the second son of Ignaz Lamm and his wife Martha, née Pinczower. His brother Heinrich was born on January 19, 1908. Only shortly before that, their parents had moved from Buttenwiesen in Swabia to the residence city of Munich, where Ignaz Lamm was one of the royal purveyors to the court as the owner of a metal smelter. In their childhood, Hans and his brother not only learned the basics of the Jewish faith, in which their parents had been raised, but were also introduced to the Bavarian traditions. At the insistence of his brother, Hans Lamm decided to follow him to the United States in 1938. After his arrival in Kansas City, Missouri, he worked at the Jewish children's home and thus financed his studies in sociology and social work. In 1943, a position with the American Zionist Emergency Council brought him to New York. One year before the end of World War II, Lamm became an American citizen.

After the end of World War II, Hans Lamm experienced a double return to his old homeland: first, he returned from exile in 1945 for a period of seven years, before the second, permanent remigration took place in 1955—after three more years in the United States. He crossed the border for the first time in 1945 as an envoy of the American Jewish Conference and subsequently made a name for himself in the Federal Republic as an interpreter at the Nuremberg Trials, a journalist, and the founder of the Ner-Tamid publishing house for Judaica. During this time he also completed his doctorate at the University of Erlangen. After his second return, he became known throughout Germany and far beyond in his functions as head of the cultural department of the Central Council of Jews in Germany (1956–1960), which was founded in 1950, and as president of the Jewish Community in Munich (1970–1985). However, it was only his employment as head of department at Munich's Volkshochschule (1961–1978) that finally enabled him to return to his hometown.

Hans Lamm died on April 23, 1985, in Munich. Until his death, he worked in his various functions to promote the coexistence of Jews and non-Jews in Germany. Only in the later phase of his life did the Munich-born writer integrate his experience as a "wanderer between two worlds" into his journalistic writing and attempt to explain the situation for Jews in Germany after the Holocaust. He already had discussed the former topic in letters to friends, which he wrote during his time in American exile. The collection of letters printed here in excerpts, written first in German and later in English, was preserved by his childhood friend Schalom Ben-Chorin (1913–1999)—a Zionist, born Fritz Rosenthal, who had left Munich for Palestine in 1935 and built a new home in the State of Israel. Despite the great distance during the years of exile, they maintained a lively exchange and remained friends into old age, overcoming disagreements and their different choices of residence after the collapse of the "Third Reich." Schalom Ben-Chorin's widow, Avital (Erika) Ben-Chorin (1923–2017), donated the letters to the Munich City Archives in 2009.[1]

Figure 16.1   Hans Lamm, 1932. *Source:* Private Collection.

Circular Letter from Hans Lamm
[written in German] May 14, 1938

Dear friends,

Once again, such a frightening mountain [of mail] before me demands an answer; thus, I take refuge in the already once well-tried system of the circular letter. All the things that concern me and are supposedly of more or less interest to you [will be included]. I then only have to write once instead of 12 times.

I have deliberately noted the exact addresses here [. . .][2] because most of the recipients live on holy ground and thus (in American terms, which I should now acquire soon) close to each other: it would be nice if you could visit each other and get to know each other—then, this letter would at least have a meaning. [. . .]

The undersigned himself is already in a bit of a mood for departure: last Tuesday, he had the dubious pleasure of presenting his affidavits to the honorable Consul of the USA, and at the end of July (after the papers seem to have found favor in His eyes), he will finally be mustered in . . . Then it should start as soon as possible. A once-considered plan to make a small detour via Palestine to get to the USA is again as good as abandoned, for various reasons. It would have been too beautiful, and therefore it was not meant to be. My Palestinian friends, all of whom I have visited before, may pay me a return visit in my new "Heimat" [home] in the near future!

Seriously, I would be incredibly happy, and I'm sure many others in the USA would be too. What I will do over there is still completely unclear, and I don't even care. I feel (forgive the unheroic openness!) very bad about going to the USA; but since I have not only my brother and his family[3] there but also hope for a minimal livelihood, and unfortunately I don't see any activity or similar possibility for me in Palestine, I have seized the chance to immigrate now and will enter there in a few months, full of prejudice and fear that I will never feel at home over there. Really, never have I felt more Zionist than today, when the decision to emigrate has been made, and envied you in Palestine, wherever you live. I believe that I am looking at your life, which I got to know myself during the bad unrest two years ago,[4] quite illusion-less, and [I do] not to heroize it as a "brochure believer."—Nevertheless, I find your way infinitely more meaningful and [believe it embodies] the maximum chance for happiness compared to ours; may it now be carried to the USA or Australia or somewhere else. We (or at least I) will never learn to submerge and to rise again, as it was possible in former times [to do], and I doubt the possibility of Jewish Galut-work, which is [admittedly] worthy (at least, again for me, who is Jewishly quite timid and not very positive). Well, by the way, I am trying to make the last weeks here as meaningful as possible: not infrequently going to theaters and the like. [. . .] By the way, I spend my short days here not only with theater visits and lazing around, but I also do some work on educational institutions and libraries (a pity that I will never and nowhere else have to do with such ideal libraries) and mainly historical things, which are partly fun, partly boring, and time-consuming trouble. In addition, I let myself be drilled in English four evenings a week for three hours each in an intensive course of Lehrhaus[5] and Reichsvertretung,[6] which will hopefully prove to be not only useful but also interesting and amusing in the long run.

[. . .] Let me hear from you all again soon, the more detailed the better. As difficult as it often is for me to keep up with my correspondence, it is gratifying and important to me, and hopefully also to you a little.

Best regards to all of you,
H.

Postcard from Hans Lamm to Schalom Ben-Chorin
[written in German] June 28, 1938

[. . .] The day after tomorrow I will be at the Consul, then I will go home immediately and—if everything works out—on July 16 to the USA. You will always be able to reach me through my brother [. . .], and I confidently hope that our connection will not be diminished by anything. How small my expectations are for over there, my recent letter will have proved to you. After all, the only good thing about it is that you can only be pleasantly disappointed. [. . .]

Letter from Hans Lamm to Schalom Ben-Chorin
[written in German] August 8, 1938

Dear Ben-Chorins,

[. . .] So, I've been in the US for 10 days now, not quite as horrified as I feared, but not suddenly thrilled either. It is a very foreign country to us and above all a people even more foreign to us, and I wonder very much whether we will ever feel different here than as guests. The chain of bad news from your country, which hardly breaks, depresses me very much, and I would be obliged if you would give me a more detailed description and assessment of the situation.

At the moment, I am still looking for a job: with my naturally still inadequate language skills, it is not at all possible to think of doing a job similar to the one I have done so far. Rather, only one in a commercial enterprise can be considered. And I would be very happy if I had such a job in sight. I would like to earn some extra income (or, as long as I am still unemployed, sole income) through journalistic work, and now I can again cooperate with Jewish newspapers outside Germany. I am convinced that you will be happy to help me. I ask you to pass on a small manuscript, which I am sending to you, to an editorial office that seems suitable to you. For the rest, I would be indebted to you for the indication of newspapers that come to mind, to which I will ask for short descriptions. Who pays well, who less? [. . .]

Circular Letter from Hans Lamm
[written in German] July 4, 1939

Dear Friends,

This will not be a real letter but is just to prove to you that I still walk on this earth and have not forgotten yours. [. . .]

So, first of all, thank you all very much, and let me assure you (believe it or not) that I am very happy to be in contact with you. I am so isolated here that letters are my only companions.

There's not much to report about my meagerness. Four weeks ago, I finished my first semester; in another four weeks, I'll do so with the 2nd and be $150.00 poorer and richer by the fancy title of a B.A.[7] Practically, this doesn't mean very much, but it gives me the right to do graduate studies; whether I will be able to cope with this (probably as a social worker) is still a very unsolved financial problem. If not, I will have to try to get through in some other, less nice way. In the meantime, hopefully my father[8] and aunt[9] will arrive in the USA; they will live in South Texas (on the Mexican border) with my brother's family (he practices there quite successfully). The children's home,[10] where I work (!), will probably be closed down in the foreseeable future (not exactly because of that), which will increase my living expenses but will no longer bind me to this godforsaken "heartland of America." On the Jewish or other activity of the people here, I can report little: on the one hand, because I am too much engaged in my work, and on the other hand, because this middle town in the Midwest is typical for the USA and does not produce any high performance. We feel depressed to have to watch the development in Erez [Israel] so idly; it is not at all only pleasure to live in a country that feels relatively "safe" from direct danger of war, when one knows so many loved ones in danger zones. Of the homeland, we better keep silent [. . .]. I'll close for today. I'm too tingly and will hardly get any rest in the next four working weeks. But then, and hopefully your answer is already available, I will try to answer with leisure and eloquence.

Please forgive and warm regards,
[Add on:]

Dear Fritz,—the Jewish papers of this country are so terrible that it is not possible to work with them. I could not place anything up to now, in spite of intense efforts. [. . .]

> Letter from Hans Lamm to Schalom Ben-Chorin
> [written in German] October 3, 1940

[. . .] It is a pity that—not only by our own fault—we almost completely lost contact. . . It is more necessary than ever today (as the connections become more and more difficult and sparse anyway) to save the few bonds that still exist until more peaceful times (will they ever come?). Of so many, one has no idea where and how they are. Recently, for example, I received a letter from a friend who was able to escape from Brussels to a camp in the south of France, and is now trying to escape to this country. Heaven knows how this might be possible. . .. My life continues in relatively unchanged cloudiness, insecurity, and loneliness, and the last two will not be lost anytime soon. I am attending a social work school,[11] but I will hardly be able to finish my studies because my children's home will probably close before then. But nowadays, even "in the heartland of America," there are more important problems than such personal issues. [. . .] What do you hear from your sister?[12] (My uncle Benno,[13] whom you may remember from Munich, is also in Buenos Aires,— or is your sister in Rio?) My father and his sister live with my brother's family in La Feria, Texas. [. . .]

> Letter from Hans Lamm to Schalom Ben-Chorin
> [written in German] June 1, 1941

Dear Fritz,

Your card from January 19 arrived a few days ago, and since I was in the middle of my final exams, I postponed answering it a bit. Now it's—oh, how important!—all behind me. I am a formally uniformed Master of Arts (which, as you know, has nothing to do with the arts; I, for example, am an M.A. in Sociology) and relatively much free time is at my disposal.

It is good to get overseas mail these days; one fears so much for one's friends abroad and dares not think of what may transpire before we hear from them again, if we ever will. . ... The events of the times touch not only yours truly very deeply; the average American here in the heartland of the continent is not unaffected. Although one does not want to go to war (who really does?), it is generally expected that we will soon be even more and perhaps formally in it.[14] America, in its overwhelming majority, is not willing to let the dark forces win.

[. . .] I don't have any more time for journalistic work, and it is also a strenuous thing to write in a non-native language; it will probably always remain a writing on crutches. [. . .] There is not much epochal to report about me. After earning a few useless degrees at the University of Kansas City, I have been studying since last September at the Washington Graduate School for Social Work, a highly developed science in this country. It involves practical work, and the insights into the way of life of many Americans—black and white—makes one wonder even more. . ..—one wonders whether such a system is capable and worthy of improvement. Or whether one should wish for its imminent and complete demise in order to make possible the rebuilding of a better one. My folks in Texas are doing well; brother and sister-in-law are quite successful country doctors. [. . .]

Greet all friends, [. . .] your family and yourself, and may you remain in peace.

Always faithfully yours,
Hans

Letter from Hans Lamm to Schalom Ben-Chorin
[first letter written in English] April 3, 1943

[. . .] What shall I tell you about my life? Since last June, I've been holding the position of an assistant and research director with this agency,[15] and I appreciate my good luck. If I am not 100% happy—is anybody?—I won't blame it on my external circumstances. Perhaps, I would feel a little more useful if I had a more direct connection with the war effort. [. . .]

Letter from Hans Lamm to Schalom Ben-Chorin
[written in English] January 8, 1944

[. . .] My main reason for not having written earlier was my anticipated change of position. Since the 16th of December, I am with the American Zionist Emergency Council[16] [. . .] for purposes of an obvious nature. My work is similar to that research and administrative activity which I carried on in Kansas City, and is interesting. It is good to know that one's effort may contribute to the achievement of a very desirable end. I need not tell you that I am looking forward to letters of yours with an increased and not only private interest. There are no essential changes which I could report about my personal life. I have not married even once yet and I don't know whether and when I shall ever do it. [. . .] I do share your longing for a renewal of personal conversations. [. . .]

Letter from Hans Lamm to Schalom Ben-Chorin
[written in German] June 24, 1944

[. . .] I have your letter of March 7 before me and am trying to correspond according to your wish and to write German. You may smile, but this is really so unfamiliar to me. Since I almost never write or speak German anymore, I cannot guarantee how successfully I will master the mother-turned-foreign tongue. Thank you for your congratulations on my new "job," which I now already have held more than half a year. I have always enjoyed organizing, and since the new position gives me enough opportunity to pursue my own ideas and there is always something new to do, I am not dissatisfied. But, there is still a possibility that I will accept another position in the not too distant future. In that case, I will inform you immediately. [. . .] Before I respond to your letter further, I must inform you that my father passed away three weeks ago in Texas. He suffered a lot during the last months, and we knew that there was no hope for his recovery. Death really came as a relief. Still, I have hardly been able to get used to the irrevocable fact. A few months ago, he was my guest in Kansas City, healthy and cheerful. With special—almost local-patriotic—interest, he has always followed your steady progress. Your assumption that I have now become a 100% Zionist is not entirely justified. I have more and more doubts that the Jewish question in the whole world could be solved by the Jewish state. When you see how complicated the problem is in America, from the outside and from the inside, you have to doubt that there is a SINGLE solution. At least, one may hope that the "Jewish Commonwealth in Palestine" for which we are working very intensively here, will contribute to a large extent to the alleviation of the Jewish plight. [. . .] Yes, I am still without a wife. However, we can leave it aside whether the only reason is that I am "a cold person" "who has never been strongly affected by women" as you suppose. That is only one aspect of the reality. [. . .]

Probably this letter is very disappointing. I am aware that it gives only "external data" and that it hardly tells what is really going on inside me. I have never been very good at talking about myself, and I have not learned anything. Where should I start, and where should I stop? I would have to write a whole book, and then I would not be sure how far I have made myself understood, and certainly, it would be highly doubtful whether it was worth writing all this down. At the moment, I would like to be able to tell you at least about this strange country and its problems. I have been here for almost six years now and have been an official citizen for three weeks; however, the people and the country are still a difficult and highly complex problem to understand. I doubt very much that you—as much as you may read about it—can form a proper picture. It is not your fault if you are failing. America is just too big and too colorful. You would like it very much here, for it is still a bold, contradictory, and opportunity-rich country. Hopefully, you will come here for at least one visit after the war. In my next letter, I hope to explain to you why this epistle is slightly confused. Things that are still quite in flux will then be clear and decided. [. . .]

Letter from Hans Lamm to Schalom Ben-Chorin
[written in English] November 1, 1945

[. . .] Now, I am about to leave next week for Germany and Austria, where I am to go to Displaced Persons' Camps, and I would very much like to hear from you. [. . .] I go as a representative of the American Jewish Conference.[17] [. . .]

Circular Letter from Hans Lamm
[written in English] December 9, 1945

[. . .] I left the States on November 7th on a fairly small victory ship bound for Le Havre, where it picked up 2000 returning servicemen. We were only 39 passengers with about twice as many crew on board, and I had a thoroughly enjoyable time. The first few days, the sea was amazingly calm, and we took in baths. Later it became somewhat rougher and a few people were seasick. I exhibited a startling inability to become ill and enjoyed the delicious meals. [. . .] After only a few hours in Le Havre and Paris, I left Saturday night for Wiesbaden[18] where I arrived three weeks ago. Saarbrücken and Mainz looked pretty badly hit. Frankfurt, where I caught the bus to Wiesbaden, offered a ghastly appearance; there is probably no street entirely undamaged and many are almost completely destroyed. I am not entering into an argument here whether this was what "they were asking for," or whether this "will teach them a lesson" (two phrases in all too common use here), but I must say that the destruction as such is a depressing and ugly sight. If it does nothing else, it hurts one's sense of beauty, and an inevitable afterthought is the feeling of utter insanity of a civilization that brings such devastation upon itself. Wiesbaden is less severely hit, although it, too, lost many of its prominent buildings and simple homes. I have now spent a number of days here, and I can't say whether

I am used to the sights it offers. One develops a certain matter-of-factness even towards the most abnormal circumstances after being exposed to them for some time, but at times one is shocked into realizing its true nature. I visited Frankfurt a number of times, where about 600 Jews are living: 300 former German Jews, 300 Displaced Persons (DPs).[19] Their situation is not easy; in many cases, they have hardly more to eat than have the Germans, their ration being only 1500 calories (after January 1, 1550 calories). At the DP camp at Zeilsheim, near Frankfurt,[20] I attended the dedication of a monument to the six million Jews who were killed from 1933–45. This camp is of rather recent date and houses about 3000 DPs, mostly newcomers from Poland who fled for their lives from new pogroms. . .[21] Up to now, I had no chance to see any other DP camp in Germany. Most of them are near Munich, and I only passed through there on my way to Vienna. Munich, too, is only a shell of its former self, and since it was so beautiful its downfall is particularly depressing. I met a few friends of olden days, and this was really moving in each occurrence. It was hard to conceal my shock when I saw the changes in their appearance. [. . .]

Circular Letter from Hans Lamm
[written in English] May 5, 1953

Dear Friends,[22]

This letter is a difficult one to write; it goes to friends scattered all over the globe: the United States and Hawaii (which may have become our 49th State by the time this message reaches you, but, which is at present still a Territory), Israel and Germany, Australia and Austria, Egypt and Spain, the United Kingdom (which some people, incorrectly, call England), the Netherlands and some other places. Some of those who are on my mailing-list have not seen me (nor heard from me) for years; others met me fairly recently either in Europe or here—yet, all are going to receive this same missive. This is a decision which I, myself, don't cherish, but I know of no simpler way of keeping in touch with all my friends, and even though this is not the accustomed personal method of communicating with you, which I should prefer, it will—I hope—be accepted as a compromise and as a demonstration of good will.

Now, what has happened to me? Beginning in 1946, I worked as an interpreter for various courts in Nuremberg, the last being the US Court of Restitution Appeals.[23] After terminating that assignment in June 1952, I returned to the US a few weeks later, met in New York City with my brother's family—incidentally, they are flying to Europe in June—and looked there for a job for quite a while. This was not easy: in the Jewish field, where interest and training have led me initially, the organizations have severely restricted their activities and reduced their staffs in recent years, and in many another realms the same situation prevails. While there is but little unemployment in the States, it is still often difficult to find a desirable position. It was, therefore, a fortunate incident, that in December a joint position was offered to me by the Community Chest of Scranton-Dunmore and the Welfare Council of Lackawanna County, as Public Relations Director of the former, and as Research Director of the latter. Here, I must stop and catch my breath; because I know that most of you, especially in foreign lands, will not know what a Community Chest or a Welfare Council is. Let me explain: After the First World War, a movement was started in many communities to unite the numerous appeals for local charitable institutions, social welfare agencies, group work organizations, etc., so that their fund-raising would not strain the patience and pocket-books of the citizens too much and that one united appeal on their behalf would take care once and for all of all their needs. This led to the creation of the Community Chests, entirely voluntary combinations of the philanthropic undertakings of a community. Hand in hand with that, Councils of Social Agencies came into being, which do joint planning and coordinating of the various organizations in the field; the latter expanded into even broader Welfare Councils like the one for which I am working now. "Public Relations" is a combination of simple propaganda for giving—it is most intensive during the Chest campaign in October—and of year-round education of the public on the work and needs of the family and childcare services, the hospitals, the group work and recreational agencies, etc. The "research" for the Council is an assembling of facts and data on the social and health services and assisting the community in drawing conclusions therefrom. This mixture of publicity and research pleases me very much, because it precludes the possibility of my work becoming too one-sided and boring.

Scranton is a city of about 140,000 people; the entire county has about 250,000 residents. The anthracite (mining) industry has been the basis of the local economy for about a century, and it's almost complete collapse in recent years has brought about a crisis which has not been overcome yet. This, and a serious loss of (mostly young) people within the last ten or twenty years, has created a situation, tragic, abnormal, yet challenging. No doubt, it is an interesting experience to work very close to the core of the community, a city, highly complex, full of traditions, religious and social stratifications. [. . .]

So far, the objective picture. Subjectively, it is premature to summarize. The job is interesting and brimful of novel situations from day to day; the executives and my colleagues, my secretarial staff are all—practically without exception—exceedingly kind and cooperative. Though, the adjustment of a bachelor (which I unfortunately still am) appears very difficult; I would be dishonest if I said that I'm sure I will ever feel fully at home here. However, I can't say whether this is actually the "fault" of Scranton, or probably mine. Weeks and months or even years will show how this problem will develop.

The fact that I have spent such stimulating years in Europe and left so many good and local friends, actually complicates matters, and the thought that I may never meet them again is very difficult if at all possible to accept.

A generation ago, some German writer wrote a book, "Wanderer between Two Worlds," and sometimes I am reminded of that title when reflecting upon myself. The fact that I lived in Germany up to '38, and again from '45 to '52 and that, on the other hand, I spent many years and received a major part of my training here, makes me feel "at home" both here and abroad—though with a difference of emotional undertone. This, being a globe-trotter, is of course, not always an asset. . . [. . .]

That's that, and I hope you will bear with me. Write soon; communications with my friends are more important to me than ever, and accept my very cordial wishes and regards.

Cordially yours,
Hans

Circular Letter from Hans Lamm
[written in English] August 25, 1954

Dear Friends,[24]

It was in May last year that I sent my most recent circular letter, and, having established that there is simply no other way to keep in touch with all of you, I resort to this means of communication. Enough water has flown down the Hudson, the Jordan, and the Isar to justify such a new missive.

The major news, of course, is that I have returned to New York in February after a stay of more than a year in Scranton, Pennsylvania. While I don't wish to say anything unkind about the latter community, I do want to sing the praises of New York City. Maybe one can fully appreciate its peculiar charm only after having resided for a while in the provinces.

People not living in New York City think of it first as the world's biggest city. That does not at all come to my mind. Actually, I leave the borough of Manhattan very infrequently; Manhattan has less inhabitants than Brooklyn or the Bronx, and the space covered by it on this long narrow island is much less than that of many middle-sized cities anywhere else. Yet, New York City (as the Post Office calls Manhattan) has within it such a wealth of contrasts that I can't help being in love with it. Let me illustrate it with the way I spent a recent Saturday evening. A friend of mine and I took a subway down from 59th Street to 4th Street (an express train made it in 10 minutes), and we strolled into the Amato Opera House in Greenwich Village,[25] that part of Manhattan being a mixture of Montmartre,[26] Schwabing,[27] and an Italian city. They produced Lucia di Lammermoor,[28] and though they sang well, we walked out of it after the first act since it was cooler outside than in. Then we had a bite to eat in a garden restaurant, and I dare to doubt that food can taste better in Naples than in this Neapolitan place. Having fortified ourselves that way, we inspected a number of quaint little stores—a Mexican one, a Scandinavian one, and one with pottery of all nations, etc.—and admired their goods, without spending a penny (the young lady with me was kind enough to enjoy just looking at these beautiful things), and we finally wound up in a book-store; the craziness of its books was only exceeded by that of its owner and customers. But while Greenwich Village is in so many ways non-conformist, it is also basically liberal, permitting each creature to enjoy him-or-herself as they like. There are little theatres, some of which present "originals only," and others the proven successes; there are missionaries preaching on one square to a group peacefully listening, while around the corner young people sing folk-songs without disturbing the checker players for whom the city has put up solid stone tables which are used at all hours of the day or night. And all that is permeated by a leisurely quietness which even in Europe is rare; but which in the heart of bustling-busy New York is certainly a pleasant surprise. [. . .]

That hymnical introduction may sound as if I had become a snob or a bohemian. Actually, I don't spend most of my time in Greenwich Village. I live uptown, very close to the place where I work, which has the advantage of my being able to walk to it in a few minutes. [. . .]

Actually, I am not even so much of a "Lokalpatriot" [local patriot] to claim that NYC is the only or best place in the US to live in. [. . .] Actually, I am very far from overlooking the shadows in the picture of New York. I never lived in a city with so much cruelty and crime, drunkenness and destituteness, lunacy and loneliness—yet, lights and shadows are close together, and while I don't pretend that one could not exist without the other, that seems to be life, and we seem to be unable to effect any profound changes.

In spite of the fact that 8,000,000 humans live in New York City, I happen again and again to meet old friends [. . .].

Never before did I enjoy as much as this year the wealth of good music offered here, in open air concerts in Lewisohn Stadium,[29] on the lawn of Washington Square Park (mainly European chamber music) and in Tanglewood, an American version of Salzburg (without the drama or opera).[30] No, America is not only jazz. . . . .

The fact that I mention my job so late in this letter should not create the impression that it is unimportant or unpleasant to me. I head the Office of Historical Information, jointly maintained by the American Jewish Historical Society and The American Jewish Tercentenary (an organization established to observe 300 years of Jews living in the US), and though the title is more imposing and impressive sounding than the actual position, it is, both as far as my interests and background are concerned, "down my alley," and the assignments I get never lack variety and other challenging features. The people working here are a fine bunch, indeed.

These are the external stations of my life since I last wrote you, and they were fairly easy to describe. My subjective situation, of course, is harder to be put in cold words, and I would not care to do so in a circular letter anyhow. But I may express myself on one point which I had raised last year and which was rather hotly discussed in a number of letters that some good friends sent me subsequently. I had used the phrase "Wanderer between two worlds." And that worried many friends. After having lived in the US again for more than two years, I see a far more positive aspect of that problem than it appeared in the spring of 1953. The fact that I lived long in Europe and that I obtained much of my education and most of my experience in America appears to me now not a draw-back, not a situation placing me between two chairs, but actually makes me now realize that this is an enriching background, which makes me at home here and there, and the fact that Judaism is a third molding force, which I gladly acknowledge, makes life only more interesting and more intriguing. While it certainly has practical and possibly emotional disadvantages not to be "native-born," the advantage of sharing in two or three traditions might be yet greater than the draw-backs.

My future plans are (as usual) uncertain. The Tercentenary Year is to end on June 30, 1955, and that will end my present position in its present form automatically. I am not sure yet what will happen then, but I don't worry too much. Frankly, I can't imagine myself right now in a job which I would want to hold until the end of my days. In the meantime, I dream of a vacation trip in 1955, but I don't know yet whether and when it will take place, nor where it will take me.

In the meantime, I enjoy a summer in New York, attend cool evening outdoor concerts and theaters, visit friends in the country on weekends, and shall look forward to hearing from all of you in the weeks to come.

Every year or every other year when I send such a circular letter, I feel apologetic about my inability to write to each and every one of you personally. Yet, I desire so much to keep in touch with and to hear from you that I again avail myself of this prosaic though convenient way. As this is so close to Rosh-ha-Shana I hasten to add my sincere wishes for the holidays and the New Year. If any of you ever should get to New York, don't fail to call me (Office: MO 6-7741; home: UN 4-6640).

All the best to all of you.

Cordially yours,
Hans Lamm

NOTES

1. Unless otherwise noted, the letters printed here are part of the personal collection of Schalom Ben-Chorin, Stadtarchiv München, JUD-V-001. Letters originally written in German have been translated by the editors. For more biographical Information see Andrea Sinn, *"Und ich lebe wieder an der Isar:" Exil und Rückkehr des Münchner Juden Hans Lamm* (Munich: Oldenbourg, 2008).

2. This letter was sent to Fritz Aronstein; Sh. Barilan (Fritz Birnbaum); Schalom Ben-Chorin (Fritz Rosenthal); Heinz Israelski; Max Leiter; Günther Lichtenstein; Familie Otto Mittler; Gusti Rindner und Lotte und Alfred Landauer; Lolli Schmidt; Peter Selz; and Irene Wertheimer.

3. Heinrich Lamm (1908–1974), a physician, met the doctor and his future wife Annie Thea Hirschel (1907–1976) in Breslau; they had two children, born in 1936 and 1938. With the help of uncle Louis Lamm, born Lazarus Lamm (1858–1951), who was already living in the United States, the family emigrated via Antwerp, Belgium, to the United States, arriving in New York on June 16, 1937. (On December 31, 1885, Louis Lamm married Sally Lamm (1867–1932), sister of Heinrich's father, in Jackson, Missouri.)

4. This probably refers to the tensions and violent clashes in the course of the nationalist uprising of Palestinian Arabs in Mandate Palestine against the British administration, which took place in Palestine from 1936 to 1939 and later became known as "The Great Revolt."

5. *Lehrhaus*, German, Jewish adult education institution. This refers to the Hochschule (then called the Lehranstalt) für die Wissenschaft des Judentums (Academy for the Science of Judaism) in Berlin.

6. The *Reichsvertretung der Deutschen Juden* (Reich Representation of German Jews), founded on September 17, 1933, was an umbrella organization of Jewish political and religious groups, coordinated and supported Jewish self-help, and was to be the political representative of German Jews vis-à-vis government authorities and to represent the interests of the Jewish population in Germany. It ceased to exist in June 1943.

7. From 1939 through 1941, Lamm studied Sociology at the University of Kansas City, earning BA and MA degrees.

8. Ignatz Lamm (1875–1844) was married to Martha Pinczower (1884–1931); he emigrated to the United States on the *Statendam* via Rotterdam, Netherlands, in August 1939.

9. This refers to Cilly Lamm (1873–1957), Ignatz Lamm's sister, who lived in the household of her brother and family in Munich since the 1920s and emigrated with him to the United States in August 1939.

10. Lamm held the position of boy's supervisor and secretary to the president in the Jewish Children's Home, Kansas City.

11. From 1940 through 1942, Lamm studied Social Work at the George Warren Brown School of Social Work, Washington University, Saint Louis, Missouri, earning an MA degree.

12. Jeanne Juana Selma Bachmann, née Rosenthal (1907–1972), sister of Schalom Ben-Chorin and wife of Hellmuth Bachmann (1901–1957), emigrated to Buenos Aires, Argentina, in February 1933.

13. Benno Lamm (1878–1967), brother of Lamm's father Ignatz Lamm.

14. The United States formally entered the European Theater of World War II on December 11, 1941, just a few days after the surprise attack on the US naval base at Pearl Harbor on Oahu Island, Hawaii, by Japan, an ally of Nazi Germany, on December 7, 1941.

15. Hans Lamm was Director of Research at the Jewish Welfare Federation of Greater Kansas City, 1942–1943.

16. From 1943 through 1945, Lamm was assistant to the director at the American Zionist Emergency Council (AZEC), New York, an organization created at the beginning of World War II to represent Zionist leadership in the United States. In 1949, AZEC became the American Zionist Council.

17. The American Jewish Conference, founded at the meeting of the leaders of 32 American Jewish organizations in the late summer of 1943, was concerned with the rescue of the Jews in Europe and the rights of the Jewish people in regards to Palestine, and from 1945 until its dissolution in 1949, also with the rights and the position of the Jews in the postwar world.

18. Wiesbaden, one of the oldest spa towns in Europe, is the capital of the state of Hesse in western Germany.

19. Administrative Memorandum Number 39 (Revised-16 April 1945) of the Supreme Headquarters Allied Expeditionary Forces on Displaced Persons and Refugees in Germany, I.5 (b), reprinted in Malcolm J. Proudfoot, *European Refugees 1939–1952: A Study in Forced Population Movement* (London: Faber & Faber, 1957), 446.

20. DP camps were facilities for the temporary accommodation of displaced persons (DPs)—especially former inmates of concentration camps—after the end of World War II in Germany, Austria, France, and Italy. In 1945, one such camp for DPs was set up in the former forced labor barracks at Farbwerke Hoechst in Zeilsheim.

21. Polish Jews returning to their hometowns after liberation encountered antisemitism that was horrific in its fury and brutality. The most shocking such episode was a violent attack in July 1946 by Polish residents of Kielce against returned survivors, in which 42 Jews were murdered.

22. Stadtarchiv München, NL Lamm, Akt 29.

23. Lamm served as court interpreter in the service of the American authorities in Nuremberg from 1946 to 1952, first at the International Military Tribunal I, then the US Military Court, and finally the US Court of Restitution Appeals.

24. Stadtarchiv München, NL Lamm, Akt 29.

25. The Amato Opera existed from 1948 to 2009.

26. Montmartre is the name of a hill in the north of Paris and a former village located there, best known for its art history and the white-vaulted basilica of Sacré-Cœur on its summit.

27. Schwabing is a district in the north of Munich.

28. "Lucia di Lammermoor" is a tragic opera in three acts by the Italian composer Gaetano Donizetti (1797–1848).

29. Lewisohn Stadium was an amphitheater and athletics facility on the campus of the City College of New York; it existed from 1915 to 1973.

30. Tanglewood is a music venue. By 1941, the festival attracted nearly 100,000 visitors annually.

Appendix 1

Glossary

Affidavit (of Support)

Affidavit of an American citizen who was willing, if necessary, to pay for the support of the immigrant to the United States so that the immigrant would not be a burden on the public welfare of the United States; prerequisite for applying for a visa to enter the United States.

Agudat Jisroel (Hebrew)

Union of Israel. Non-Zionist, conservative movement of Torah observant, Orthodox Jews founded in Katowice in 1912.

Alija(h) (Hebrew)

Ascending, Moving Up. Jewish immigration to Palestine. The Youth Aliyah was founded in 1933 as a department of the Jewish Agency with the aim of rescuing Jewish children and young people from Germany. After World War II, it cared for children who had survived.

Anschluss (German)

Joinder, Connection, or Unification. Contemporary term describing the incorporation of Austria into Germany. Some sources describe the *Anschluss* as an "annexation" rather than a union.

"Aryanization"

Contemporary term for the transfer of assets from Jewish to "Aryan" owners. The "Aryanization" was the largest state-organized robbery of a population group in history.

Aschkenasi, Plur. Aschkenasim (Hebrew)

Term for the Central and Eastern European Jews and their descendants in Central and Eastern Europe.

Auschwitz

Concentration and extermination camp complex established by the SS in 1940 near the Polish town of Oświęcim. According to serious estimates, more than 1.1 million people were murdered here.

Bar Mizwa/Mitzwa/Mitzvah (Hebrew)

Son of God's commandment. At the bar mitzvah celebration, a 13-year-old and thus commandment-bound male Jew is called to perform Torah reading for the first time.

Bat Mizwa/Mitzwa/Mitzvah (Hebrew)

Daughter of God's commandment. Rite of passage for Jewish girls created in the style of the bar mitzvah (especially in non-Orthodox communities).

Bergen-Belsen

Initially a camp for Allied prisoners of war near the city of Celle, Germany; became a concentration camp after being turned over to the SS in 1943.

Bet ha-Knesset (Hebrew)

House of Assembly. Synagogue.

Betsaal (German)

Prayer room. Small synagogue room.

Bimah

Pulpit. A raised platform or stage in a synagogue from which the Torah is read and services are led.

British Home Office

British Immigration Office.

Buchenwald

The Buchenwald concentration camp, not far from the city of Weimar, was established in 1937. The largest concentration camp on German soil included a total complex of almost 140 camps, in which about 250,000 people were imprisoned.

Bund Deutscher Mädel (BDM)

National Socialist youth organization for girls between the ages of 10 and 18; part of the Hitler Youth.

Cantor

Congregational official, a modern term for the precentor and prayer leader in the synagogue (see Chasan).

Centralverein deutscher Staatsbürger jüdischen Glaubens (German)

Central Association of German Citizens of Jewish Faith, CV or *Centralverein.* The organization was founded in Berlin on March 26, 1893, by German Jews to counter the rising antisemitism in the German Reich. During the Nazi period, the CV had to change its name several times; after *Kristallnacht,* the CV had to stop publishing its newspaper and the association was banned a short time later.

Chasan/Hazzan (Hebrew)

Overseer. Prayer leader in the synagogue. In English, often referred to as cantor.

Chełmno

One of six killing facilities established by the SS to carry out the mass murder of European Jewry, dedicated primarily to the extermination of people in gas chambers. It was the first stationary facility where poison gas was used for the mass murder of Jews. The SS and police conducted killing operations in Chełmno from December 1941 until March 1943 and then again for a brief period in June and July 1944.

D-Day

Expression specifically for June 6, 1944, the start of the landing of Allied troops in Normandy in World War II.

Dachau

First concentration camp, set up on the outskirts of the city of Dachau, Germany, in March 1933 on the orders of Munich Police President Heinrich Himmler. The "Dachau model" developed into the model for the National Socialist concentration camp system.

Der Stürmer (German)

The Attacker. The antisemitic weekly newspaper *Der Stürmer* was published in Nuremberg from April 20, 1923, to February 2, 1945. Its founder and editor was the Nazi party member and Gauleiter (regional leader) of Franconia, Julius Streicher (1885–1946).

Displaced Person (DP)

After the end of World War II, the term "DP" was used in the Western occupation zones to describe a civilian who was outside their home country as a result of the war and who wished to return or find a new home but was unable to do so without assistance.

Enemy Alien

Term used in Anglo-American law for nationals of a state with which the country in which that person is present is in conflict—not necessarily war.

Erev Rosch ha-Schana (Hebrew)

First evening of the Jewish New Year. See Rosh ha-Shanah.

Erez Israel (Hebrew)

The Land of Israel, the Promised Land, Palestine. Erez Israel was also the Hebrew name for the land ruled under the British Mandate from 1919 to 1948.

Gestapo (= Geheime Staatspolizei)

The *Geheime Staatspolizei* (Secret State Police) was Germany's political police during the Nazi era and possessed extensive powers in combating political opponents. It was declared a criminal organization at the Nuremberg Trials.

Gleichschaltung (German)

Coordination, Nazification of state and society, or bringing into line. The term refers to the forced incorporation of all social, economic, political, and cultural forces into the uniform organization of a dictatorship, which ideologically appropriates and controls them. The Nazis used the word for the process of successively establishing a system of totalitarian control and coordination over all aspects of German society and societies occupied by Nazi Germany.

Gymnasium

A secondary school in Germany, Scandinavia, or central Europe that prepares pupils for higher education at a university.

Hachschara (Hebrew)

Preparation. This refers to agricultural or craft training in preparation for emigration, usually in the form of compact training courses.

Hanukkah/Hanukah (Hebrew)

Consecration. The Jewish Festival of Lights. The eight-day festival (25th Kislev-2nd Tewet) commemorates the rededication of the second Jewish temple in Jerusalem in 164 BCE after the Maccabean revolt. According to tradition, due to the conquest by the Syrians, there was only one jar of consecrated oil left to feed the eternal light of the menorah. By a miracle, this oil had burned for eight days until new was made.

Haschomer Hazair (Hebrew)

Young Watchmen. Founded before World War I, the oldest Jewish socialist-Zionist youth organization whose goals were emigration to Palestine and the establishment of kibbutzim. The movement was influenced by the Boy Scout idea and propagated a collective lifestyle.

Hasid, Plur. Hasidim (Hebrew)

The pious. Members of a Jewish mystical sect founded in Poland about 1750; widespread in Eastern Europe since the middle of the 18th century.

Hasidism (from Hebrew Hasid, the pious)

Jewish religious renewal movement founded in the 18th century in Eastern Europe that combines mysticism and piety with a life-affirming cheerfulness.

HIAS

Jewish-American nonprofit organization, founded as the Hebrew Immigrant Aid Society to provide humanitarian aid and assistance to refugees. Originally founded in 1881 to help Jewish refugees, the organization has been assisting refugees of all nationalities, religions, and ethnic origins since 1975.

Hitlerjugend (HJ)

Hitler Youth. National Socialist youth organization served to collect and indoctrinate young people. Compulsory membership (since 1939) applied to 10- to 18-year-olds.

Immigration Quota

Immigration to the United States was regulated by a law passed in 1921 and tightened in 1924. According to the quota system stipulated in 1921, a maximum of 3 percent of the inhabitants of the United States originating from a country in 1910 were allowed to immigrate from that country each year. As of 1924, only 2 percent of the respective population living in the United States in 1890 was allowed to enter.

Joint

American Jewish Joint Distribution Committee (JDC). US relief organization that provided financial and material support to Jews in Eastern Europe until the start of the war between Germany and the United States. After the end of World War II, the organization sent many teams to the American occupation zone to help Jewish Holocaust survivors.

Judenhaus (German)

Jew House. This refers to real estate (houses and apartments), mostly Jewish-owned, into which Jewish men, women, and children were officially assigned after being evicted from their homes since 1939.

Jüdische Volksschule (German)

Jewish elementary school. The Jewish elementary school Munich was located in Herzog-Rudolf-Straße in the immediate vicinity of the Orthodox synagogue Ohel Jakob.

Kennkarten-Doppel (German)

ID Card Duplicate. The identity card was introduced in the German Reich in July 1938 as a "general police domestic identity card." The ordinance came into force on October 1, 1938. Applying for and carrying of an identity card was obligatory for adult male Germans; for Jews, however, both sexes had to apply for an identity card. These "Jewish ID cards" were identified by an imprinted capital "J." The identity cards were issued in duplicate; one copy (Kennkarten-Doppel) remained with the authority.

Kibbu(t)z, Plur. Kibbu(t)zim (Hebrew)

Collection, Assembly, Commune. Rural collective settlement in Israel with common property. The first kibbutz was founded in 1909/1910.

Kindertransport (German)

Children's transport. Relief action by the British government after the *Kristallnacht* of November 1938 to rescue Jewish children from Germany. More than 10,000 children—mainly from Germany and Austria—were brought to safety in this way.

kosher (Hebrew)

Law, fit. In accordance with the rabbinical ritual regulations (e.g., kosher food).

Kristallnacht

Literally "Night of Crystal," often referred to as the "Night of Broken Glass." Wave of violent anti-Jewish pogroms which took place on November 9 and 10, 1938 throughout Germany, annexed Austria, and in areas of Sudentenland in Czechoslovakia recently occupied by German troops.

Lift (also Liftvan)

Containers in which the removable goods of emigrants were stored.

Moschav, Plur. Moschavim (Hebrew)

Settlement, village. Cooperatively organized form of settlement in Israel in which properties are owned both collectively and privately. The first moshav was established in 1921.

Nuremberg Laws

On September 15, 1935, the Nuremberg Laws came into force. These racial laws defined who was a Jew. These laws also prohibited marriages between Jews and "Aryans."

"Ostjuden"/ "Ost-Juden" (German)

Designation of Jews in or from Eastern European countries, especially Russia, Ukraine, the Baltic States, Poland, Romania, Hungary.

Passover/Pessach (Hebrew)

Passing. Spring Festival, one of the three pilgrimage festivals, commemorating the Exodus from Egypt some 3,300 years ago, is celebrated on 14–21 Nissan.

Purim (Hebrew)

Lots. Carnival-like festival of joy, commemorates the salvation of the Jewish-Persian diaspora in the 6th century BC from the attack of the Grand Vizier Haman (Esther narrative), is celebrated on 14 Adar.

Quota(system)

see Immigration Quota

Rabbi (Hebrew)

Rabbi = My teacher. Religiously and academically trained as well as ordained scholar who, as a congregational employee, represents the religious head of a congregation; judge in religious and ritual matters; has no priestly function.

Rebbe, Plur. Rebbes (Yiddish)

Rabbis in Hasidic communities.

Reichsfluchtsteuer (German)

German Reich Flight Tax. As of December 8, 1931, all emigrants who gave up their domestic residence and whose assets exceeded RM 200,000 or whose annual income exceeded RM 20,000 had to pay 25 percent of their assets as Reich Flight Tax. In 1934, the exemption limit was reduced to RM 50,000.

Rosh ha-Shanah/Rosch Haschana (Hebrew)

Beginning of the year. Jewish New Year occurs in September or early October of the Gregorian calendar; marks the beginning of a ten-day penitential period.

Rosh HaYeshiva (Hebrew)

Title for the dean of a yeshiva.

SA (= Sturmabteilung)

Storm Troopers. The SA was a paramilitary fighting organization of the Nazi Party that existed from 1921 until it was banned in 1945. After the elimination of the leadership in the Röhm putsch in mid-1934, the organization lost much of its importance.

Sachsenhausen

The Sachsenhausen concentration camp, not far from the Reich capital Berlin, was established in 1936. In addition to imprisoning politically disfavored persons and people persecuted on racial and/or social grounds, Sachsenhausen also served as a training camp for SS members and prospective concentration camp commanders and SS guards.

Schtetl (Yiddish)

Settlement. Designation for Jewish communities in Eastern Europe.

Schti(e)bel (Yiddish)

Parlor. ("Eastern Jewish") prayer room.

Seder (Hebrew)

Order. The Jewish Passover festival begins with the Seder. It commemorates the exodus of the Jews from Egypt by gathering with the family and sharing a ritualized feast.

Sefer Torah (Hebrew)

Book of Torah. Torah scroll.

Sephardi, Plur. Sephardim (Hebrew)

Term for the Jews and their descendants who lived in the Iberian Peninsula until their expulsion in 1492 and 1513.

Shabbat (Hebrew)

Rest day. Seventh day of the week (work rest), lasts from Friday evening to Saturday evening.

Shoah/Schoa (Hebrew)

Hebrew word for "calamity" or "great catastrophe"; denotes the Nazi genocide of the Jews.

SS (= Schutzstaffel)

Protection Squadron. The SS was a paramilitary organization of the Nazi Party that existed from 1925 until it was banned in 1945. It exercised control over policing in the "Third Reich" and was responsible for the operation of concentration camps from 1934 onwards.

Synagogue

Place of assembly, learning, and worship in Judaism.

Talmud (Hebrew)

Instruction. Summary of the teachings and traditions of post-biblical Judaism.

Theresienstadt/Terezín (German/Czech)

Ghetto for Jews established by the Nazi occupiers in 1941 on the territory of the "Protectorate of Bohemia and Moravia." According to current estimates, more than 140,000 men, women, and children were interned there. Most of them were deported to extermination camps; about 33,000 people lost their lives in Theresienstadt.

Torah (Hebrew)

Teaching. The Pentateuch (five books of Moses—Genesis, Exodus, Leviticus, Numbers, Deuteronomy) written by the sofer (Torah scribe) on a Torah scroll (Sefer Torah) made of parchment and rolled up on two sticks, held together by the mappa (band) and wrapped in a Torah mantle. The staffs are studded with rimmonim (pomegranates) and a keter Torah (Torah crown), respectively. Over this, on the front of the Torah mantle, the tas (shield) and the jad (pointer) are hung as a reading aid.

Treblinka

Major Nazi German forced labor camp and extermination camp, established by the SS during the German occupation of Poland in World War II near the village of Treblinka, 50 miles (80 km) northeast of Warsaw. From late July 1942 to September 1943, camp personnel murdered an estimated 925,000 Jews at the Treblinka killing center. They also killed an unknown number of Poles, Roma, and Soviet prisoners of war.

Ulpan, Plur. Ulpanim (Hebrew)

Instruction. Intensive Hebrew course; for new immigrants to Israel important cornerstone for learning the language and integrating into Israeli society.

Völkischer Beobachter

From 1920 to April 30, 1945, the *Völkischer Beobachter* was the Nazi Party's journalistic mouthpiece and the flagship of National Socialist propaganda. From 1933, it was a quasi-government organ, published daily.

Volksgemeinschaft (German)

"People's Community" or "National Community." According to Nazi ideology, the *Volksgemeinschaft* was a "pure," ideal, and harmonious German society which rejected old religions, ideologies, and class divisions, instead forming a united German identity based around ideas of race, struggle, and state leadership. Accordingly, only the German "Aryan" who was also committed to the community in party and state organizations could be part of the *Volksgemeinschaft*. Inclusion and exclusion are therefore the two inseparable sides of the National Socialist "Volksgemeinschaft."

Wiedergutmachung *(German)*

"To make good again." Term for the legal confrontation in Germany with the injustice of the Nazi regime and for the state's efforts to provide material compensation for this injustice.

Yeshiva, Plur. Yeshivot *(Hebrew)*

Higher Jewish theological teaching institution (Talmud school) for the training of scholars and rabbis.

Yom Kippur *(Hebrew)*

Day of Atonement. Day of Atonement, celebrated on the 10th of Tishri, a strict day of fasting and repentance, highest Jewish holiday. It marks the end of the ten days of repentance and conversion that begin on Rosh ha-Shanah, New Year's Day.

Yom Tov *(Hebrew)*

Good day, feast day, holiday. Designation for the Jewish holidays on which no work may be performed: Rosh ha-Shanah, Yom Kippur, the first day(s) of Sukkot, Shmini Azeret, Simchat Torah, the first and last days of Passover, and Shavuot.

Zionism

National Jewish movement that emerged at the end of the 19th century, aiming at the creation of a Jewish national state in Palestine.

Appendix 2
Credits and Copyright

The editors gratefully acknowledge the permissions granted to reproduce the copyright materials in this book. Every effort has been made to trace copyright holders and to obtain their permission for the use of copyright material. The editors apologize for any errors or omissions in the list and would be grateful if notified of any corrections that should be incorporated in future reprints or editions of this book.

MEMOIRS

Lotte Bamberger, A Family History: For my Children and Grandchildren
LBI New York, ME 1403, MM III 14, 000201867, DTLPID: 430182.
Unpublished manuscript, hardcover, 325 pages; written in English in 1990.
Selection: pp. 183–188; 209–225, with occasional omissions.
© Lotte Bamberger/LBI New York. Courtesy of Leo Baeck Institute New York.

Fred Bissinger, The Jaws of the Swastika Tighten
StadtAM, JUD-M-24.
Unpublished computer printout, 9 pages; written in English in June 1997.
Selection: Full reprint with occasional omissions.
© Fred Bissinger/Stadtarchiv München.

Charlotte Haas Schueller, Tossed by the Storms of History: Experiences of a Survivor
StadtAM, JUD-M-27.

Typewritten English-language manuscript, 110 pages; given to the Munich City Archives by the author during a visit to Munich in 2004.
Selection: pp. 45–72, with omissions.
© Charlotte Haas Schueller/Stadtarchiv München.

Erich Hartmann, The Munich Years (Münchener Jahre)
StadtAM, JUD-M-15.
Hard copy, 13 pages; written in German, 1997; English translation by the editors.
Selection: Reprint with two omissions (pp. 2–4, 8).
© Erich Hartmann.

Ernest B. Hofeller, Munich, 1933–1938
StadtAM, JUD-M-16.
Hard copy, 98 pages; written in English in the late 1990s.
Selections: pp. 1; 4–7; 21–23; 32–37; 56–58; 64–70; 83–84; 90–96 (with occasional omissions).
© Ernest B. Hofeller/Stadtarchiv München.

Hugo Holzmann, An Emotional Handicap
StadtAM, JUD-P-Holzmann, Hugo (27.3.1929 in Mü.).
Hard copy, 1 page; written in English, around 2016.
This essay was first published in *The Hidden Child 25th Anniversary Issue: Infant Survivors of the Holocaust—The Last Witnesses. A Publication of Hidden Child Foundation/ADL* XXIV (2016): 33 (https://www.adl.org/media/13110/download).
Selection: Reprint in full.
© Hugo Holzmann/Hidden Child Foundation/ADL.

Hanns Peter Merzbacher, Memories (Erinnerungen)
StadtAM, JUD-M-32.
Printout, hardcover, 92 pages with photos and documents; written in German in 1996; English translation by the editors.
Selection: pp. 39–80, with occasional omissions.
© Hanns Peter Merzbacher/Stadtarchiv München.

Inge Moss, My New Life in the U.S.
StadtAM, JUD-M-11.
Unpublished computer printout, 4 pages; written in English, 1999.
Selection: pp. 2–4.
© Inge Moss/Stadtarchiv München.

Christine Roth-Schurtman, A Student's Fate, 1933–1945
StadtAM, JUD-M-33.
Essay "Ein Schülerschicksal, 1933–1945" written for *München Mosaik* in English translation, typed manuscript, 9 pages; written in German in 1984; English translation by the author.
Selection: Full reprint with occasional omissions, supplemented with selected sections from "I live my life in Widening Circles" (hard copy, 4 pages; written in 2004), and "Sweet Sixteen" (hard copy, 4 pages; written in 2006), taken from the same City Archives file.
© Christine Roth-Schurtman/Stadtarchiv München.

Pesach Schindler, A Jewish Childhood in Nazi Germany
StadtAM, JUD-M-36.
Computer printout, 25 pages; written in English in September 2004.
Selection: Full reprint with occasional omissions.
© Pesach Schindler/Stadtarchiv München.
Permission to use the photograph of Pesach Schindler was given by Daniel Kalman Epstein, author/photographer of Portraits in Faith ©2021, to the author(s) on August 22, 2021.

Ilse E. Scholle, Tossed by the Wind: A Proud Journey from 1920 to 1994
StadtAM, JUD-M-66.
Hard copy, 100 pages with photo appendix; written in English in 1994, digital revised version of 2020.
Selection: pp. 37–42, 46–49, with occasional omissions.
© Ilse Scholle.

Charlotte Stein-Pick, The Lost Home (Die verlorene Heimat)
Leo Baeck Institute, ME 619, MM 73, 000201092, DTLPID: 416859.
Typewritten manuscript entitled "Die verlorene Heimat," 82 pages, written in German in 1964; English translation by the editors.
Selection: pp. 64–74, 79–82, with occasional omissions.
© Charlotte Stein-Pick/LBI New York. Courtesy of Leo Baeck Institute New York.

LETTERS

Family Schwager, ". . . What One Leaves Behind"
StadtAM, DE-1992-JUD-V-0191.
Digitalized letters by various members of the Schwager family, originally written in German, later typed and translated into English by Erwin Schwager.

Selection: Excerpts of 14 letters, all written in 1938.
© Dianne Schwager and Gary Schwager.

Family Blechner "I'm Alive: It's a Miracle!"
StadtAM, JUD-V-99.
Copies of the collection of typed letters of various members of the Blechner
Family, written in German; English translation by the editors.
Selection: Excerpts of seven letters, all written in 1939.
© Courtesy of Anthony and Mark Blechner, the Blechner family Boston,
London, Zuerich.

Family Koppel, The Tragedy of Emigration
StadtAM, NL Koppel, DE-1992-JUD-V-0158-10.
Published version of letters originally handwritten or typed by various mem-
bers of the Koppel family, written in German, published in Alfred Koppel,
"Dies ist mein letzter Brief...": *Eine Münchner Familie vor der Deporta-
tion im November 1941*, ed. Ilse Macek and Friedbert Mühldorfer (Munich:
Volk, 2014); English translation by the editors.
Selection: Excerpts of nine letters written by Carla Koppel and one letter
written by Carl Koppel in German in late 1941.
© Koppel Family/Ilse Macek.

Hans Lamm, Wanderer between Two Worlds
StadtAM, JUD-V-001 and StadtAM, NL Lamm, Akt 29.
Unsorted collection of letters written with typewriter; originals and carbon
copies; written in German and English; English translation for German let-
ters provided by the editors.
Selection: Excerpts of eleven letters and one postcard, written between 1938
and 1954.
© Hans Lamm/Stadtarchiv München.

ILLUSTRATIONS

Leo Baeck Institute, New York
Private Collection
Staatsarchiv München
Stadtarchiv München

Bibliography

ARCHIVES

Bayerisches Hauptstaatsarchiv (BayHStA, Bavarian Main State Archive), Munich.
Harvard College Library (HCL), Cambridge, MA.
Leo Baeck Institute (LBI), New York.
Staatsarchiv München (StAM, State Archive Munich), Munich.
Stadtarchiv München (StadtAM, City Archive Munich), Munich.
The U.S. National Archives and Records Administration (NARA), Washington, DC.
The Wiener Holocaust Library (WHL), London.

BIBLIOGRAPHY

Arad, Yitzhak, Israel Gutman, and Abraham Margaliot, eds. *Documents on the Holocaust: Selected Sources on the Destruction of the Jews of Germany and Austria, Poland, and the Soviet Union*. Lincoln: Univ. of Nebraska Press, 1999.

Barkai, Avraham. *From Boykott to Annihilation: The Economic Struggle of German Jews, 1933–1943*. Hanover: Univ. Press of New England, 1989.

Barkai, Avraham. "German Interests in the Haavara-Transfer Agreement 1933–1939." *Leo Baeck Institute Yearbook* 35 (1990): 245–266.

Bauer, Yehuda. *Jews for Sale? Nazi-Jewish Negotiations, 1933–1945*. New Haven: Yale Univ. Press, 1994.

Baumann, Angelika and Andreas Heusler, eds. *München arisiert: Entrechtung und Enteignung der Juden in der NS-Zeit*. Munich: Beck, 2004.

Baumel-Schwartz, Judy Tydor. "The Rescue of Jewish Girls and Teenage Women to England and the USA during the Holocaust: A Gendered Perspective." *Jewish History* 26, no. 1–2 (2012): 223–245

Ben-Chorin, Schalom. *Jugend an der Isar*. Munich: List, 1974.

Bendersky, Joseph W. *A Concise History of Nazi Germany.* 5th ed. Lanham: Rowman & Littlefield Publishers, 2020.

Benz, Wolfgang. *Das Exil der kleinen Leute: Alltagserfahrungen deutscher Juden in der Emigration.* Munich: Beck, 1991.

Benz, Wolfgang and Angelika Königseder, eds. *Das Konzentrationslager Dachau: Geschichte und Wirkung nationalsozialistischer Repression. Festschrift für Barbara Distel.* Berlin: Metropol, 2008.

Berenbaum, Michael, ed. *Witness to the Holocaust.* New York: HarperCollins Publishers, 1997.

Berghahn, Marion. *Continental Britons: German-Jewish Refugees from Nazi Germany.* Rev. ed. Oxford: Berghahn, 2007.

Bergmann, Katharina. *Jüdische Emigration aus München: Entscheidungsfindung und Auswanderungswege (1933–1941).* Munich: DeGruyter Oldenbourg 2021.

Blickle, Peter. *Heimat: A Critical Theory of the German Idea of Homeland.* Rochester: Camden House, 2002.

Blutinger, Jeffrey C. "Bearing Witness: Teaching the Holocaust from a Victim-Centered Perspective." *The History Teacher* 42, no. 3 (2009): 269–279.

Boehling, Rebecca and Uta Larkey. *Life and Loss in the Shadow of the Holocaust: A Jewish Family's Untold Story.* Cambridge: Cambridge Univ. Press, 2011.

Breitmann, Richard and Alan M. Kraut. *American Refugee Policy and European Jewry, 1933–1945.* Bloomington: Indiana Univ. Press, 1987.

Brinkmann, Tobias. "Transnational Ties: The Longue Durée of Jewish Migrations to the United States." *American Jewish History* 101, no. 4 (October 2017): 563–567.

Caestecker, Frank and Bob Moore, eds. *Refugees from Nazi Germany and the Liberal European States.* New York: Berghahn, 2010.

Cahnman, Werner J. "The Decline of the Munich Jewish Community, 1933–1938." *Jewish Social Studies* 3, no. 3 (July 1941): 285–300.

Childers, Thomas. *The Third Reich: The History of Nazi Germany.* New York: Simon & Schuster, 2017.

Curio, Claudia. "Were Unaccompanied Child Refugees a Privileged Class of Refugees in the Liberal States of Europe?" In *Refugees from Nazi Germany and the Liberal European States*, edited by Frank Caestecker and Bob Moore, 169–189. New York: Berghahn, 2010.

Davie, Maurice R. and Samuel Koenig. *The Refugees are now Americans.* New York: Public Affairs Committee, Inc., 1945.

Distel, Barbara. *The Dachau Concentration Camp, 1933 to 1945: Text and Photo Documents from the Exhibition.* Munich: Lipp, 2005.

Dörfler, Hans-Diether. "Von Bamberger & Hertz zu HIRMER: Ein respektables Stück Wirtschaftsgeschichte." Accessed June 21, 2021. https://www.hirmer -gruppe.de/download/presse/pressemappe/hirmer_gruppe_geschichte.pdf.

Dwork, Debóra and Robert Jan van Pelt. *Fight from the Reich: Refugee Jews, 1933–1946.* New York: Norton, 2009.

Eddy, Beverley Driver. *Ritchie Boy Secrets: How a Force of Immigrants and Refugees Helped Win World War II.* Guilford: Stackpole Books, 2021.

Edelman, Joseph. "The Centenary of Jewish Immigration to the United States: 1881–1981." *Judaism* 32, no. 2 (1983): 215–229.

Ehrenreich, Robert M. and Tim Cole. "The Perpetrator-Bystander-Victim Constellation: Rethinking Genocidal Relationships." *Human Organization* 64, no. 3 (2005): 213–224.

Eigler, Friederike and Jens Kugele, eds. *Heimat: At the Intersection of Memory and Space*. Berlin: DeGruyter, 2012.

Embacher, Helga. "Die USA als Aufnahmeland von jüdischen Verfolgten des NS-Regimes und Holocaustüberlebenden." In *"Nach Amerika nämlich!" Jüdische Migrationen in die Amerikas im 19. und 20. Jahrhundert*, edited by Ulla Kriebernegg et al., 111–134. Göttingen: Wallstein 2012.

Essner, Cornelia. *Die "Nürnberger Gesetze" oder Die Verwaltung des Rassenwahns 1933–1945*. Paderborn: Schöningh, 2002.

Fast, Vera. *Children's Exodus: A History of the Kindertransport*. London: I. B. Tauris, 2010.

Friedländer, Saul. *Nazi Germany and the Jews: The Years of Persecution, 1933–1939*. New York: HarperCollins, 1997.

Friedländer, Saul. *Nazi Germany and the Jews: The Years of Extermination, 1939–1945*. New York: HarperCollins, 2007.

Fulbrook, Mary and Ulinka Rublack. "In Relation: The 'Social Self' and Ego-Documents." *German History* 28, no. 3 (2010): 263–272.

Garland, Libby. "State of the Field: New Directions for American Jewish Migration Histories." *American Jewish History* 102, no. 3 (2018): 423–440.

Geller, Jay Howard. *Jews in Post-Holocaust Germany, 1945–1953*. Cambridge: Cambridge Univ. Press, 2005.

Goschler, Constantin. *Schuld und Schulden: Die Politik der Wiedergutmachung für NS-Verfolgte seit 1945*. Göttingen: Wallstein, 2005.

Gottlieb, Moshe. "The First of April Boycott and the Reaction of the American Jewish Community." *American Jewish Historical Quarterly* 57, no. 4 (June 1968): 516–517, 519–556.

Grinberg, Léon and Rebecca Grinberg. *Psychoanalytic Perspectives on Migration and Exile*. New Haven: Yale Univ. Press, 1989.

Haus der Bayerischen Geschichte: Bavariathek. "Atlas zum Wiederaufbau: München." Accessed June 17, 2021. https://www.bavariathek.bayern/wiederaufbau/orte/detail/muenchen/2.

Hammel, Andrea, ed., *The Kindertransport to Britain 1938/1939: New Perspectives*. Amsterdam: Rodopi, 2012.

Hanke, Peter. *Zur Geschichte der Juden in München zwischen 1933 und 1945*. Munich: Bauknecht, Wölfle, 1967.

Henderson, Bruce. *Sons and Soldiers: The Untold Story of the Jews Who Escaped the Nazis and Returned with the U.S. Army to Fight Hitler*. New York: William Morrow, 2017.

Hett, Benjamin Carter. *Burning the Reichstag: An Investigation into the Third Reich's Enduring Mystery*. Oxford: Oxford Univ. Press, 2014.

Heusler, Andreas. *Das Braune Haus: Wie München zur "Hauptstadt der Bewegung" wurde*. Munich: DVA, 2008.

Heusler, Andreas and Tobias Weger. *"Kristallnacht": Gewalt gegen die Münchner Juden im November 1938*. Munich: Buchendorfer Verlag, 1998.

Heydt, Maria von der. "Möglichkeiten und Grenzen der Auswanderung von 'jüdischen Mischlingen,' 1938–1941." In *"Wer bleibt, opfert seine Jahre, vielleicht sein Leben:" Deutsche Juden 1938–1941*, edited by Susanne Heim, Beate Meyer and Francis R. Nicosia, 77–95. Göttingen: Wallstein 2010.

Hilberg, Raul. *Perpetrators, Victims, Bystanders: The Jewish Catastrophe, 1933–1945*. New York: HarperCollins, 1992.

Hill, Jeff. *The Holocaust*. Detroit: Omnigraphics, 2006.

Hilton, Laura J. and Avinoam J. Patt, eds. *Understanding and Teaching the Holocaust*. Madison: Univ. of Wisconsin Press, 2020.

History, Art & Archives, U.S. House of Representatives. "House Select Committee Investigates Japanese Evacuation and Relocation." Accessed June 19, 2021. https://history.house.gov/Blog/2018/May/5-8-tolan-committee/.

Hochstadt, Steve. *Sources of the Holocaust*. New York: Palgrave Macmillan, 2004.

Hockerts, Hans Günter. "Wiedergutmachung in Deutschland: Eine historische Bilanz 1945–2000." *Vierteljahrshefte für Zeitgeschichte* 49 (2001): 167–214.

Hohnschopp, Christine ed. *Exil in Brasilien: Die deutschsprachige Emigration, 1933–1945*. Leipzig: Deutsche Bibliothek 1994.

Jüdisches Leben in München: Lesebuch zur Geschichte des Münchner Alltags (Geschichtswettbewerb 1993/94), published by the City of Munich. Munich: Buchendorfer Verlag, 1995.

Kaplan, Marion A. *Between Dignity and Despair: Jewish Life in Nazi Germany*. New York: Oxford Univ. Press, 1999.

Kaplan, Marion A. *Hitler's Jewish Refugees: Hope and Anxiety in Portugal*. New Haven: Yale Univ. Press, 2020.

Kaplan, Marion A. *Zuflucht in der Karibik: Die jüdische Flüchtlingssiedlung in der dominikanischen Republik, 1940–1945*. Göttingen: Wallstein, 2010.

Kershaw, Ian. *Hitler*, 2nd ed. Harlow: Longman, 2001.

Kellerhoff, Sven Felix. *Der Reichstagsbrand: Die Karriere eines Kriminalfalls*. Berlin: be.bra Verlag, 2008.

Klemperer, Victor. *Ich will Zeugnis ablegen bis zum letzten: Tagebücher, 1933–1945*. Berlin: Aufbau, 2015.

Koessler, Maximilian. "Enemy Alien Internment: With Special Reference to Great Britain and France." *Political Science Quarterly* 57, no. 1 (1942): 98–127.

Koppel, Alfred. *"Dies ist mein letzter Brief…": Eine Münchner Familie vor der Deportation im November 1941*. Edited by Ilse Macek and Friedbert Mühldorfer. Munich: Volk, 2014.

Koppel, Alfred. *My Heroic Mother: Voices from the Holocaust*. Victoria, BE: Trafford Publishing, 2010.

Kossert, Andreas. *Flucht: Eine Menschheitsgeschichte*, 2nd ed. Munich: Siedler, 2020.

Krauss, Marita. *Heimkehr in ein fremdes Land: Geschichte der Remigration nach 1945*. Munich: Beck, 2001.

Krauss, Marita and Erich Kasberger, eds. *Rechte Karrieren in München von den Weimarer Jahren bis in die Nachkriegszeit*. Munich: Volk, 2010.

Kreutzmüller, Christoph. *Final Sale in Berlin: The Destruction of Jewish Commercial Activity 1930–1945*. New York: Berghahn, 2015.

Kriebernegg, Ulla et al., eds. *"Nach Amerika nämlich:" Jüdische Migration in die Amerikas im 19. und 20. Jahrhundert.* Göttingen: Wallstein, 2012.

Lavsky, Hagit. *The Creation of the German-Jewish Diaspora: Interwar German-Jewish Immigration to Palestine, the USA, and England.* Berlin: DeGruyter, 2017.

LeMay, Michael C. *U.S. Immigration Policy, Ethnicity, and Religion in American History.* Santa Barbara: Praeger, 2018.

Lesser, Jeffrey. *Welcoming the Undesirables: Brazil and the Jewish Question.* Berkeley: Univ. of California Press, 1995.

Lixl-Purcell, Andreas. "Memoirs as History." *Leo Baeck Institute Year Book* 39 (1994): 227–238.

Lixl-Purcell, Andreas, ed. *Women of Exile: German-Jewish Autobiographies since 1933.* New York: Greenwood Press, 1988.

Loberg, Molly. *The Struggle for the Streets of Berlin: Politics, Consumption, and Urban Space, 1914–1945.* Cambridge: Cambridge Univ. Press, 2018.

London, Louise. *Whitehall and the Jews, 1933–1948: British Immigration Policy, Jewish Refugees, and the Holocaust.* Cambridge: Cambridge Univ. Press, 2000.

Longerich, Peter. *The Nazi Persecution and Murder of the Jews.* Oxford: Oxford Univ. Press, 2010.

Löw, Andrea, Doris L. Bergen and Anna Hájková, eds. *Alltag im Holocaust: Jüdisches Leben im Großdeutschen Reich 1941–1945.* Munich: Oldenbourg, 2013.

MacDonald, Kevin. "Jewish Involvement in Shaping American Immigration Policy, 1881–1965: A Historical Review." *Population & Environment* 19, no. 4 (1998): 295–356.

Maòr, Harry. *Über den Wiederaufbau der jüdischen Gemeinden in Deutschland seit 1945.* Diss. Phil., Mainz : [s.n.], 1961.

Marcuse, Harold. *Legacies of Dachau: The Uses and Abuses of a Concentration Camp.* Cambridge: Cambridge Univ. Press, 2001.

Marrenbach, Nicole. "Memoiren Münchner Juden als Quelle für die 'Arisierungs' Forschung." *zeitenblicke* 3, no. 2 (2004). Last modified September 13, 2004. http://www.zeitenblicke.historicum.net/2004/02/marrenbach/index.html.

Marrus, Michael R. *The Nuremberg War Crimes Trial, 1945–46: A Brief History with Documents.* 2nd ed. Boston: Bedford/St. Martin's, Macmillan Learning, 2018.

Marrus, Michael R. *The Unwanted: European Refugees in the Twentieth Century.* New York: Oxford Univ. Press, 1985.

Marx, Emanuel. "Messages from a Present Past: The Kristallnacht as Symbolic Turning Point in Nazi Rule." In *Marking Evil: Holocaust Memory in the Global Age*, edited by Amos Goldberg and Haim Hazan, 319–344. New York: Berghahn Books, 2015.

Mascuch, Michael, Rudolf Dekker, and Arianne Baggerman. "Egodocuments and History: A Short Account of the Longue Durée." *Historian* 78, no. 1 (2016): 11–56.

Matthäus, Jürgen and Emil Kerenji, eds. *Jewish Responses to Persecution, 1933–1946: A Source Reader.* London: Rowman & Littlefield, 2017.

Meinen, Insa. *Verfolgt von Land zu Land: Jüdische Flüchtlinge in Westeuropa, 1938–1944.* Paderborn: Schöningh, 2013.

Mendel, Meron. "The Policy for the Past in West Germany and Israel: The Case of Jewish Remigration." *Leo Baeck Institute Yearbook* 49 (2004): 121–136.

Mendelsohn, John, ed. *The Holocaust: Selected Documents in Eighteen Volumes.* New York: Garland, 1982.

Meyer, Michael A. "Looking Back: American Jews' Relationship to Their Places of Origin." *Modern Judaism* 37, no. 2 (2019): 143–164.

Monroe, Kristen Renwick. "Cracking the Code of Genocide: The Moral Psychology of Rescuers, Bystanders, and Nazis during the Holocaust." *Political Psychology* 29, no. 5 (2008): 699–736.

Mosse, Werner E., ed. *Second Chance: Two Centuries of German-Speaking Jews in the United Kingdom.* Tübingen: Mohr, 1991.

Münchener Stadtmuseum, ed. *München – "Hauptstadt der Bewegung" [Exhibition in Munich's City Museum, October 22, 1993–March 27, 1994]* Munich: self-published, 1993.

Nikou, Lina. *Besuche in der alten Heimat. Einladungsprogramme für ehemals Verfolgte des Nationalsozialismus in München, Frankfurt am Main und Berlin.* Berlin: Neofelis Verlag, 2020.

Ofer, Dalia. "Personal Letters in Research and Education on the Holocaust." *Holocaust and Genocide Studies* 4, no. 3 (1989): 341–355.

Ophir, Baruch Z. and Falk Wiesemann, eds. *Die jüdischen Gemeinden in Bayern 1918–1945: Geschichte und Zerstörung.* Munich: Oldenbourg, 1979.

Orlow, Dietrich. *The Nazi Party, 1919–1945: A Complete History.* New York: Enigma, 2010.

Popkin, Jeremy D. "Holocaust Memories, Historians' Memoirs: First-Person Narrative and the Memory of the Holocaust." *History & Memory* 15, no. 1 (2003): 49–84.

Priemel, Kim Christian. *The Betrayal: The Nuremberg Trials and German Divergence.* New York: Oxford Univ. Press, 2016.

Quack, Sibylle. "Changing Gender Roles and Emigration: The Example of German Jewish Women and Their Emigration to the United States, 1933–1945." In *People in Transit: German Migrations in Comparative Perspective, 1820–1930,* edited by Dirk Hoerder and Jörg Nagler, 379–397. Washington: German Historical Institute, 1995.

Richarz, Monika. "Juden in der Bundesrepublik Deutschland und in der Deutschen Demokratischen Republik seit 1945." In *Jüdisches Leben in Deutschland seit 1945,* edited by Micha Brumlik et al., 13–30. Frankfurt /Main: Jüd. Verl. bei Athenäum, 1988.

Rosenthal, Fritz. *Zur religiösen Lage in Palästina: Ein Beitrag zur religiösen Anthropologie der Gegenwart.* Tel-Aviv: Verl. "Matara," 1940.

Roth John K. et al., eds. *Remembering for the Future: The Holocaust in an Age of Genocide, Vol. 3: Memory.* Basingstoke: Palgrave, 2001.

Rozett, Robert. "Published Memoirs of Holocaust Survivors." In *Remembering for the Future: The Holocaust in an Age of Genocide, Vol. 3: Memory,* edited by John K. Roth et al., 167–171. Basingstoke: Palgrave, 2001.

Sanden, Heinrich. "'Das Foto ist von mir ...'." In *Die Gleichschaltung der Bilder: Zur Geschichte der Pressefotografie 1930–1936,* edited by Diethard Krebs, Walter Uka and Brigitte Walz-Richter, 122–126. Berlin: Fröhlich & Kaufmann, 1983.

Schlör, Joachim. *Endlich im Gelobten Land? Deutsche Juden unterwegs in eine neue Heimat.* Berlin: Aufbau, 2003.

Schöck-Quinteros, Eva, Matthias Loeber, and Simon Rau, eds. *Keine Zuflucht. Nirgends: Die Konferenz von Evian und die Fahrt der St. Louis, 1938/39.* 2nd corr. and exp. ed. Bremen: Institut für Geschichtswissenschaft, 2019.

Schrafstetter, Susanna. *Flucht und Versteck: Untergetauchte Juden in München – Verfolgungserfahrung und Nachkriegsalltag.* Göttingen: Wallstein, 2015.

Schulze, Winfried, ed. *Ego-Dokumente: Annäherung an den Menschen in der Geschichte.* Berlin: DeGruyter, 1996.

Shakespeare, William. *Henry V: The Oxford Shakespeare.* Edited by Gary Taylor. New York: Oxford Univ. Press, 2008.

Sherman, Ari J. *Island Refuge: Britain and Refugees from the Third Reich, 1933–1939.* 2nd ed. London: Frank Cass, 1994.

Sinn, Andrea. *"Und ich lebe wieder an der Isar:" Exil und Rückkehr des Münchner Juden Hans Lamm.* Munich: Oldenbourg, 2008.

Sinn, Andrea A. "We Have the Right to Exist Here: Jewish Politics and The Challenge of *Wiedergutmachung* in Post-Holocaust Germany." In *Rebuilding Jewish Life in Germany,* edited by Jay Howard Geller and Michael Meng, 30–47. New Brunswick: Rutgers Univ. Press, 2020.

Stadtarchiv München, ed. *Beth ha-Knesseth: Zur Geschichte der Münchner Synagogen, ihrer Rabbiner und Kantoren.* Munich: Buchendorfer Verlag, 1999.

Stadtarchiv München, ed. *Biographisches Gedenkbuch der Münchner Juden 1933–1945,* 2 Vol. Munich: EOS Verlag, 2007. Online: https://gedenkbuch.muenchen.de/.

Stadtarchiv München, ed. *"… verzogen, unbekannt wohin:" Die erste Deportation von Münchner Juden im November 1941.* Zurich: Pendo, 2000.

Steinweis, Alan E. *Kristallnacht 1938.* Cambridge: Harvard Univ. Press, 2009.

Stoltzfus, Nathan. "The Limits of Policy: Social Protection of Intermarried German Jews in Nazi Germany." In *Social Outsiders in Nazi Germany,* edited by Robert Gellately and Nathan Stoltzfus, 117–144. Princeton: Princeton Univ. Press, 2001.

Strauss, Herbert A. "Introductions: Jews in German History. Persecution, Emigration, Acculturation." In *International Biographical Dictionary of Central European Emigres 1933–1945, Vol. II/Part 1 (A–K): The Arts, Sciences, and Literature,* edited by Herbert Strauss and Werner Röder, XI–XXVI. Munich: Saur, 1983.

Strauss, Herbert A. "The Immigration and Acculturation of the German Jew in the United States of America." *Leo Baeck Institute Year Book* 16, 1 (1971): 63–94.

Strnad, Maximilian. *Privileg Mischehe? Handlungsräume "jüdisch versippter" Familien 1933–1949.* Göttingen: Wallstein, 2021.

Strnad, Maximilian. *Zwischenstation "Judensiedlung:" Verfolgung und Deportation der jüdischen Münchner 1941–1945.* Munich: Oldenbourg, 2011.

Thies, Jochen. *Évian 1938: Als die Welt die Juden verriet.* Essen: Klartext Verlag, 2017.

Trachtenberg, Barry. *The United States and the Nazi Holocaust: Race, Refugee, and Remembrance.* London: Bloomsbury, 2018.

Treitschke, Heinrich von. "Unsere Aussichten." *Preußische Jahrbücher* 44 (1879): 559–576.

Trevor, John Bond. *An Analysis of the American Immigration Act of 1924*. New York: Carnegie Endowment for International Peace, 1924.

Ullrich, Anna. *Von "jüdischem Optimismus" und "unausbleiblicher Enttäuschung": Erwartungsmanagement deutsch-jüdischer Vereine und gesellschaftlicher Antisemitismus 1914–1938*. Berlin: De Gruyter Oldenbourg, 2018.

Wilson, A. N. *Hitler: A Short Biography*. London: HarperPress, 2012.

Wimmer, Florian. *Die völkische Ordnung von Armut: Kommunale Sozialpolitik im nationalsozialistischen München*. Göttingen: Wallstein, 2014.

Wingenroth, Carl D. "Das Jahrhundert der Flüchtlinge." *Außenpolitik* 10 (1959): 491–499.

Wolff, Frank. "Global Walls and Global Movement: New Destinations in Jewish Migration, 1918–1939." *East European Jewish Affairs* 44, no. 2–3 (2014): 187–204.

Zucker, Bat-Ami. "American Refugee Policy in the 1930s." In *Refugees from Nazi Germany and the Liberal European States*, edited by Frank Caestecker and Bob Moore, 151–168. New York: Berghahn, 2010.

Zucker, Bat-Ami. *In Search of Refuge: Jews and US Consuls in Nazi Germany, 1933–1941*. London: Valentin Mitchell, 2001.

Index

198nn41, 50, 199, 208, 210–11;
Broadway, 76, 191; Bronx, 72,
74–75, 77–79, 83, 210; Brooklyn,
55, 100, 107, 109–10, 111n4,
116, 197n40, 210; Greenwich
Village, 210–11; Lower East Side,
55; Manhattan, 37, 83, 109, 137,
139nn30–31, 210; Washington
Heights, 109–10; West Side, 116;
Yorkville, 137, 139n31
New York (state), 17, 28
Nice, France, 92–93, 101n7, 113, 121
North Sea, 64
Nuremberg, Germany, xvii, xxi, xxx,
xxxixn21, xlivnn71, 4, 15n11, 21,
26n24, 32, 51, 52nn5–6, 57, 61,
78–79, 112n13, 149, 178n10, 199,
208, 214n23, 218, 221

Oahu Island, Hawaii, 125n14, 139n28,
214n14
Oakland, California, 169
Oberammergau, Germany, 43
Oberaudorf, Germany, 28
Oberdorfer, Toni Anna, 193, 198n45
Oesterreich. *See* Austria
Oettinger, Helene (Lene), née Koppel,
192, 197n39
Oles, Eva, née Schindler, 65n8

Palatka, Florida, 108
Palestine, xvii–xix, xxii, xxv, xxxixn25,
xliin55, 22, 39, 69–70, 73, 78, 85n6,
86n18, 105, 200–1, 206, 213n4,
214n17, 215, 218–19, 225. *See also*
Erez Israel; Israel
Palm Beach, Florida, 90, 108
Paris, France, 41, 47n23, 60, 66n15,
173, 177, 207, 214n26
Pasadena, California, 161
Passau, Germany, 17, 19–21, 23, 24n3,
25n11, 49, 113, 124n4
Pembroke Pines, Florida, 3
Philadelphia, Pennsylvania, 50–51,
52n4, 125n9, 164

Piaski, forced labor camp and/or ghetto
site, 52n8, 197n27
Pick, Ludwig Hermann Arthur, 178n2
Pittsburgh, Pennsylvania, 69
Poirier, Robert, 35n14
Poland, 55–57, 59, 66n14, 89, 93, 96,
100, 101n15, 103n35, 198n44, 208,
219, 221
Portland, Maine, 164, 171
Portugal, 3, 114, 195n4
Prague, Czech Republic, xlin45
Providence, Rhode Island, 46n13

Rajcza (Rzeszow), Poland, 57
Ramstein Air Base, Germany, 37
Rath, Ernst vom, 47n23, 66n15
Regensburg, Germany, 85n9
Reis, Dr. Fritz, 81, 86n27
Reiss, Isaak, 193, 198n44
Reiss, Marta Magda, née Griesbach,
193, 198n44
Rhineland, Germany, 29
Rhode Island, 46n13
Riga, Latvia, 32, 34
Rindner, Gusti, 213n2
Rio de Janeiro, Brazil, 141–43, 151,
155n2
Riverside, California, 159, 166n2
Rödelheimer, Hans, 36n22
Rödelheimer, Ilse, 36n22
Rödelheimer, Johanna, 31–32, 36n22
Rödelheimer, Julius, 36n22
Rödelheimer, Marianne, 31–32, 36n22
Rödelheimer, Regina, née Stiefel,
31–32, 36n22
Rokeach, Aaron, 59, 66n11
Rokeach, Shalom, 65n3
Rolandia, Brazil, 141, 144–48, 150
Roosevelt, Franklin D., xxvi, 78–79,
143
Rorschach, Switzerland, 91,
101n4
Rosenack, Ignaz, 191
Rosenberg, Anneliese (Iche), née
Wallach, 81, 86nn24–5

About the Editors

Andrea A. Sinn received her doctorate at Ludwig-Maximilians-Universität München with a study on Jewish Politics and Press in the Early Federal Republic. Today, she is O'Briant Developing Professor and Associate Professor of History at Elon University, NC. Previously, she served as DAAD Visiting Professor at the University of California, Berkeley. Her research focuses on modern Jewish history with special interest in 20th-century German and migration history. She has published widely on German-Jewish responses to the great traumas of the 20th century as well as the rebuilding of Jewish life in the Federal Republic of Germany. Her list of publications comprises studies in interdisciplinary journals on German and Jewish history, such as the *Leo Baeck Institute Year Book*, *Studies in Contemporary Jewry*, *Journal of Modern Jewish Studies*, *European Judaism*, and *Central European History*, as well as contributions to edited volumes, exhibition catalogs, two authored books, and one coedited volume.

Andreas Heusler received his doctorate at Ludwig-Maximilians-Universität München with a study on the National Socialist war economy. After more than 25 years as head of the Contemporary History/Jewish History Department at the Munich City Archives, he is, since 2022, head of the Institute for Urban History and Remembrance Culture, Munich. His research interests are primarily in the fields of Nazi history, exile research, municipal cultural history, and recent contemporary history. His current research focuses on questions of memory culture and contemporary forms of collective remembrance. With a large number of publications and exhibition projects, he has provided striking impulses for the examination of suppressed or forgotten historical themes. In one of his last publications, he examined the biography of the writer Lion Feuchtwanger; Germany's transition to modern democracy is the subject of a coauthored publication on the 1918/1919 revolution; and current migration phenomena are the subject of a publication on Munich's urban history after 1945.

www.ingramcontent.com/pod-product-compliance
Lightning Source LLC
Chambersburg PA
CBHW071537110726
47908CB00007B/1921